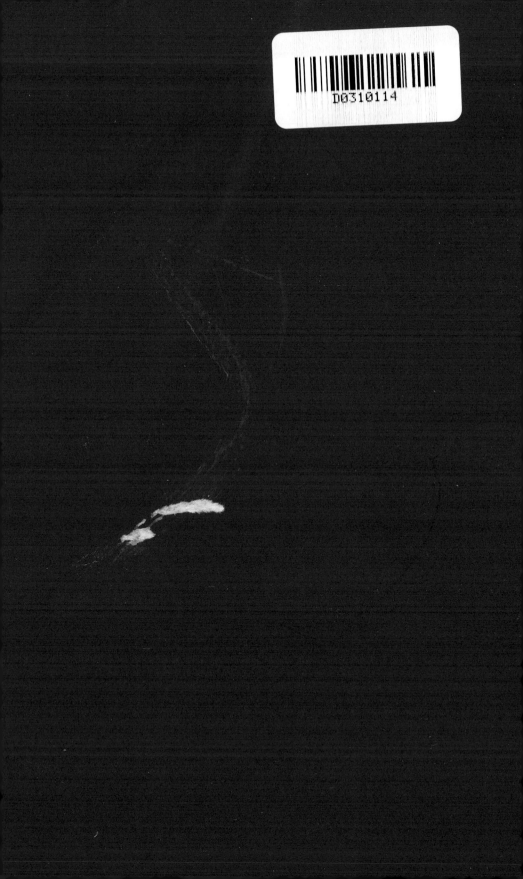

Party Animals

Paddling to Jerusalem: An Aquatic Tour of Our Small Country
Voodoo Histories: The Role of the Conspiracy Theory in
Shaping Modern History

Party Animals

My Family and Other Communists

DAVID AARONOVITCH

JONATHAN CAPE
LONDON

3 5 7 9 10 8 6 4

Jonathan Cape, an imprint of Vintage Publishing,
20 Vauxhall Bridge Road,
London SW1V 2SA

Jonathan Cape is part of the Penguin Random House group of companies
whose addresses can be found at global.penguinrandomhouse.com

First published by Jonathan Cape in 2016

www.vintage-books.co.uk

A CIP catalogue record for this book is available from the British Library

ISBN 9780224074711

Typeset in India by Thomson Digital Pvt Ltd, Noida, Delhi

Printed and bound in Great Britain by Clays Ltd, St Ives PLC

Penguin Random House is committed to a sustainable future for our business,
our readers and our planet. This book is made from
Forest Stewardship Council® certified paper.

For Lavender and Sam. Reunited in this, at least

'Who's going to be interested in any of it, silly boy? It's about us, it's between us. It won't mean a thing to anybody else.'

Leah Wesker to her son Arnold on his play *Chicken Soup with Barley*

Contents

PART I

COMRADES COME RALLY

Party Like It's 1961

**Five for the years of the five-year plan
And four for the four years taken!**

Red Fly the Banners O!

In the summer of 1961 the Communists of Parliament Hill Fields celebrated. Nellie Rathbone sang to herself as she picked up the milk and the *Daily Worker* from her doorstep in Makepeace Avenue. Old Andrew Rothstein's lips lifted the white moustache below his black homburg as he walked down Hillway on his way to the Marx Memorial Library. In the dentist's surgery in St Albans Road, Rose Uren, the Party orthodontist, gripped the drill a little more lightly and may even have permitted her victims the use of an anaesthetic. Or so I imagine. I was only seven at the time, but my infant sensors could distinguish between primary emotions, and what was going on among the comrades was something close to happiness.

The cause of this good humour was the visit to Britain of the world's first cosmonaut (which I wrongly took to be a word created by amalgamating 'communist' and 'astronaut'). Handsome, wholesome Yuri Gagarin was everything a British Communist wanted a Russian to be: the son of a peasant family, a proletarian apprentice in a foundry, then an officer in the Red Air Force. On 12 April 1961, Gagarin had become the first man in space. Bunched up in a tiny capsule called Vostok 1, screwed on to the end of a huge rocket, he had been blasted into the stratosphere – where his smile had been picked up on grainy film – and then he had been almost magically wafted to earth somewhere in the vastness of Soviet Central Asia. It was a triumph for socialism.

Three months later, on a wet and rather cold British summer's day, Yuri Gagarin arrived in Manchester. It is said that small children wearing home-made cosmonaut outfits lined the terraced streets to wave to him. He appeared before crowds in Trafford Park and was noisily feted by teenage girls who – weeks earlier – might have been screaming for a coiffed idol with a guitar. Gagarin was sexy – an attribute not often associated with Russia, with its women shot-putters and fleshy General Secretaries. In the *Sunday Express* the chronicler-cartoonist Giles drew a group of young women in a milk bar, swooning over a picture of the twenty-seven-year-old cosmonaut while their scowling boyfriends looked on. 'Good night, Elvis Presley,' one was saying, 'good night Cliff Richard, come in Yuri Gagarin'.

He came – Communism came – offering peace and progress, after years of isolation and Cold War. When Gagarin addressed an audience at the office of the foundry workers' union he was the model of what Communists insisted Communism was all about. 'Although only one person was aboard the spaceship,' he said, through his interpreter, 'it took tens of thousands of people to make it a success. Over seven thousand scientists, workers and engineers just like yourselves were decorated for contributing to the success of the flight.' Major Gagarin smiled. 'There is plenty of room for all in outer space,' he said. 'I visualise the great day when a Soviet spaceship landing on the moon will disembark a party of scientists, who will join British and American scientists working in observatories in a spirit of peaceful co-operation and competition rather than thinking on military lines.' The crowd, apparently, stood to applaud. Peace instead of war, progress instead of backwardness, rationality instead of prejudice, planning instead of chaos.

Then Gagarin came to London. Every time a Soviet leader or hero visited they would take a big black limousine and go on a pilgrimage to the granite memorial to Karl Marx in Highgate Cemetery. There they would bow, and place flowers in front of the giant leonine head. If you stood on the dustbin by our side

gate on Bromwich Avenue and peered over the fence on the
afternoon of 14 July, you could see the cars slowly climbing the
steep hill towards the entrance 200 yards away.

At the memorial, standing within a semicircle of local digni-
taries and embassy officials, the elegant Major stood to attention
and saluted the founder of Communism. And if any of the local
comrades thought it was an irony that the capitalists of Britain
had connived in the erection of such a large bust of the great
anti-capitalist, then I never heard them say so. They lined the
streets and I stood on the dustbin and we tried to discern Gagarin
and then again, two years later, the first woman in space, Valentina
Tereshkova, followed by Alexei Leonov, the first man to walk in
space, and Popovich, whom we named a puppy after, as they
looked out of the windows of their black cars – the socialist future
come at last to pay tribute to the prophetic past.

On our mantelpieces and at our Communist Party bazaars the
space memorabilia, shipped over from the Soviet Union, took up
residence. We had a silver-coloured Sputnik – the first satellite,
sent into orbit in 1957 – lifting off on a plastic whoosh from the
gilt earth. And then after Gagarin's triumph we added a Vostok
rocket, attached by an orbiting wire to a planet, its point of origin
marked with 'CCCP' – the Union of Soviet Socialist Republics,
the Sovetsky Soyuz, the 'socialist eighth of the earth'.

The wire holding the rocket to its origins was also a metaphor
for what attached the orbiting Parliament Hill Fields Communists
to Russia, to socialism, to the causes of peace, progress and the
international working class. Random post-war tides had deposited
them in this semi-urban part of North London, slipped rather
comfortably into the gap between Hampstead Heath and Islington.
They had come there from Lanark and Edinburgh, from Vienna
and Berlin, from Russia and Esher, from jobs on the railways and
in universities, and fetched up in London NW5 and N6, with (in
those romantic days before digits took over entirely) phone
addresses that began Gulliver or Fitzroy and phones that sometimes

clicked oddly when they were answered. Among the Tories, Liberals, right-wing Labourites and nothing-much-at-all-folk dwelt the Davises, the Schons, the Kessels, the Frankels, the Whitakers, the Boatmans (or the Boatmen as my mother inevitably called them), the Formans (but not the Formen), the Loefflers, Pete and Elvira Richards, old Irma Petrov and the impoverished Ken Herbert, with his glasses sellotaped together, the lenses thick with dust. And sprinkled among them the senior Party people, the Gollans, Jock and Bridget Nicholson and the Aaronovitches.

Like other Party children I had – though it took me the first decade of my life to realise it – been born at a 90-degree angle to the rest of society. I simply lived that life, knowing no other, but the Party people around me had chosen at some point to exist like that. So most things the world around us thought were good, we thought were bad. Much we held to be virtuous was considered pernicious by everyone else. For us the churches were sinks of superstition, the royal family was a feudal remnant, the police were oppressors, the Americans were crass warmongers, the army was a tool of imperialism, the management of major companies were exploiters and the press, the BBC and many teachers were purveyors of lies and propaganda. We were indifferent to if not contemptuous of crooners, Hollywood epics and musicals.

We were overtly anti-war, anti-fascist, anti-racist, anti-apartheid, anti rent rises, anti-landlord, anti-bomb, anti-imperialist, anti-colonialist; anti-neo-colonialist, even. But we weren't miserable because there were plenty of things we were pro too. We liked trade unions (and the more militant the better), we quietly loved the Soviet Union, were warm to Irish Republicanism, supported national liberation movements from just about anywhere, upped the workers, worked for the cause of peace (or Peace, as I thought of it), enjoyed world cinema and took the collectivist's odd pleasure in male voice choirs and folk-dancing.

Much that we cared about seemed exotic or remote to the people around us. At the age of seven I knew, to take a far-flung example, where Guyana was and that the forces of imperialism had displaced the good leader Cheddi Jagan with the wicked Forbes Burnham. It was confusing later to discover that Burnham was black. Black people were good. They were oppressed in America, discriminated against in Britain, shot down in South Africa and butchered in the Congo. In that sense, though we Communists were behind history when it came to democracy and individualism, when it came to race and, I'd say too, to feminism, we were well ahead.

What I think I understood was that, once – during a war that was only sixteen years gone – we and the British people had been on the same side. United against the Nazis, whose unique brutalities I could find in dreadful photographs in books my parents thought I couldn't reach. United with the heroic Red Army, who had 'really' won the war. We were in communion. But before that war, and after it again, we were almost pariahs. In every war and 'struggle' (never 'a' struggle, but always 'the' struggle) following that glorious moment when the Allies shook hands on the Elbe and Will embraced Sasha we were on the other side.

When the Iron Curtain descended we were stranded, representative not of allies but of alien lands of moustached and grim men, tanks and hefty, badly dressed women. This isolation was hard, but perpetual opposition is a habit with its own consolations too. It cemented the solidarity of comrades – hardened in adversity, loyal to each other, *contra mundum*, bloody but unbowed.

Yet, for all that, any sign of our own respectability was seized upon. And beginning in 1957 after the launch of Sputnik, suddenly we – so poor in every other way – were associated with success. We were Communists and it was Communists who were launching rockets, sending dogs, monkeys and then men into space. They were able to do this because their system, a system of rational planning rather than the chaotic *sauve qui peut* of capitalism, was allowing human advances such as had never been seen before. Five-Year Plans decided what was needed and who would produce it, so there would be no waste. Planners created whole cities near the fabled Urals dedicated to scientific and technological progress. There was Akademgorodok – the city of scholars. And Magnitogorsk, city of magnets (I supposed).

Supersonic MiG jets defended Soviet skies, Tupolev airliners whizzed comrade citizens between the steppe-separated Russian cities, jet hydrofoils sped hull-high from port to port, nuclear ice-breakers broke the ice literally and – for us – metaphorically, red-scarved pioneers smiled through summer camps while their parents rested in workers' rest homes on the sunny Black Sea. In modern, sunlit sanatoria Soviet doctors and nurses treated the sick without distinction between professional, intellectual and proletarian.

In this updated, uprated version of *Babar the Elephant* – one of my favourite childhood books – Babar the General Secretary presided over a Celesteville in which everything was new and everything had its own building and its specialised elephant. And when the hewer had hewed his day's wood and the drawer had drawn her day's water, they would board an electric tram or take the Metro to the theatre, the opera or the library to be filled up with the best culture the world could offer. 'Ahh,' sighed the bolshy shop steward Fred Kite in the 1959 film *I'm All Right Jack*, 'Russia! All them corn fields – and ballet in the evening!' Nothing was too good for the working class.

After the years of toil and sacrifice real socialism was paying off. The General Secretary was not actually Babar, but the equally paternalistic Nikita Khrushchev, with his smiles, boasts and folksy language. In 1959, when Dwight Eisenhower's vice president, Richard Nixon, visited Moscow for a much-photographed encounter at the American national exhibition, Mr K told him what the North London comrades all wanted so badly to believe. 'America has existed for one hundred and fifty years and this' – Khrushchev gestured at the fridges and TVs, 'is the level she has reached. We have existed not quite forty-two years and in another seven we will be on the same level as America.' And then he added, 'When we catch you up, in passing you by, we will wave to you.'

Seven years later was 1966. Around that time, when I was eleven years old, a boy asked me what my parents were. I told him they were Communists. 'Communists?' he said, disbelievingly, 'I thought they'd all been shot.' And I wondered what it would be like to be shot, and so insouciantly, *routinely* shot, at that. But when I glimpsed Gagarin on his pilgrimage to Highgate, shooting was out and history, as Fidel Castro, the new leader of Cuba, had said, was 'on our side'. Once again we were the people of the future. We briefly touched the golden face of fashion.

2

The Party: a Brief Biography

The hall rose, thundering. How far they had soared, these Bolsheviki, from a despised and hunted sect less than four months ago, to this supreme place, the helm of great Russia in full tide of insurrection!

John Reed, *Ten Days That Shook the World*

'The Party' to anyone who wasn't in another party – and even to many who were – meant the Communist Party. To be a Liberal, or even a Labourite, was usually a mere affiliation and committed the member to as much or as little activity and support as they liked. To be a Communist was different. A Party member was described as 'card-carrying' – the real thing, as opposed to the mere fellow traveller or armchair revolutionary. It was a statement of fundamental being and moral seriousness. In this sense it was religious. Like a post-communion Catholic, a Communist really meant to try and live a life of faith.

What guided Communists in their Great Task was Marxism – or, as they thought of it, scientific socialism. Far from being just a belief or a desire, Marxism they understood to be a way of understanding human society and human history – a system for organising the world in your head. The philosophy of dialectical materialism was to the twentieth-century Marxist what the Quran was to the devout Muslim: the final word on how to comprehend life. And it was a 'tool', part magic, part science – like Dr Who's sonic screwdriver – available to Communists alone.

The year I caught a glimpse of Gagarin, 1961, the Communist Party of Great Britain turned forty-one – young adulthood in the life of a political party, its members old enough to have children who were old enough to be members. It had been founded in 1920, three years after the Bolshevik revolution and two years after the end of the Great War, as a response to both. A Unity Convention of various small socialist and working-class groups was held that summer in the Cannon Street Hotel, the architect E. M. Barry's glorious adjunct to Cannon Street station to which T. S. Eliot's narrator in *The Waste Land* was invited for luncheon at around that time, by a Mr Eugenides, 'the Smyrna merchant Unshaven, with a pocket full of currants'. After a day at the doubtless rather bourgeois and expensive hotel the delegates adjourned a mile or so north-west to a socialist hall not far from Old Street, which features in no poem I can find.

The eight score men and a few women who gathered – members of the British Socialist Party, the Workers' Socialist Federation, and the Socialist Labour Party; readers and writers of the *Call*, the *International* and the *Workers' Dreadnought*; Scottish ship-workers and Welsh miners from the militant areas of the Clyde and Rhondda; anti-imperialists; conscientious objectors to the war; William-Morris-type intellectuals; several suffragettes – were often courageous, invariably dedicated and consequently isolated, agitating on the far political coast. Inland of them there was the vast continental mass of the world's oldest and most sophisticated working-class party – the Labour Party – which had recently won sixty seats in Parliament and would surely soon put a worker's shoes on the portraited stairs inside Number 10 Downing Street.

The budding Communists thought that the Labour Party had become a 'reformist' organisation, getting its men into positions of power where they would make capitalism more palatable, rather than ushering in the new dawn of a completely different system called socialism. In their view, reformism had led to Labour figures collaborating in the deaths of millions of workers in the catastrophe of the First World War. The new Communists believed that the alternative working-class power should be exercised through workers' councils (or soviets, as the Russians called them) where workers or their delegates would meet, debate and vote. And the Communist Party itself – as prescribed by Karl Marx in *The Communist Manifesto*, and by Lenin in a series of works written both in exile and then in government – was to be the vanguard of the vanguard, the cleverest and most strategic section of the revolutionary class. The *crème de la crème* of the great seething pudding. The jutting jaw on the craggy face of the stoneworker.

A contingent among them simply wanted Labour to be destroyed; they wanted to make its compromises and failures their main target and to supplant it in the affections of the workers. They were animated by the second Russian Revolution of 1917 when Lenin's numerically small Bolshevik faction had seized control of a huge peasant nation in the name of the industrial working classes, withdrawn from the war and turned the world upside down. Turned it upside down and then defended their revolution and the revolutionary classes against everything the imperialist world and the old order could bring to bear against them. From the Polish border to Vladivostok and from Archangel to Odessa the Russian Civil War had raged, and as the fire died down Lenin's Party was seen through the smoke, still standing.

One influential voice against such a strategy, however, was the man of iron, V. I. Lenin himself. Somehow dealing with Russia's staggering problems still left enough time for the world's top Bolshevik to engage with the politics of small revolutionary parties in far-off countries. As the invitations were going out for the Cannon Street Hotel congress, Lenin was publishing one of his pamphlets – *Left Wing Communism: An Infantile Disorder* – dealing with those whose instincts were to work against Labour.

Lenin's logic was direct and ruthless. 'At present,' he wrote, 'the British Communists very often find it hard to approach the masses and even to get a hearing from them.' If, on the other hand, Communists argued that the workers should vote for the Labour Party of Arthur Henderson and Philip Snowden, rather than for the Liberals of Lloyd George, they would certainly be listened to. But, in Lenin's famous, icy phrase, this would be a vote 'to support Henderson in the same way as the rope supports a hanged man'. Once Henderson was in power he could be dealt with in the same way that his 'kindred spirits' were in Russia and Germany – supplanted by the revolutionaries to his left.

To the new Communists such war was the natural state of things. History was composed, they believed, of the victories of one class over another. First there had been a slave society but slavery had been inefficient and had been replaced by feudalism. The land-owning, feudal classes had in their turn been superseded by the merchants and capitalists (the bourgeoisie), whose frenetic activities had created industrial capitalism. But in building indus-trial society the bourgeoisie had also manufactured a new class of people to service it: the immiserated industrial proletariat. This class – which would become the most numerous in society – was the revolutionary class, the class that was destined first to supplant the 'dictatorship' of the capitalist class with the 'dictator-ship of the proletariat', and then to usher in the era of classlessness, the nirvana of Communism, where, in the words of Robbie Burns, 'man to man, the world o'er, shall brothers be, for a' that.'

By the time of the Cannon Street Hotel congress, the world movement already had its anthem – the Internationale. The lyrics were originally in French, and the music had been composed by a Belgian in 1888. In English its verses probably sounded odd even in 1920, with 'servile masses' and 'starvelings' spurning dust to win the prize. The chorus however was perfectly immediate. 'Then comrades come rally and the last fight let us face,' it enjoined before declaring, 'The Internationale unites the human race!'

That 'Internationale' was the Third International. There was still theoretically a Second Socialist International which the Labour Party belonged to, but that grouping had not morally survived the experience of the First World War in which its members had willingly slaughtered each other in the names of their respective empires. The Third (Communist) International had created a proper, centralised organisation – the Communist International (Comintern for short) – to which the British Party was to be formally affiliated. The Party's members' true identification was with the world proletariat, not with the nation state, which, with time, would wither away, ushering in the era of true Communism. The CP's destiny was to act as a local branch of a World Party; taking responsibility both for itself, and for the workers of all the world, whose chains it would help to strike off, from Vancouver to Vietnam. From the very beginning, and almost uniquely, the Communist Party took up the causes of the black, brown and yellow colonial peoples of the Empire as its own.

That brotherhood, however, lay on the other side of the global Red Revolution. To the men and women at the Cannon Street Hotel, Labour's present-day conception of 'One Nation' would have seemed a diversionary nonsense devised by the ruling classes to hide the very existence of their own power and thus gull workers into quiescence. The 'state' was not some neutral mechanism for the delivery of services and protection to all of a country's citizens. Nor were parliaments in capitalist countries expressions of the people's will. They were inevitably part of the apparatus of the bourgeois state, actively on the side of the ruling classes. The state belonged to them, and to think anything else was to suffer from a delusion. The state could not be reformed or captured through election – it could only be smashed and then remade through revolution.

Even so, after something of a battle, the new Communist Party decided that it would try at first to work through Labour rather than against it. Labour was a problem but also an opportunity: a block but also possibly a conduit. The Party would ask to affiliate to Labour, seek influence through its work in trade unions, and encourage its members to become Labour candidates. Like almost every other subsequent group to the left of Labour, the Party's strategy towards Labour was to become parasitical on its bigness.

Amazingly, for some time this was actually tolerated by the Labour Party. Though the new Communist Party was not allowed to affiliate formally, active CP members were permitted to be active Labour Party members too. In the general election of 1922 an open Communist, Shapurji Saklatvala, stood for Labour in the North Battersea constituency and was elected. In the same year, in Motherwell in Scotland, Walton Newbold stood as a Communist candidate with local Labour Party support and also won.

It didn't last. By the time of the 1926 General Strike Labour was wise to the ways of the Party. As CP membership waxed in the wake of its often courageous leadership of the strike, reaching 10,000 at the year's end, so its influence in the Labour Party declined. By the '30s the Communist Party was outside Labour and increasingly hostile to it. The Communist Party was a party whose leaders would find themselves periodically in prison for what the law considered acts of sedition or agitation. Labour, on the other hand, was intent on becoming and remaining a party of government, and needed no Bolshevik noose to support it.

Measured by the conventional yardsticks of democratic politics – members and votes – the Communist Party of Great Britain was a failure from its inception to its demise. But the degree of its failure varied and with this variation so rose and fell the hopes, illusions and disappointments of its members. After its peak of 10,000 members, Party membership fell to 2,500 in November 1930. At the same time the German Communist Party, the KPD, claimed around 350,000.

However, instead of closing itself down, the CPGB transformed its 'organ', the Weekly Worker, into the Daily Worker and doubled membership in a year. The Party was a great spawner of bodies such as industrial 'advisories' or sectoral committees. There was an economic committee, a women's committee, an international committee, an electrical industry advisory, an agricultural advisory and dozens more. An active Party member could easily spend her entire non-working existence in a state of circulation between one committee, advisory, campaigning group and another. The threat of fascism, the Civil War in Spain and Communist association with militant campaigns against unemployment also boosted the Party's puny fortunes. By 1939 it had 16,000 members, a charismatic General Secretary called Harry Pollitt and one MP, Willie Gallacher, the member for West Fife in Scotland.

The basic unit of organisation was the Party branch. Most branches were based in a locality, the size of which depended on the number of Communists in the vicinity. There were also student branches, university branches and factory and workplace branches. A number of branches composed an area, which might have a Party 'full-timer' as Organiser, and a number of areas composed the District, the second most important party structure, led by a District Secretary. Each year branch delegates would attend Party Congress in London and elect an Executive Committee – its members invariably chosen from what was known as 'the recommended list' drawn up by a special committee. But true power rested with the Party's Political Committee (its Politburo) made up of full-timers working in the Party's headquarters in Covent Garden.

Since the Nazi seizure of power in 1933 the Party had preached the politics of the 'popular front' against fascism. This had been one of its principal attractions, not least to intellectuals and, of course, to Jews. Such a stance was encouraged by the Communist International and by the Soviet Communists, since it was anticipated that – as soon as he could – Hitler would go to war with Russia for the 'Lebensraum' that formed such a large part of his personal ideology. When France and Britain declined to help Czechoslovakia against partition and eventual annexation in 1938, Communists saw this as a Western willingness (if not a desire) that Germany should go on to destroy the first workers' state. The Party became frantic with anti-fascist prophecy.

Then, on 23 August 1939 – as Germany threatened Poland – the Nazi Foreign Minister Joachim von Ribbentrop and the Soviet Commissar for Foreign Affairs, Vyacheslav Molotov, signed the Nazi–Soviet Non-Aggression Pact in Moscow. The British Party could just about defend this act as an attempt by the Soviet Union to buy time before an inevitable onslaught in which it could rely on no allies. When Poland was indeed invaded nine days later, Britain and France declared war on Germany, and the CPGB declared its support for the war on fascism – until, infamously, it changed its mind. Or, rather, had its mind changed for it by Stalin. The 'line' coming from Moscow now was that the war was an imperialist one – like the First World War. The Party's top committee met and reversed itself, and the pro-war General Secretary Harry Pollitt stood aside. Almost overnight, Communists apparently were to switch from being militant anti-fascists to being militant pacifists. Thus commenced one of the most notorious passages in the Party's history.

Over the next several years, the *Daily Worker* gave voice to the Party's stance against the war. So effectively, in fact, that in January 1941 the paper was banned, by order of the Home Secretary, Labour's Herbert Morrison. In an editorial, the *Manchester Guardian* supported the banning of a fellow newspaper:

> The 'Daily Worker' began the war as a supporter of resistance to Hitler; it changed its tune when it found that Stalin wanted to be friends with Hitler. Day after day since it has vilified the British Government and its leaders to the exclusion of any condemnation of Hitler . . . More recently the paper has largely devoted its columns to derogatory accounts of Service conditions on the one hand and to the encouragement of agitation among munition workers on the other. This might be excusable if the motive were honest, if it were really desired to help the country in its struggle to keep democracy alive in Europe. But the 'Daily Worker' did not believe either in the war or in democracy; its only aim was to confuse and weaken. We can well spare it.

When Hitler invaded Russia five months later, the imperialist war became the war against fascism writ huge. Harry Pollitt resumed his duties, and the greatest of those was to spur the effort in assisting Britain's great, courageous and essential new ally – the Union of Soviet Socialist Republics. Of a sudden the aims of the Party and of broad opinion in Britain were synchronous. As Russia became more important to the winning of the war, the British Communist Party seemed an important part of the war effort. So, far from being punished for its epic volte-face, the Party ended the war with 56,000 members, two MPs and scores of local councillors established in cities, towns, civic organisations and trade unions throughout Britain. This was the high-water mark not just for British Communism, but for every political force to the left of the Labour Party.

Then the Cold War set in. Stalin went from friend to tyrant, from ally to potential deadly adversary. Party membership declined, though not precipitously. The Party lost its MPs and many of its councillors. After the Soviet invasion of Hungary and the revelations by the new Soviet leader, Khrushchev, about Stalin's reign, many of its intellectuals departed too. During the bleak '50s the Party went into a state of militant isolation. Its influence in trade unions became its most important connection with British society.

By 1961, where we began, the worst of the Cold War was over; Party membership was around 35,000, and slowly rising again under General Secretary Johnny Gollan, a Scots signwriter. Seventy-five per cent of Party members were working class – the same as the country as a whole but most unusual for a political organisation. Then, in 1962, Wogan Philipps, the most celebrated example of an upper-class Communist, had the choice to join the House of Lords after his father, the first Baron Milford, passed away.

Because the Party from its foundation was to be a workers' party – the party of those who toiled and strove – it became very attractive to those of the gentler classes who wished to break their own softer chains. Philipps had been given a conventional upper-class education before going into the family shipping business in the City. His private life, however, was bohemian. He painted nudes in full possession of pubic hair, mixed with artists, went out drinking with the notorious painter Augustus John, married the novelist Rosamond Lehmann and formed with her part of the Bloomsbury set. While some of his Eton contemporaries helped to run the pickets during the 1926 General Strike, Philipps's sympathies were with the strikers. A decade later he went as an ambulance driver to Spain and served on the Republican side for eighteen months of the most bloody fighting, being wounded in 1937. On his return to Britain he joined the Communist Party.

He and Lehmann divorced and he remarried, this time an Italian aristocrat – Cristina, Countess of Huntingdon – who was also a Communist. Philipps became a Party farmer, buying a 180-acre farm in Gloucestershire, where he raised sheep, pigs and cattle and grew corn. In 1946, he stood for the rural district council and became the only non-Tory sitting on it. He served on the Agricultural Committee of the Party and was the editor of the *Country Standard*, the Party's agricultural and rural journal. 'There were few sights as inspiring as Philipps, a very tall and ravishingly handsome man, swinging a scythe,' a local newspaper noted. 'He was Tolstoy's Levin, one thought.'

At the 1950 election the Party decided, somewhat quixotically, to stand Philipps as the Communist candidate for the safe Conservative seat of Cirencester and Tewkesbury. This led to a spectacle of Party activists holding meetings, distributing leaflets and selling *Daily Workers* to possibly the most resistant electors in the country. Some of the locals – including a few former British Union of Fascists stalwarts – followed the campaigners round the constituency, heckling and throwing eggs, tomatoes and (more painfully, perhaps) potatoes. Philipps's car was assaulted with a turkey thrown from another vehicle, which then attempted to force him off the road. The eventual result, for all this effort, was 423 votes.

Now in 1962, Philipps consulted the Party and it was decided that more could be gained by taking his father's place in the House

of Lords, than not. His maiden speech, turned into a Party
pamphlet, was a call for the abolition of the place. 'My Lords,'
he asked his peers, 'what, in fact, are we supposed to inherit? Is
it some special ability which enables us to function as legislators?
No. What we inherit is wealth, and privilege based on wealth – a
principle which cuts right across every conception of democracy . . . As long as [the House of Lords] lasts, its functions will
be – as they always have been – to stem the advance of democracy,
to protect wealth and privilege. For this reason, I am for the
complete abolition of this Chamber which is such a bulwark
against progress.'

Philipps's – who gave up farming when his second wife died,
remarried, and finished his days in Hampstead in North London –
was one kind of story among several. His was a particular kind
of what Vivian Gornick has called 'the Romance of Communism'.
At various times the appeal of Communism touched the sensibili-
ties of numbers of intellectuals, artists, philosophers and scientists.
Perhaps this was partly because the Party, like some other British
working-class organisations, put a huge – almost Edwardian –
emphasis on the power of learning. Many of the Party's members
were advocates of persistent self-improvement through self-educa-
tion. There were classes in Marxism, in dialectical materialism
and economics. Party weekend schools were held in woodland
camps and trade union country centres. For Party children there
was the Socialist Sunday School. There was also a youth wing –
the Young Communist League, or YCL, which held its own
Congress, published a journal called *Challenge* and which was
several thousand strong in the 1960s.

Films were shown, plays performed. Party actors played in
dramas written by Party writers in the Party's own Unity Theatre.
For, like one of those mini states much loved by '50s and '60s
British cinemagoers (Burgundy in *Passport to Pimlico* or the Duchy
of Grand Fenwick in *The Mouse That Roared*) the British Communist
Party ran parallel mini institutions. For example (there were so
many) it published a history journal called *Past and Present*, a

journal for teachers and another for economists. It also had a film company called Forum Films, a travel company called Progressive Tours, a central London bookshop called Collet's and a publishing house, Lawrence & Wishart. It was a little world within a world.

Allow me a digression which begins at a student discotheque at the old Oxford Polytechnic in the mid 1970s. I was a few days into a short career at Oxford University and earlier that day had been along to what they called a 'Freshers Fair' where the university's myriad clubs and societies literally set out their stalls and attempted to seduce people into membership. One stall was that of the Socialist Society (SocSoc), personned by a striking-looking young woman with dark eyes and full lips. Let's call her Ms C.

I was a socialist, so I went to the stall, joined the society and was rewarded with smiles from the young woman and an invitation to that night's Oxpoly disco. I said au revoir, visited a few more stalls, joined the Communist Society and the History Society too, and felt this was all very congenial.

As the disco blared some hours later I spotted Ms C and went to say hello. If I had lazily imagined a physical response from her, it wasn't the one I got, which was a slap across the face. 'Stalinist!' she hissed. Until the moment of that slap I had wrongly thought that all socialists were more or less the same sort of breed and that Communists were a particular stripe – as if all were terriers, but Party members Jack Russells. I said something like this to her, perhaps in a slightly aggrieved (and certainly surprised) tone of voice. 'Rivers of blood,' said Ms C, 'run between you and me.'

Ms C, it turned out, was a member of the International Marxist Group – a rather trendy Trotskyist outfit with an entirely middle-class membership of whom the snooty-voiced but romantic Anglo-Pakistani Tariq Ali was the most celebrated figure. She was hitting me that night because of what Stalin did to Trotsky in 1940 and what Communists had done to Trotskyists in years long gone.

This was my first encounter with what used to be called 'sectarianism' – in essence the political expression of what Sigmund Freud called 'the narcissism of minor difference'. Our very similarities meant that any disagreement at all was unbearable. Or, to put it in a very practical way, it was more likely that she'd bed a member of the League of Empire Loyalists that night than consent to making me a phenomenally successful fresher. The slap also opened the door on the world of the large number of sometimes minuscule left-wing groups who also thought they were 'the Party'.

Indeed the play *The Party* by Trevor Griffiths, first performed at the National Theatre in the year that I got my face slapped, was not about the *real* Party at all. It depicts the influence on a group of middle-class and rather credulous people of a political guru called John Tagg, National Organiser of the fictitious Revolutionary Socialist Party. Tagg, first played by Sir Laurence Olivier, is a working-class bully and a browbeater. He speaks like a cult leader and his method is the same. In a speech to the assembled delicatos in an urban living room he stresses sacrifice and renunciation:

> 'The party means discipline. It means self-scrutiny, criticism, responsibility, it means a great many things that run counter to the traditions and values of Western bourgeois intellectuals. It means being bound in and by a common purpose. But above all it means severing from the prior claims on your time and moral commitment of personal relationships, career, advancement, reputation and prestige.'

Tagg was a fictionalised version of Gerry Healy, leader of a second Trotskyist organisation that metamorphosed from something called the Club, to the Socialist Labour League and eventually became the Workers Revolutionary Party. It was famously a party of revolutionary actors, scooping up Vanessa and Corin Redgrave and several of their friends. The party split in the mid '80s when it turned out that Healy had exercised a kind of revolutionary *droit de seigneur* with women members. In the matter of who the leader had sex with, as in others, leftist cults resembled their religious counterparts.

A third major Trotskyist strand was represented by the International Socialists (of which both the Hitchens brothers, Christopher and Peter, were youthful members), which later became the Socialist Workers Party. The IS at Oxford later made me happy by chanting at the face-slapping Ms C during some unity event or other, 'IMG, IMG, idle sons of the bourgeoisie'.

A fourth group worked secretly inside the Labour Party pretending to be a newspaper called *Militant*. In fact you could tell if someone was a member of the Revolutionary Socialist League (and therefore a comrade of the Liverpool wide-boy, Derek Hatton) because only its actual members would deny that the RSL existed at all. At its mendacious and well-publicised zenith in the 1980s 'Militant' had three Labour MPs.

These were but four. There was also Workers' Fight, Big Flame, the Revolutionary Communist Party, the pro-Chinese Communist Party of Britain (Marxist–Leninist), the Socialist Alliance, Respect, Socialist Action (an outcrop of the IMG to which several of London mayor Ken Livingstone's advisors clandestinely belonged) and many more. All of them, when they were founded, formed the kernel of the new organisation of the vanguard of the working class. And all were perfectly sincere. All of them wanted to be, but weren't, the Party.

3

Party Man and Party Wife

SAM

My father's Communism has a place in high literature. The narrator of Doris Lessing's *The Golden Notebook*, Anna Wulf, not long arrived in late '40s London from Rhodesia, is thinking about joining the Communist Party. A friend who is already a member of the Party telephones Anna and tells her that a 'Comrade Bill', the party official responsible for culture, wants to interview her. 'You don't have to see him of course, if you don't feel like it,' says the friend, 'but he said he would be interested to meet the first intellectual prepared to join the Party since the cold war started.'

Intrigued, Anna makes her way to the CP headquarters in London's Covent Garden. The windows and doors have reinforced glass, the interior is one of dark narrow stairs and small, austere offices. In one of which sits the Cultural Secretary.

> Comrade Bill turned out to be a very young man, Jewish, spectacled, intelligent, working-class. His attitude towards me brisk and wary, his voice cool, brisk, tinged with contempt. I was interested that, at the contempt, which he was not aware he was showing, I felt in myself the beginnings of a need to apologize, almost a need to stammer.

Anna Wulf is, of course, Lessing herself. Comrade Bill is my father, Sam, then aged around thirty. In the second volume of her autobiography, *Walking in the Shade*, published thirty-five years after *The Golden Notebook*, Lessing adds to his portrait – this time naming him. She thought him

Lean, stern, military in style, with the grim, sardonic humour
of the times. He had been a very poor boy from the East
End. The Young Communist League had been his education,
but not his nursery, because he was a Jew and one of the
people of the Book.

My father was eight weeks younger than Lessing – born on
Boxing Day 1919 in the borough of Stepney, in what was then
the Jewish East End. The one surviving photograph of him in
childhood – taken against a grimy brick background – shows a

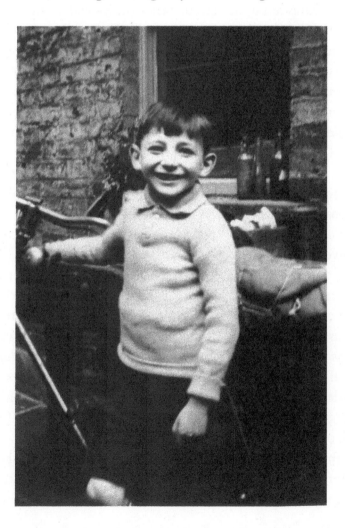

six- or seven-year-old wearing a grubby jumper, with big ears and
big mouth displaying a very big grin. In objective terms, as
Marxists might put it, he had little to grin about since he was
indeed a 'very poor boy' belonging to a group people did not
much like.

His father and mother, Morris and Kate (originally Moishe and
Gitel – and Lord knows what their true surname was, 'Aaronovitch'
being a patronymic probably donated by a Tsarist bureaucrat or
a British immigration official), had come from a mostly Jewish
village near the city of Vilnius (or Vilna or Wilno), then in the
Russian Empire but at various times the capital of Lithuania or
part of Poland. The area lay in what was called the Pale of
Settlement outside which Jews were not allowed to live without
permission. By the time they were born in the early 1880s four
of every ten Vilnians were Jewish and the surrounding countryside
contained many Jewish shtetls. As the Jewish population grew, so
too did bureaucratic and popular persecution and economic pressure. Those relatively few Jews who had emigrated to the United
States, South Africa, South America and other countries sent word
back to their beleaguered co-religionists that these were lands full
of jobs and security. In the thirty years before the Great War as
many as two million East European Jews heard the call and
followed it.

I seemed to remember my father telling me that his parents
had arrived by ship at the Port of London in about 1903 or 1904,
but I could find no sign of any Aaronovitches at all in the 1911
census. One reason for thinking that Sam was right was the
Aliens Act, which became law on 1 January 1906. Following the
arrival of some 100,000 East European Jews in the previous two
decades (including 3,000 Jews who arrived in Britain in 1900
having walked from Rumania), the Act severely restricted further
right of entry.

Although this piece of lawmaking – which became the first
proper legislation in Britain aimed at limiting immigration – was
not declared as being aimed at Jews, everyone had understood

that it was. The Conservative Prime Minister, Arthur Balfour himself, took part in the debate around the Bill. Britain had the right 'to keep out everybody who does not add to the strength of the community – the industrial, social, and intellectual strength of the community'. The alien migrants were 'largely Jewish' and this in itself was a problem because 'it would not be to the advantage of the civilization of the country that there should be an immense body of persons who, however patriotic, able, and industrious, however much they threw themselves into the national life, still, by their own action, remained a people apart, and not merely held a religion differing from the vast majority of their fellow-countrymen, but only inter-married among themselves.'

Morris and Kate did not add much, in any obvious way, to 'the industrial, social and intellectual strength' of Britain. They were both illiterate and unskilled: to the end of her life in a hospital ward in Dalston in 1969, my grandmother spoke almost nothing but Yiddish. (I only found this out later. Her habit of not putting in her false teeth made incomprehensible almost any word she uttered in whatever language.)

My half-sister, Frances, solved the mystery of my grandparents' missing years. Realising that customs officers and census takers had sometimes been a little hasty when dealing with incomprehensible foreigners, she entered a whole series of variants on 'Aaronovitch' into the census database. She found the family – parents, Uncle Joe and my aunt Rachel (the red-headed one who died before I was born) – entered under the name 'Aronofitch'. In 1911 they were living at 4, St George's Square in the Stepney parish of St George's in the east. The square (which later became Swedenborg Square but has now disappeared into council estates) had been built for the well-off tradesmen who had supplied the masted ships of the nineteenth century. By the time Kate and Morris moved there it was a run-down area of largely Jewish immigrants subletting rooms in its once-commodious houses.

It was just as well they were there. Had the Aaronovitches not arrived in Britain before 1906 it's more likely that they would either be pushing up pine needles in some mass grave in a Lithuanian forest, or that some version of me would be writing this on the Upper West Side from the library of his $20 million penthouse. But arrive they did, and went to live in a teeming, filthy-bricked house on one of London's most notorious thoroughfares, Cable Street, where my father Sam was born, and from where my grandfather went out to work as a needleman in the rag trade.

For several years Morris was employed in various clothing factories, such as Polikoff's on London Lane. Then, some time in the '20s – probably because he had been laid off – he left the low-paid security of the plants and set up a clothes repair workshop in the two rooms that the family of five then inhabited in a small turning off Cable Street itself. This was nothing unusual in the East End. When searching the 1911 census for East London Aaronovitches I came across one family of four with a similar name living in two rooms in Morgan Street in Mile End. The place still stands and I went and visited it. Gentrified now, you wouldn't fit a family of five into that small two-storey terraced house. In 1911, besides the wrong Aaronovitch family, there were sixteen other people there.

The kind of work my grandfather did was repairing the buttonholes on jackets – paid by the piece – for second-hand suits. My father once told me that he had been present on several occasions when Morris – who earned nearly nothing for his efforts – faced haggling from the wealthier members of the Jewish community, 'men with fur on their collars', who owned the clothes shops. I have only ever seen one photograph with my grandfather in it. Judging by the flower in his buttonhole and my grandmother's fur stole, it was taken at a wedding, probably in the late 1930s. My grandfather stands upright, head up, has a small moustache and looks like a grimmer Clement Attlee. My mother remembered him as a modest, soft-spoken man.

Morris had a hard life, and now Sam had one too. For the whole of my father's childhood and adolescence the family lived in the sort of poverty where there was often not enough to eat, spending months at a time dependent on handouts from Jewish charities and the 'Public Assistance Committees' – the latterday Bumbles who had taken over from the Poor Law Boards of Guardians.

There were no compensations. This was not one of those semi-mythic Jewish homes of Arnold Wesker's play *Chicken Soup with Barley*, where newspapers were avidly read and discussed by a procession of friends and relatives. From what little I could gather from my father in later life, this was a depressed household, almost pulverised by poverty. It may even have been that my grand-mother – paranoid about strange people and strange ideas – was mentally unwell for much of her life. Intellectually there wasn't much going on at home.

But my father was different from the rest of the family. From early childhood he was articulate, and impatient with his constrained and difficult life. In his book *Far from the Tree* the American writer Andrew Solomon examines the phenomenon of

children who, in one way or another, are not like their fathers or
mothers. Solomon argues they have two identities, the first vertical
and the second horizontal. The vertical identity is passed on from
parents to children by virtue of upbringing, geography and group
allegiance. So my father was Jewish: circumcised, observing *shabat*,
attending the synagogue, and reciting the prayers. He was uneducated: bookless, unread to, badly taught. He was poor and immo-
bile, had never travelled, going only as far as he could by grabbing
on to the back of a lorry or a cart along a few streets. And these
attributes he shared with his parents and many of the people
living around him.

The inherent, differentiating trait that my father seemed to
possess, Solomon's horizontal identity, was a ferocious determination to learn. As far as I can tell he put childish things behind him
before his teens, left the others to their street sports and slum
mischief, and as soon as he could took off down Cable Street,
turning right where it became Royal Mint Street, passing under
the railway bridge, and walking the 400 yards down Leman Street,
where a rightward kink brought him to the Whitechapel Library,
above Aldgate East underground station.

This unexpectedly elegant red-brick building, put up in 1892 by
a gentile philanthropist, was then nicknamed the University of
the Ghetto. Outside was the world of uneducated people shoved
together in tiny houses on dirty streets. Inside, the sons and
daughters of migrants from the Pale read books and newspapers
and tried not to disturb the sleeping tramps. Another East End
Jew, the playwright and poet Bernard Kops, feeling that he too
was 'different from my brothers and sisters, and I don't know
why', many years later wrote a poem about what the University
of the Ghetto meant.

> The reference library, where my thoughts were to rage,
> I ate book after book, page after page.
> I scoffed poetry for breakfast and novels for tea.
> And plays for my supper. No more poverty.

Welcome young poet, in here you are free
to follow your star to where you should be.

That door of the library was the door into me

And Lorca and Shelley said 'Come to the feast.'
Whitechapel Library, Aldgate East.

The Library hadn't come soon enough to help my father's formal education. In 1930 Sam had failed the grammar school entrance examination, that unforgiving, irrevocable and absurd sorting out of little sheep and goats that dominated the English educational system then. And failure meant being schooled with the kids who weren't expected to shine academically or to read books, but to bide their time impatiently before joining a stagnant labour market and contributing a few quid to the family finances.

At fourteen he ran away, my father's apple rolling further from the orchard, picking up speed as it went. He had heard stories of the mining communities of the Welsh valleys and decided to go and see these fabled singing proletarians for himself. Hitch-hiking there and back, he slept in barns and under hedges, living like any itinerant in that depressed time. He probably followed the route of the old A4 through Marlborough, past Silbury Hill and then made the detour round the estuary of the Severn through Gloucester and into Wales.

He arrived there, I know, though we never got around to talking about what he found and who he met, or even how long he stayed. Probably only a few weeks. But on the journey somewhere he picked up a group-A streptococcal bacterial infection, which translated itself into rheumatic fever. In the days before antibiotics such infections could kill or permanently damage the body. In Sam's case it meant six months in hospital back in London, six months off school, and a weakened heart. And six months of reading and thinking.

In her memoirs Doris Lessing asks the question about my father
that had clearly worried her younger self:

> Why had the party chosen a young man who had read
> nothing of modern literature, and was not interested in the
> arts, to represent culture?

She was right about the modern literature, but for the rest she
couldn't have been more wrong. Autodidacts – completely self-
taught men or women – begin with nothing but an understanding
of their own ignorance and a determination to overcome it. The
self-taught have had the assistance of no conversations at home
about novels or writers, no intriguing books with inviting covers
on the shelves; they haven't been read to, spoken to, taken to
exhibitions, concerts, theatres or museums. They have had
nothing given to them and they live at first in what they deduce
must be an almost unbridgeable gap between themselves and the
educated world. What does the scholar know that they don't?
How can they know it too? So they set about the business of
learning. The self-taught have to storm the castle of knowledge,
to wrestle baffling information to the ground, and they live in
the learn-it-by-rote world of encyclopaedias. So they usually start,
not with the fashionable and possibly ephemeral, but with the
classics.

That's why my father didn't spend his time on modern literature, or indulge an easy 'interest in the arts'. By the time he met
Lessing – had she but known it – he had read Goethe, Schiller,
Dickens, Tolstoy, Cervantes, Balzac and Shelley. He had taught
himself German and some Russian. (At eighteen, imagining a life
building socialism on the edge of the Gobi Desert, he had even
taught himself some Mongolian out of a German–Mongolian
dictionary. The war, of course, put an end to that scheme.
Otherwise I think he might actually have gone through with it
and I might be vending yak-milk in a suburb of Ulan Bator. If
Ulan Bator has suburbs.) In his late teens Sam, when he wasn't

selling cheap tat door-to-door on the Isle of Dogs, was a regular in the Reading Room at the British Museum.

He had no interest in popular culture. It was of no use to him in trying to catch up with the educated, with the unmet Doris Lessings. No musicals, no flicks, no football or any other kind of sport. Later in life he permitted himself the occasional TV sitcom, but he became known to his grandchildren as the septuagenarian who would drive in a day from Urbino to Stuttgart to see just one painting by Lucas Cranach in the Staatsgalerie.

His family hardly understood, let alone encouraged this eccentricity. As Andrew Solomon, the writer of *Far from the Tree*, puts it, 'ostensibly desirable variances are often daunting', and they were daunted. The more so because Sam decided that though he couldn't help being Jewish and therefore hated by the local Irish boys, some of the newspapers, and the small but noisy and growing fascist movement led by Oswald Mosley, he could help being religious. Judaism was superstition and superstition was, to him, anti-knowledge. He'd have none of it.

It was the scarlet banner that replaced the Mogen David, since the other 'horizontal' identity Sam acquired was that of Communist. He had already seen some of the brightest and most animated of the young Jews in the East End selling the *Daily Worker*, and holding street meetings about fascism and poverty, the young orator standing on a crate or a stepladder. The dirty brick of the factory and railway walls and even the pavements were daubed, cleaned and re-daubed with whitewashed slogans. Another East End poet, Charles Poulsen, was a slightly older Young Communist in Stepney, and it was often his work Sam would be looking at. Poulsen wrote a poem called 'The Whitewash Squad'.

> So the street or the wall is our canvas, our paint is whitewash
> Our theme is class conflict, our love is expressed as hatred:
> Oh workers of all lands unite, no power can be stronger,
> And here is the place of our meeting. We need each other.

'Our love is expressed as hatred'. At the end of 1934, at the age of fourteen, my father joined the Stepney branch of the Young Communist League. Ten years later, at the end of the war, Sam explained to a Party committee what had motivated his membership. 'Hatred of Fascism,' he replied. 'Hatred of capitalists who squeezed the blood out of my father and made Stepney the slum it is.'

But love expressed as love was there to be had as well. The YCL was a place where friendships and romances were made. One boy my father admired was Harold Rosen, the father of the poet and children's writer Michael Rosen. Harold came from a raucous, disputatious and political family, had passed his 11-plus and gone to grammar school, so was already an intellectual in Sam's eyes. And there was one girl too: the punchy Bertha Sokoloff, with braided hair, brown-skinned and eloquent, who – though still in her teens – became one of the leaders of a famous rent strike by local Stepney tenants.

In his memoir of his youth, Charles Poulsen described a meeting of the Stepney branch of the YCL held in a cellar under a Bethnal Green tobacconist's shop. 'There were about a dozen of us; we sat on old boxes from the fruit market, and an oblong orange crate provided the chairman's table. It was lit by a bare electric bulb, and no sooner were we seated than it went out, leaving us with no light but the gleam that filtered in through the pavement light.'

Michael Rosen, however, was told that his mother and father 'met up by a table-tennis table at the YCL', so perhaps some more expansive premises had been found by then from which to plot the revolution.

Whatever the Cable Street school authorities thought of my father's activities, which included selling the *Daily Worker* both inside and outside the school, they didn't have to put up with them for very long. At just fifteen he exited the gates and was now in the world of work. Which, in 1935 in East London, was mostly the world of out-of-work, with 11,000 unemployed in Stepney alone. 'My father,' he wrote later to a Party appointment

panel, 'resolutely opposed my taking a trade because of unemployment, especially in tailoring, and I drifted into dead end jobs
with long periods of unemployment.' He touted for errands, ran
messages for anyone who'd employ him and went to the library.
Anything to keep out of the family's two rooms with their close-
closeted smells of cabbage, commodes and unhappiness.

In 1936, when the British Union of Fascists and National
Socialists decided to route one of their blackshirt parades down
Cable Street, Sam acted as a runner for the comrades who were
putting up barricades. The Fascists, famously, had to give up their
procession. He was caught by the police while out with the
whitewash squad and fined – his one conviction. With many of
his older comrades leaving for Spain to fight on the Republican
side in the Civil War (eight Stepney men died in Spain), he leaf-
leted and raised money for the anti-fascist cause.

Around this time – probably in 1937 – Sam declared his love for
Bertha. I have to try to imagine the conversation that went on
between him and Bertha before he wrote this letter in January 1938,
when he was barely eighteen. It was probably written from a ward
in the London-County-Council-run St George-in-the-East Hospital
where he was suffering a recurrence of the effects of rheumatic
fever. Had she mentioned something about his clothes, or his smell?

If it's dirt (!) you are protesting against – remember it's on
my hands and not in my heart. Apparently my father still
isn't working and I hardly know on what my parents are
subsisting.

Do you think I grumble over-much at my condition? Tell
me if you think so for one hasn't much time for self-pity in
the struggle. But the thought of returning home tenses my
nerves like bow-strings.

Yours sincerely, Samuel.

A week or so later he recounted to Bertha how he spent his
time around the ward:

I and the nurse have been having great arguments on religion, for I have declared to her my atheism. Ugh! Ignorant cow! Ignorant of literature, ignorant in her belief, vulgar in her sophistication . . .

One wonders what the nurse thought of these exchanges. But then there's a passage which, in retrospect, explains much that happened later:

I wasn't over-keen on coming here. But I was dreadfully weak and depressed, quite incapable of doing anything useful. For three days I trekked from Labour Exchange to Labour Exchange and from one employer to another till I was sick with humiliation . . . Do not bring any fruit – some novels if you want.

By the end of February Sam was in Kent, in Ward 1a of Queen Mary's Hospital, Sidcup – an LCC convalescent hospital. Ward 1a was a large room full of beds containing rheumatic fever patients. Next door was another with a complement of men with TB. And beyond that was a ward full of sufferers from St Vitus's dance. The regimen was fresh air, and the large windows were always open to the icy weather of late winter. 'This morning a heavy mist overhung the ground and you could barely see the sun, a weak ineffectual, coloured disc, peering out of the east,' wrote Sam, who was obviously recovering his spirits. He then launched into an attack on East End philanthropists, such as the famous Quaker, Mary Hughes, whose work for East Enders went poorly rewarded here:

Though I have much affection for Mary Hughes and her Quakerism, the old feeling of hate for religion is returning to me. It's hard to forget that Mary is a giver of Charity and what should one hate more than this? Once it was in my mind to write a little book of sketches of East End life . . . Perhaps I should start off something like this:

The East End is to rich spinsters and well-meaning men what the Pacific Islands are to the anthropologist . . . Our pleasures are fast being spiritualised and now one goes a-slumming and not so frequently a-hunting. One plunges into the East End as one would into a mudbath in a Mayfair Beauty Clinic.

I have the feeling that in this letter my father was picking a political fight with his lover, testing out his own arguments. Many years later Bertha wrote a book – something of a eulogy – about Edith Ramsay, the middle-class daughter of a Highgate clergyman, who 'plunged' (in young Samuel's words) into the poverty of the East End in 1920. It's probable that Bertha, even then, would have felt warmly towards Mary Hughes, of whom Ramsay was a protégé. One senses a young lovers' tiff by proxy. 'You must love AND HATE to live', my father added, possibly as an explanation. 'Nothing insipid for me, thank you . . .'

There are only three photographs of him from this period. Two were taken in 1938 on a ramble in the countryside on what was obviously a cold day, perhaps weeks after leaving the hospital. The first is out of focus. In the second a group of four have stopped to eat. Sam, spectral pale, intense and thin, sits looking directly into the camera lens, a sandwich in his hand.

The third is very different. It's clearly a warm day, he's in his
shirtsleeves and allowing himself a smile. His arm is draped over
the shoulder of a tanned, pretty woman with sturdy legs. On her
other side is a young chap whose smart raffishness reminds me
of Pinkie in the film of *Brighton Rock*. But the difference is not
just in the weather and the smile. My dad in 1938 was somehow
beaten down. The back of this photograph, made into a postcard,
reads 'June 30, 1940. Brighton'. Sam Aaronovitch in that wartime
summer has become a more confident man. To me he looks as
though – through Bertha and politics (he had joined the Party
proper a year earlier) – he was beginning to find his joy.

If I'd been him I might rather have been terrified. France had
just fallen. On Guernsey on the same day that the photograph

was taken, 113 nautical miles away from Brighton (and what other kind of miles are there between the two places?) German planes landed to begin the occupation of the Channel Islands. The beach at Brighton had been closed earlier in the month and barbed wire and concrete blocks now ran down the strand, so the trio hadn't been walking on the shingle. If the feared and expected Nazi invasion had happened, Sam, as a Jewish Communist, would have been one of the first on the list for detention and destruction.

Yet he smiled. Three months earlier Sam – now married to Bertha – had been rejected as physically unfit for military service by the Army Medical Board. But this meant that, at last, he could enter the world of the true proletariat, as jobs appeared in factories deprived of workers or building the machinery of war. Now he could leave the world of the piece worker, the rag trade and Yiddishkeit and become a British working man.

In 1940 he was given a job with Armstrong Whitworth in Coventry, missing the infamous bombing raid by a few hours. And then in early 1941, 'under pressure from my wife' (as he later told a Party board), Sam applied for a job at the Rolls-Royce engine works in Glasgow, possibly the most politically radical city in Britain. He and Bertha made a home in Glasgow, sharing lodgings and even a room with Scottish comrades whom he had found through the Party grapevine.

Sam loved Scotland. The country was, he later told an interviewer, 'like wine, like alcohol to me'. Unlike the East End whose people were either escaping from the past or living in another, ancient homeland in their collective mind, Scotland had a present history. And the factories and shipyards of the Clyde were a great and recent part of it.

Between 1941 and 1942 – in which time Russia went from being a tyrannical ally of Hitler's to being a heroic ally of Britain's – the Party group at the Rolls-Royce plant grew from 50 to 250. Sam, who had discovered an aptitude for speaking in public and explaining the virtues of Marxism to tentative revolutionaries, was seen by the local Party leaders as a new political talent.

Now Sam met a couple who were to be a big part of our family life. The District Secretary of the Scottish Communist Party at the time was a gaunt Edinburgh man, the former signwriter Johnny Gollan. Gollan, eight years older, was ascetic, and another autodidact. 'He was like me,' Sam said after Gollan's death in 1977. 'We were both people who had a struggle to learn and we learned largely by doing things, or writing about things – but what we never had was any systematic education.' Gollan's elegant and temperamental middle-class English wife, Elsie, acted as the Scottish District Treasurer and – the Party being an organisation which respected hierarchy and proletarian discipline – was the only person who could shout Johnny down; 'to everybody's pleasure,' Sam said later.

In April 1942 Gollan asked my father to become 'Lit Organiser' for the Scottish Party. 'Lit' was a party word. It meant all the material that the Party or Party sympathisers published for distribution or sale: leaflets, pamphlets, short tracts by the greats of Marxism, booklets, magazines and even – if the buyer was keen enough – the clunky Soviet-printed *Collected Works of Marx and Engels*. So Lit organisation was the practical arm of the Party's propaganda work, and was central to everything that an agitational organisation did. Without it the masses wouldn't even know that the Party was there, and the members would never progress into being the vanguard of the proleteriat.

Besides, Party members venerated adult education. This was a trade union tradition (the bigger unions held 'schools' in country houses ironically bought cheap as the aristocracy declined) in which uneducated men and some women first learned the business of chairing meetings, taking minutes, writing agendas and even public speaking, and progressed to reading the classics and learning languages with the help of organisations like the Workers' Educational Association, founded in 1903. Members wanted things to read and to discuss. Sam made sure they got them.

Though still working at Rolls-Royce, Sam, just twenty-two, set about Lit with an almost heroic vigour. Had there been a Party

Distinguished Service Medal he would have earned it in a nine-month spell in which, among other things, he gave birth to several Party bookshops including Clyde Books in Glasgow, and a Party publishing company, Caledonian Books. He was the Icarus of Party activism, soaring on home-made wings towards a proper Party job – and in 1942 he got it.

The war had left civil organisations, including the Communist Party, short of men. Sam now applied to be exempted from war work in the factory so that he could take up the post of Propaganda Secretary of the Scottish Party. In an extraordinary display of bourgeois tolerance (or of clever calculation about where he would be less of a nuisance) the authorities agreed. So he became what he was to be for the next twenty-five years – a Party 'full timer', a man whose life was entirely given over to revolutionary and left-wing politics. 'And that,' as he said later, 'was really how I arrived.'

I can imagine him in his time of liberation, unshackled from poverty, home and Jewishness, connected now to the romances of Scotland and the Scottish working class, and with a job to do. A paid job. 'From John O'Groats to the pits in Dumfriesshire; from outside factory gates in Govan and beside the shipyards of Harland and Wolff', Sam would get on a box holding a loudhailer and preach about the workers of the world uniting and the need for a Second Front to help Russia. And not just workers. In an archive I found a letter of his to the film-maker and Communist Ivor Montagu from December 1944 mentioning speaking on Russia at a meeting of the Milngavie Literary Association, where, with characteristic precision, he mentioned that 370 people had been present, 'mostly suburban democrats'.

Amongst comrades like Willie Gallacher, the Communist MP for the mining constituency of Fife, and Johnny Campbell, the veteran imprisoned in 1924 for sedition, Sam was schooled in what he called 'the University of Scottish Communists'. And though the English Socialist William Morris was my father's original literary hero, Robert Burns became his poetic inspiration:

> *Then let us pray that come it may,*
> *As come it will for a' that,*
> *That Sense and Worth, o'er a' the earth,*
> *Shall bear the gree, an' a' that.*
> *For a' that, an' a' that,*
> *It's coming yet, for a' that,*
> *That man to man, the world o'er,*
> *Shall brothers be for a' that.*

Sam was determined that it would come. The war ended and around that time so did his marriage to Bertha, who had gone back to Stepney. (They had married too young, she told me many years later. They both still had too much exploring to do.) Sam returned to London at the end of 1945 with the intention of taking up Party work in the capital. He acted as election agent for two successful Communist candidates in the London County Council elections.

By 1946, in Labour Britain, Sam was to be found living in salubrious digs on an 1890s Boehmer and Gibbs Art and Crafts estate on the southern edge of Hampstead Heath. John Betjeman had been born there and Lissenden Gardens was more E. M. Forster than Robert Tressell. My father cannot possibly have afforded the rent himself so it may be that his second wife – whom he married at around this time – owned or rented the flat. This was an age of lodgers, and an elderly Welsh Communist wrote to me a few years ago to say that he and his newly wed wife had also shared the smallish flat.

Until very recently I knew astonishingly little about my father's second wife, the mother of my half-sister Frances. She was born Kirstine Uren (a Cornish name), sister to Ormond Uren, whom you will be hearing more of, and sister-in-law to his wife Rose, the French dentist whom you met briefly in Chapter 1. I don't know exactly how they met and I never got to hear Sam's version of why they later divorced. Records tell me that they were married in Edmonton in 1946. I also know that together they wrote a book called *Crisis in Kenya*, published by the Party publishing house in 1947, a condemnation of the economic consequences of settler rule in a British colony.

Sam had no background in economics and, of course, he had never been abroad, let alone to Africa. Back before the war he had helped a man called Surat Ali in organising what were called 'lascar' seamen in the Port of London. These Indian, Chinese and African sailors aboard merchant vessels were discriminated against, poorly paid and often abused by their employers, and as the Second World War began they went on strike. So my father, who had delivered strike leaflets to them in their quarters aboard ship, was already interested in the colonies and their peoples, but that was as far as his prior knowledge will have gone. He made contact with sympathetic academics and even civil servants, but I can easily imagine him – at all possible hours – in the British Library, searching for the data on land usage in the Maasai Mara or Happy Valley.

About the time he and Kirstine were finishing writing the book Sam was appointed by the Political Committee of the Party to a new job, and one that was to last nearly a decade. Operating from the HQ in King Street, Covent Garden described by Doris Lessing, he became first a full-timer on 'cultural work' and then Cultural Secretary of the Party. His was to be the tricky job of herding historians, thespians and novelists in the service of Marxism and in the direction of Communism.

In the Party's archive, held in the People's Museum in Manchester, I came across one of Sam's great attempts at conquering the world with information. He wrote to Party members, 'comrades', in all the cultural professions, requesting details and figures. How many journalists were employed on British national newspapers? How many on regional papers? What proportion was in the National Union of Journalists? What did a standard Equity contract contain? How many students of architecture were there in British universities? How many documentary films were made in Britain in a particular year? And then he compiled the results for future use because, in his mind, if you had the data and a Marxist analysis, then the rest would follow. Work, work, work. Rigour, rigour, rigour. My father was the king of Empirical Capture. He remained like that for the rest of his life.

Did this make him dark? Doris Lessing, writing of their meeting around this time, says that he was grim and sardonic.

He heard me out like an officer interviewing a rookie, and said he was intrigued to meet an intellectual who wanted to join the Party, when most of them were leaving it, and he looked forward to reading my denunciations of it when I left.

Internal party documents bearing his signature from this time are mildly hectoring and gently tedious. 'My immediate aims,' he writes in a personal statement to Party officials, 'are to contribute to a large scale development of the Marxist training and ideological work of the Party.' Later he is set upon 'improving our ideological work' which is 'lagging behind' the Party's activism and he wishes to 'improve our practice as Party writers, artists, historians, architects etc.' Why? 'Because as cultural activity is taken up by wider circles, the solution of the problems which arise out of this very activity require continuous ideological discussion and leadership.' In other words, there has to be rigour and intellectual discipline.

To get his argument over required what might be called the Stalin-Socratic dialogue. 'Why is it essential to overcome this weakness?' he asks the comrades about their ideological work, replying, 'It is essential to overcome this weakness because . . .' And then he tells them.

But there was a paradox here. The ideologico-bureaucratic idiom Sam adopted for written internal communication was clearly not the one he used everywhere else – and no one who knew my father ever described him to me as being in any way 'grim'. He was, for example, a favourite at Party schools, where he persuaded, charmed and flirted. Another rare photograph shows four men holding racquets on a scruffy tennis court on a hot day. The back says 'Sam, Hastings, 1948'; the thin white stripe on the right, skinny, shirtless and grinning, is my father, and this is his one known foray into sport until, much, much later, he became an improbable distance runner.

The tennis court must have belonged to the large house near Hastings where the Party held its summer schools. The Party archive contains several group photographs in which sixty or seventy Party members in three rows smile across a lawn at the invisible cameraman; behind them the wing of a large house that is past its best. One of these pictures has Sam, in shorts, sitting at the centre of the happy group. For years before his death and afterwards I would hear from people who said how wonderful he had been, what an inspirational speaker he was, how he had a way of smiling while he spoke that made them warm to him. I don't think they were just being nice.

Despite his charm, in 1950 – just after the birth of their daughter Frances – he and Kirstine separated. The following year he met my mother. They married in January 1954 and I was born on 8 July that year. Two days earlier Sam, now a member of the Executive Committee of the Party, chaired a meeting of the Cultural Committee. In his summing up of the discussion he talked of the 'special leadership of Communists'. Hearing him out were the historians Eric Hobsbawm, Christopher Hill and A. G. Morton, the composer Alan Bush, the writers Derek Kartun, Brian Behan and Jack Lindsay, the International Brigadier Len Crome, the artists Kim James and Barbara Niven, the philosopher Maurice Cornforth and the literary critic Arnold Kettle.

By the time I began to know my father, six or seven years after this meeting, he was no longer skinny, and that obviously made him happy. The extra pounds he had put on had transformed his pigeon chest into something more like a barrel. A hairy barrel, since the thick black hair on his head was almost matched by the hair on the rest of his body. At any outdoor excuse he would throw off his shirt, puff out his chest, hold in his stomach and preen. Around the house he would move naked and confident from the bathroom to his bedroom, his circumcised penis poking like a little pink face from what D. H. Lawrence would have called his loins. This sight was a minor puzzlement to me, since he had had none of his sons circumcised, and as a child I wasn't quite sure what had happened to make him so different. Perhaps it was age. Perhaps it would happen to me. I hoped not – it didn't look comfortable.

With his clothes on – usually a jacket and tie – Sam would present himself as a good-looking, large-featured man of medium height, wearing thick-rimmed glasses to correct his astigmatism. He laughed a lot and enjoyed plays on words. He told me a joke once involving a woman being impenetrable and inconceivable, but I didn't quite understand it. His voice, retaining a gradually diminishing East End twang, had a slightly gravelly and mellifluous timbre. When he wasn't shouting (and he reserved his shouting for his home and children) it was a pleasant and an effective voice, a radio voice. Had things gone differently for him he would have made a fine presenter on BBC Radio 4, perhaps fronting statistic-heavy editions of *Analysis*.

LAVENDER

In 1950 Jock Nicholson, a Party organiser in Scotland, met Bridget Long – a single mother – at a Party school. They fell in love. She had two school-age children and was living in Belsize Park in London and so, if they were to be together, he would have to move south. In a memoir he published fifty years later with the help of his union, the National Union of Railwaymen, Nicholson recalled the telephone discussion he had with the Scottish District Secretary after requesting a transfer 'for personal reasons'. The conversation went like this:

'What is your personal reason? Is it domestic?'

'No.'

Pause.

'Is it a woman?'

'Yes.'

'Don't tell me you've got yourself involved in some trouble.'

'No, it is quite straightforward and honest.'

Long pause.

'Well, you'd better put your request before the comrades on the committee. You should be prepared to give a full explanation, otherwise it will be very difficult for the comrades to understand.'

Nicholson put his case to the comrades and it was agreed – by them at any rate – that he would stay in Fife helping the Communist MP Willie Gallacher till the forthcoming general election, and only then be allowed to depart. By the time he got down to London he and Bridget had been apart for eighteen months. But he now understood that whom a Communist full-timer cohabited with – and where – was almost a committee matter. He probably already knew that, if possible, one ought to marry within the faith.

So who did Sam choose for his third Communist wife?

My childhood memories of my mother, Lavender, are over-coloured by my spectacularly difficult relationship with her. Much of the time I feared and distrusted her and she clearly – but conflictedly – did not like me. It has taken me until now to understand it, and perhaps I haven't quite grasped it even yet. Back then I knew things were bad, I just didn't know why.

To an objective onlooker my mother probably looked more Jewish than my father. She was dark-haired and though she had worn her hair soft, full and wavy in the '40s (and was to do so again in old age), by the time I was noticing such things it was in the short early '60s bob that made women look like overgrown

boys. This cut emphasised her rather splendid beaky nose, her
small eyes, her pronounced front teeth and her excellent English
rose complexion. (I am not sure my mother ever had a spot in
her life.) Even after three children, of whom more later, Lavender
had what I think is called a good figure, full-busted, slim-waisted
and strong. She liked animals, bicycles, North Wales, films and
underdogs. And, just as my father did, when her planets were
aligned she enjoyed laughing. I remember going with her as a boy

to see a famous French comedy, *Monsieur Hulot's Holiday*, starring the lugubrious comic Jacques Tati. Every few minutes my mother would make a strangled noise, as though the air in her lungs had built up sufficiently to burst her ribcage and there was no escape. And then, just as a seizure or an explosion seemed unavoidable, a great tide of air, like the Severn Bore, rushed up her windpipe, forced its way through the chicane of her vocal cords and emerged into a startled cinema, having been transformed into a whinnying 'heeeeeeeee!' Though usually easily embarrassed, I loved that laugh. It couldn't be simulated, so it meant that for once she was happy and that nothing could go wrong.

For years I assumed that my mother's politics were a product of her relationship with my father. It turned out not to be true, but the mistake was understandable. Her background, in all material ways, could not have been more different from his. She was the result of an alliance between the younger scions of two upper-middle-class manufacturing families. Not of Jews, as you might have been expecting, but of the English shires.

My grandfather's people, the Walmsleys of Lancashire, owned a carriage works in Preston where they built first for the horse-drawn trade and then, as the nineteenth century waned, for the horseless kind. Arthur Wyndham Walmsley (hereinafter just 'Wyndham') was born in 1897 – the year of the Queen's apparently unrepeatable diamond jubilee – in Westmoreland. The 1911 census found him, aged thirteen, boarding at Dover College, a private school that seems to have turned out more than its fair share of military men and missionaries, including the officer who won a posthumous VC at the Somme for kicking footballs across no man's land.

Wyndham was destined for the army, and was sent to Sandhurst in the second year of the Great War. In 1915 he was gazetted into the Army Service Corps, essentially the unromanticised people who kept the soldiers supplied from Blighty up to the furthest forward trench. Within months, however, he was shipped over to the Channel to fight with, as he put it in a letter much later to my mother, 'one brand new pip on each shoulder and an expectation of six months'. He was in reserve with the 20th (Light) Division at the Somme, and was wounded in the slight and capricious way that seemed to mark his military career. Three miles from the front, as he rested on a reverse slope, a spent German bullet managed to pick him out and strike him in the foot between his big and second toes. There was, he said, 'much blood' and he was carted off to a field dressing station. On a stretcher next to him was a disgruntled officer called Robert Graves.

The following year Wyndham was injured again at the Battle of Cambrai when he and his dapple grey mare – nicknamed Pissing Lizzie by the squaddies – encountered an early British tank coming over a ridge. The terrified horse bolted towards German lines, stopping suddenly at some barbed wire and pitching Wyndham over the barrier into no man's land. He escaped with a broken wrist.

Perhaps it was when convalescing from this latest wound that my mother's father met my mother's mother, Ida May Greatwich. Ida was on the London stage, and – always attracted to theatricality and pulchritude – when he saw her Wyndham became a stage-door Johnny, waiting for her with flowers as she left the theatre. My grandfather, a tall and handsome young man in uniform, must have been persuasive and he and Ida were married in Chelsea in the late summer of 1917. Only just in time. My aunt Eve was born in April 1918.

Ida had been born above the Severn in Bridgnorth in Shropshire, also in 1897. Her father was a woollen yarn manufacturer in an area of carpet-making. The family was later rich enough to move a few miles down the river to a William and Mary mansion near Stourport-on-Severn called Lick Hill House. We have one photograph of the young Ida, who was full-lipped, with perfect skin, large eyes and lustrous hair.

When the war finished Wyndham decided to stay in the army. What else could a younger son do? His even younger brother Hugh had also stuck to the services, having transferred from the infantry to the Royal Flying Corps. Eventually he was to become Air Marshal Sir Hugh Walmsley, KCB, KCIE, MC and DFC, last Commanding Officer of the RAF in India. (Given connections like these it has always amused me when I have written something for a newspaper about national identity, and – as quite often happens – a dissenting correspondent has written arguing that with my foreign antecedents it isn't surprising that I don't *really* understand the English.) So began a genteel but increasingly penurious existence for the young family, as the pay for junior officers in peacetime was nowhere near as high as their social aspirations.

Their second daughter, my mother Lavender, was born towards the end of February 1923 in Murree, a hill station in what was then British India and is now Pakistan. Murree, incidentally, was also the birthplace of Sir Francis Younghusband, the Christian soldier who massacred the Tibetans, and Sir Reginald Dyer who, less than four years before Lavender was born, had even more notoriously massacred the citizens of Amritsar at the Jallianwalla bagh. (Discovering exactly where her eyes had first opened proved to be a problem because, though none of her children knew until I discovered it ninety years later, my mother was registered at birth as 'Phoebe'. The only known Phoebe in our family was a pet rat my mother bought and had christened. Her private joke, presumably.)

My grandfather was then stationed in the Punjab, making his way glacially up through the officer ranks, and Ida had gone with him, leaving Eve back in Britain. There are a few grainy pictures of my mother as a baby being carried in a basket on the back of a sherpa on the 14,000-feet-high summit of the Yamhar Pass. She even had a Gurkha ayah or nanny.

Soon the family was back in London. Wyndham was attached to Chelsea barracks and both he and Ida were attached to Chelsea society. The Walmsleys were going through hard times: Ford's mass production had killed the carriage trade and the various investments that Wyndham's father engaged in, from property to shares, turned out never to yield anything as tangible as money. Ida received no great sums from her own family, but she was not poor in connections. Possibly the most influential of her Severnside contemporaries was Diana Brinton, daughter of the chairman of Kidderminster's greatest carpet company and therefore another sprig in the great bouquet that was the West Midlands manu-facracy – an elite that was topped by the Baldwin Iron Works, of which Prime Minister Stanley Baldwin was the most famous flower.

While the males in her family went into the carpet business and played county cricket for Worcestershire, Diana became an artist. In 1922, and only in her mid-twenties, she was elected Secretary of the London Group of British artists. This was a society rivalling the Royal Academy, but particularly interested in exhibiting young artists who were overlooked by the arts estab-lishment; members included Jacob Epstein, Barbara Hepworth, Henry Moore and the Bloomsburyites Roger Fry, Duncan Grant and Vanessa Bell. In 1925 Diana Brinton began a love affair with the older artist and sculptor, Rupert Lee, who had fought in the Great War and was eventually invalided out of the forces suffering from shell shock. Together the Brinton Lees became an important part of the London art scene – and that's why in London in the mid '20s the Walmsleys, the young officer and his wife, found themselves at interesting parties in artistic places.

One of these events took place in a large house in St John's Wood into which the Brinton Lees had just moved. The occasion, Wyndham wrote in a much later letter to my mother, was a slightly chaotic one. There was:

> Rupert, a superb raconteur raconting; poets, one with long hair and a tri-sexual look about him, many artists; Val Gielgud and Lance Sieveking from the BBC, who I had met when we were on leave in Kashmir.

Anyway, Wyndham continued, so many were there that:

only a few of the guests had the desire or opportunity to sit anywhere. Thus I found myself lying half under a large table. Lying alongside me was a plumpish lady wearing a kind of smock and slightly the worse for alcohol. She studied me at close quarters for some time, then asked me to come to her studio and sit for her. I think she assumed I knew who she was. Later I asked Diana about her. It was Vanessa Bell.

Wyndham went to Mrs Bell's studio and was sketched. He had no idea what had happened to the picture, but perhaps it still exists. Anyway, Wyndham's out of barracks life had him under that table with Vanessa Bell, then at another party (he insisted) with the writers Vera Brittain and Winifred Holtby who shared a house in Cheyne Row, and on the town with the roistering and ubiquitous painter Augustus John whom he met in the Good Intent in King's Road, 'at that time a favourite place for the Chelsea lot to foregather, eat, drink and scrounge'.

This intermittent social existence made up a little for the problem that peacetime soldiering was boring and didn't pay. Still, as far as we can tell, the handsome soldier, the pretty mother and the two daughters lived happily enough in a succession of flats and rented houses in Battersea and Barnes. Lavender adored both parents.

Then, in the summer of 1930, the first signal tragedy of her life occurred. That August my mother had been sent off to stay with friends of Ida's family – the Vales – near Stourport-on-Severn while a new baby arrived. It was obviously a difficult labour, and Ida spent a fortnight or more in bed. A letter she sent to Winifred Vale expressed her frustration at being ill and also her concern for Lavender, who was clearly not relishing the idea of being ousted as her mother's youngest child. 'Was it', wondered Ida, 'a case of green eye'?

On 16 August, out of bed at last and sitting in the garden, Ida was stung by an insect. Maybe it was a Home Counties gnat, a tiny female close to the end of its own short life. My great-aunt

Dorothea Walmsley (a genial unmarried games mistress every-body called 'Dick') wrote up what happened in her economical style in her pocket diary. On Sunday 17 August, 'Ida's face very swollen.' 18, 'Ida very ill.' 19, Ida 'Taken to nursing home in St Leonard's. Operated on. Poison has gone right through her.'

On Wednesday 20 August, at the Oval, the Australian Don Bradman scored 232 runs in the fifth Test against England. That night, according to Dick, 'dear old Ida died'. The funeral was held in Bexhill three days later, and then my mother was driven to London by Wyndham and his brother. 'You did not want to go,' Dick wrote to Lavender later, 'and clung to me. Then you decided to be brave and ran downstairs and gave Wyndham a slap on the back and off you went. You can imagine the state you left me in.'

My mother returned to Stourport and the care of the Vales. The baby – my aunt Gill – went to an orphanage. Eve stayed at boarding school. My grandfather was called back to his barracks. Aunt Dick, teaching in Bexhill, would cycle out every Monday during a free period to put flowers on my grandmother's grave. It is an irony that my utterly impoverished Yiddisher grandmother survived to her late eighties, but my genteel, pretty grandmother didn't see her thirty-fourth birthday.

Her daughter Lavender was now becoming a Worcestershire girl. Robert Parsons Vale was the middle-aged son of Thomas Vale, who had started a construction company in Worcestershire, and seen it thrive. 'Uncle Bob' worked at the company, and lived with his wife Winifred ('Aunt Winnie') – the daughter of a seed merchant – in a large, slightly secluded, modernish house called The Upland, part of the village of Wilden, on the smaller Kidderminster road parallel to the Staffordshire and Worcestershire Canal that linked the Severn to Wolverhampton. They had no children of their own but had already extended their hospitality to Ida's when the occasion demanded.

Books could be written about the strange synergies that existed before the Second World War between the conservative and supremely bourgeois lives of the provincial capitalists and English bohemianism. It's there in D. H. Lawrence's *Women in Love* in the mud-death-sex struggle of the mine owner's son Gerald Crich and the artist Gudrun Brangwen. It was to be there too, in a vastly more attenuated sense, in the way that Winnie and Bob reacted to my mother. It was there in Wilden itself. The small church of All Saints, just down the road from The Upland, contains fourteen stained-glass windows by Edward Burne-Jones, produced by the William Morris company. They were commissioned by the local steel manufacturer, Alfred Baldwin, whose wife Louisa was the sister of Burne-Jones's wife, Georgiana. A third sister had married a Mr Kipling and produced an exceedingly good writer called Rudyard. A fourth was wed to Edward (later Sir Edward) Poynter, painter and President of the Royal Academy. Alfred and Louisa were the parents of the man who was both the Vales' local member of parliament and their Prime Minister, Stanley Baldwin.

And there is my second irony of the chapter. My mother would be taken to church in the 1930s and gaze upon a gold threaded altar frontal designed by William Morris and paid for by the Baldwin family. At roughly the same time my father was reading Morris's works on socialism and his fantasy of a socialist utopia, *News from Nowhere*, in which there were no slums, or capitalists, or Baldwins, but a brother- and sisterhood of craft and joy.

Life in Worcestershire was not hard. There were servants, trees to climb trees, and ponies. But Lavender expected continuously to be called back to a father and a family of sisters, to be returned. When, less than two years after Ida's death, Wyndham married a Theodora Taylor, seven years younger than he was, my mother anticipated a reunion, a call from London. It never came. For whatever reason – perhaps they felt that Ida's children were best left where they were, or maybe Theo did not want to raise someone else's family – Eve, Lavender and Gill were not called back. Instead Wyndham and Theo began their own family, mostly of boys, and contact was sporadic. It was, for my mother, a crushing rejection that scarred her psyche for ever.

Uncle and Aunt were kind, staid, limited, reserved and provincial. And my mother – perhaps slightly aware at seven of the mild bohemianism of Chelsea – grew up at a tangent to their world. In it and not of it, she simultaneously manipulated it and hid from it. Her Whitechapel Library was inside her own mind. She would sit in trees, concealed by branches and leaves, and drop pine cones on the heads of passing adults. Or, taking up station under the big table in the drawing room or behind one of the sofas, she would secretly eavesdrop on adult conversations. Some of these concerned the doings of her distant father whom she still worshipped and who, she wrote later, occasionally 'made forays into Worcestershire to see me and borrow money from Auntie and Uncle'. She realised that her guardians did not approve of Wyndham, but she decided that she was on his side.

Perhaps understandably, the isolated ward began to live a fantasy existence. At her secondary school, Kidderminster High School for Girls, she told her credulous classmates that she was an ill-used Cinderella of a child who had lost her mother. But her heroic father, who even now was fighting brigands and rebels on the North-West Frontier, was one day going to return and rescue her.

This lie, which she persisted in, created a social dilemma for her. Isolated as she was, she longed for playmates, but she couldn't ask anyone back to The Upland who might, as she put it later, 'blow the gaff' on her fabrications. There were one or two girls – like Barbara Broad the hairdresser's daughter and Betty Lewis the butcher's daughter – whom she liked and felt she 'could fool', but her aunt was something of a snob and refused to allow her to invite these tradesmen's children for tea.

There was only one way out of her own trap. 'I made up a great load of misery and poured it into poor, gullible Auntie's lap. I told her how miserable I was at school, how bullied and cruelly treated I was, and demanded to be taken away.' In pursuit of her campaign Lavender refused to eat, grew pale and meagre, until at last Auntie Winnie gave in. My mother 'entered a potty little private school and began all over again, two years older and a lot more discreet'.

The 1930s were drawing on. Lavender became a boarder at Malvern Girls' College, alma mater to, among others (but not contemporaneously), Green Party MP Caroline Lucas and Dame Barbara Cartland. There Lavender bullied other girls who were happier than she was ('I was spiteful', she said to me not long before her death, 'because I enjoyed it') and consciously passed on to them some of the misery that had been unconsciously doled out to her. But she also formed the usual passionate attachments, one of which was to an older girl called April Senior Tolson who was apparently the school rebel. Together they became 'reds' and – in the shadow of the Malvern Hills – championed the cause of the Spanish Republic in the Civil War.

Lavender may have been encouraged in this radical affiliation by her mother's old friend, the artist Diana Brinton Lee. In 1936 she and Rupert Lee had just organised the first International Surrealist Exhibition in London, the famous event at which Salvador Dali delivered a lecture while wearing full diving gear, including a brass helmet, and almost suffocated in the process. Later that year, after General Franco rather less amusingly invaded the Spanish mainland the Lees signed the English Surrealists' 'Declaration on Spain', condemning the British government's policy of non-intervention and calling for arms to be sent to 'the people of Spain'.

News of Diana's declaration would certainly have reached her family's acquaintances in Worcestershire, where the Vales were in the process of moving from The Upland to Sandbourne, a large house on the edge of the Severnside town of Bewdley. I visited gloomy Sandbourne, with its Gertrude Jekyll garden, a couple of times as a child; after its sale and demolition in 1971 to make way for a middle-class housing estate, some of its furniture and books came to my mother, and after her, to me. It isn't hard to imagine Diana turning into that gravel drive in 1937 to try and collect money for her Relief Fund to help Basque children affected by the Fascists' bombing raids.

Lavender's older sister Eve, however, offered a nearer example of radicalisation. In 1937 she had gone up as an undergraduate to the University of Reading – the only new university to be opened in England between the wars. There she was wooed by a young man who intended to become an agrarian socialist and who was studying at the university's excellent School of Agriculture. Wooed and, in 1939, married. Mike Richardson was a fiery, noisy, craggily handsome man, who – as a letter of the period implies – seriously discombobulated my grandfather by requesting his daughter's hand in marriage, 'as I presume that's what someone of your class demands'. Wyndham contemplated giving him a thrashing, but my grandfather was now over forty and, besides, a bigger conflict was imminent.

As war began, my mother's undistinguished time at Malvern was coming to an end. Various illnesses and her dislike of many of her teachers meant that she had never caught up with her academic studies, and no one seems to have regretted her departure at sixteen *sans* qualifications. They may have imagined (if they thought about it at all) that she would eventually get married and disappear into a child-heavy detached house with a large garden in a Kidderminster suburb.

Lavender – like many others who survived – had a happy, almost blissful war. She was becoming an attractive young woman, and now there were useful things for bourgeois women to do. She joined the Women's Auxiliary Air Force (or WAAF) and worked on the barrage balloon units guarding key targets in the Midlands, and then as a driver on Wellington bomber airbases. She made friends and the many pictures of her in this period show her to be, if anything, radiant. In Bewdley, on leave, she attended parties for the young Free French officers who were stationed there and thought them charming and romantic.

Perhaps she had too happy a war. Simple maths puts the moment of my half-sister Sabrina's conception at some point in late February or early March 1945. By the time of VE Day, as everyone else celebrated, Lavender probably knew that she had rather more to look forward to than most, and rather sooner. The father was a good-looking and amiable young airman whom either she did not want to marry or who did not want to marry her. To this day I have no idea what his name was.

Sabrina was born in or near Crewe in December 1945. There, perhaps because Lavender was now in disgrace with the Vales, and her sister Eve and radical brother-in-law Mike were attending the nearby Reaseheath Agricultural College. The next few months were probably spent staying with people who would have them while Lavender tried to find a place to live for her and her baby.

But then, in the spring of 1946, my single parent mother did a most extraordinary thing. One of the best-selling books of 1940 had been an account of how, between the wars, a Canadian called Thomas Firbank had taken over a Welsh sheep farm in the Snowdon range. The book begins with his description of how, the day he arrived, 'wild flurries of rain and mist shut out the skylines, and the steep, rocky slopes reared upward till they were swallowed by the clouds'.

The farm, Dyffryn, cost Firbank £5,000 for 2,400 acres of boulder, ridge and sloping meadow. There he and his feisty wife Esmé, a former actress from Surrey, learned how to survive the elements, rear lambs, castrate rams, shear and dip, and even how to open a profitable summer snack bar beside the valley road. I know that my mother read all about them in the book, and I know where. The copy I'm looking at now is inscribed to Lavender's guardian Uncle Bob, 'R.P. Vale, Sandbourne, Bewdley'.

So when the Women's Land Army, which kept going through demobilisation, needed help on a Welsh sheep farm, Lavender volunteered and was somehow chosen. To Dyffryn and to Esmé (Firbank himself had found a new lover during the war and didn't return) my mother went, carrying her little daughter with her. And there she stayed for a while, working on the farm, living in a small cottage and effectively hiding from the world. She and

Sabrina were there in shine and gale, when the electricity failed
and when the snows cut off the valley.

My favourite photograph of Lavender is of her at this time
atop a Welsh peak on a rare limpid day, rope around her shoulder,
looking over a landscape of cliff, peaks, moors and lakes. My
mother could be impulsive, adventurous even, but she liked soli-
tude. For years she insisted that she wanted her ashes scattered
from the summit of Snowdon, which stood across the far end of
the Dyffryn valley and which she had climbed many times.

But the WLA was being wound down, and Sabrina would have
to go to school, so by 1948 Lavender was back in London. She
took various lodgings in Hampstead, which in those days was a
place of fine houses subdivided into a warren of badly converted
flats, let by those who had fled from the bombs to those who
couldn't or wouldn't. She had restored her relationship with Uncle
and Aunt and after a year or two they gave her what was to be,
perhaps, the Golden Goose of the Aaronovitch family. Uncle Bob
bought a house for Lavender on the un-Hampstead side of
Hampstead Heath. It was a semi-detached 1920s affair on a tree-
lined avenue on the Holly Lodge Estate, a few hundred yards
from the trolleybus terminal at Parliament Hill Fields. (From then
on, though the family usually had no money, we had a home.
The Vales of Worcestershire subsidised the Communist Party just
as the Baldwins had employed William Morris. Baldwin, however,
got a church out of it.)

My mother went on a secretarial course, learned to type and
got a job as secretary to an official in the Engineering Union.
And she took in lodgers, one of whom – I discovered from the
electoral register for 1952 – was Ormond Uren, the brother of
my father's second wife, the Kirstine with whom he wrote the
book on Kenya.

Ironically, it must have been around the time that she became
a young homeowner that Lavender formally joined the Communist Party (the exact moment of her apotheosis is lost now, unlike
my father's). The Party branch she joined was the same one,

however, that Sam, half a mile away in Lissenden Gardens, already belonged to.

By now they had a small network of acquaintances in common, but they actually met at the flat Sam shared (Kirstine having moved out) and in late 1952 they seem to have been living together. In another rare picture, taken on a Box Brownie by a third party, Doris Lessing's grim young man stands with Lavender in the garden of her house on Bromwich Avenue, a huge smile dividing his face from ear to ear. In that moment, for all that came later, they were certainly happy. He was content to have a lover with a small daughter, since his own, Frances, was living elsewhere. Lavender was delighted and amazed to find a man – a Communist man, a moral man – who would take on both her and Sabrina.

At the beginning of 1954 in St Pancras Town Hall they were declared Party man and Party wife. In July of that year I was born. I have no idea why they chose David as my first name. But the middle name they gave me was Morris, after both my grandfather and Sam's hero, William Morris.

Wyndham re-enters the tale briefly at this moment. The story – as my mother told it to us – went that he turned up at Bromwich Avenue shortly after I was born and met my father, whom he did not like at all. Wyndham supposedly later described Sam to one of his other daughters as 'that hairy Jewish gorilla' and the description got back to my mother.

I had begun to think that this might be apocryphal – a convenient way of rationalising the twenty-year estrangement that now took place between Wyndham's family and mine (I met my grandfather only once before he died). But then I came across a letter Wyndham had sent to Lavender in the late '70s after they had been reconciled. The eighty-year-old retired Lieutenant Colonel, in the middle of one of his usually funny and rather well-written short epistles, described a visit to see a grandson at Charterhouse public school. There, he said, he and his wife Theo had 'watched students come and go; Wops, Chinks, Nips, Fuzzy Wuzzies; the lot. I only hope,' he added, 'that the overburdened, browbeaten and bedeviled English tax-payer is not footing the whole bill.'

Given where my mother was born, given his own impecuniousness and constant need to borrow, given that he must have known that his granddaughter Sabrina was right then happily bringing up two half-Greek Cypriot children – given all that, the staggering insensitivity, the unearned sense of superiority and the lack of irony in that passage tell you something important and damning about Wyndham and indeed almost his whole class. It tells you something too about what Communists thought they were fighting against.

4

Party Life

Monday 10th: Branch meeting in evening. Report on industrial discussion at congress. V. dull!
Tuesday 11th: Extended area meeting in the evening.
Thursday 13th: Evening. Went to Sam's class on surplus value. Very good, exhilarating to see light dawn on new members re profit etc!!
Friday 14th: Sold Daily Workers with Jean – 21, not bad! Another Soviet spaceman up – Colonel Bykovsky.
Saturday 15th: CND Summer Fair
Sunday 16th: Off to Burnham Beeches with the Socialist Sunday School. Cheered by the news that the Soviet Union have sent up a woman into space – Valentina Tereshkova, age 26. What a lift for us women!

Lavender Aaronovitch, diary, June 1963

Only on the Wednesday of that June week did Lavender Aaronovitch (née Walmsley), aged forty, part-time secretary and mother of three, not do something political. And if there was anything odd about those seven days in her Party life, it was that, unusually, there was no demonstration – or 'march', as we called them – held at the weekend.

Lavender began to keep a diary in January 1963, when I was eight, and continued to write for the rest of her life, starting with little, stubby pocket diaries in which she'd be lucky to fit sixty words for each day. The early entries consisted mostly of an editing together of birthdays, meals, illnesses and meetings; only later did she begin to use her writing muscle, and write in larger A5 diaries and notebooks, recording something of what she felt beyond the one most common word for her state of mind – 'depressed'. But even when they are at their most laconic and functional, her entries help make sense of my childhood impressions and revive mothballed memories – of a film, perhaps, a record, or another disastrous family holiday. My father, of course, was a paid activist, but everything my mother did she did out of conviction, love or guilt – and so we led a life that was dominated by the odd rites and practices of British Communism.

Every fortnight began, like that particular week in June, with the gathering of the comrades at the 'branch meeting', the secular mass of a Party existence. The meeting was open to every card-carrying member of the Party in an area, college or workplace – in

my parents' case, in the 'Parliament Hill Fields and St John's' district of the northern part of the London borough of St Pancras. I think in this period there were 30 or 40 of them – often husbands and wives – of whom 8 to 20 would turn up on any given branch meeting night.

Often these would be held at our house, in our sitting room, its one wonky green sofa and armchair supplemented by a flotilla of chairs of various shapes and sizes commandeered improbably – like the small boats at Dunkirk – from rooms as distinct as the kitchen and the bathroom. My siblings and I would already be in bath or bed by the time, at around seven, the comrades arrived. They might be heard at the garden gate, their different knocks suggesting whether it was an older or a younger branch member, then footsteps along the hall and the door opening, perhaps a glimpse from the landing of someone shuffling off an overcoat and putting it in the cupboard just inside the door.

The comrades might have a cup of tea, a little gossip and then would settle down to the minutes of the last meeting, a reminder of forthcoming events and finally move on to the political discussion. The subject of this last – which would be 'led' by a branch member – could be almost anything from the 'Great Rates Swindle' to the progress of the revolution in Cuba. Many nights their gentle burble and the smell of Frank Loeffler's pipe ushered in sleep for us children.

In March that year Lavender told her diary that the branch meeting had heard one of its own members – General Secretary John Gollan, back from a trip to Moscow and Peking (these were pre-Beijing times) – 'reporting on talks with Khrushchev and Lui Chou Schi'. This was a glorious thought, a serious discussion between a mouse and two elephants, since Mr K was General Secretary of the Soviet Communist Party and Liu Shaoqi was Chairman of the People's Republic of China. My mother added for that night, as on so many other nights, that my father was home 'v. late'.

If the branch meeting was a sitting-room affair, the branch committee meeting was a kitchen-table business. On alternating weeks, the officers got together to make sure that in their small part of the world democratic revolution was functioning properly. Most active branch members, unless there were very specific reasons why they couldn't, took a turn on the branch committee.

There was a branch treasurer whose responsibilities included the sale of the monthly stamps which Party members would stick in their Party cards. (To be badly in arrears with your stamps was a sign of moral weakness.) Optimally the treasurer took charge of the annual ritual of 'recarding' – a local version of the census of Caesar Augustus, except that instead of everyone going into his own city to be taxed, the branch officials would undertake the journey to each member's home to issue the next year's party card.

Then there was, of course, a lit organiser. As the Communist message of peace, socialism and solidarity with the struggles of workers worldwide was unlikely to occupy much space on the BBC or the relatively new ITV, the main way in which Party members could discern the Party line was to have it delivered to them in the form of a booklet. This was the lit the lit organiser organised and Lavender was several times appointed to the position.

Had she been more confident she might have become – at least, episodically – the true power in the branch: the Branch Secretary. The chairman, I should note, was the least important functionary of all, usually someone emollient and well spoken, who could preside over branch meetings without letting certain members become too long-winded. Despite Orwell's dystopic insight that 'he who controls the past controls the future, and he who controls the present controls the past', the secretary's puissance did not reside in the writing up of the minutes. It was the contact he or she alone enjoyed with the Party hierarchy that conferred real status. In correspondence with the Party centre, the secretary was the first to receive the circulars and bulletins concerning Party actions and statements.

In another part altogether of the writing zoosphere John le Carré captured the spirit of local Party life in his novel *The Spy Who Came in from the Cold*, published in 1963. The hero of the book is Alec Leamas, a rumpled and supposedly failed spy who is actually the key cog in a complex British plot to snare a top East German security official. As part of his cover Leamas takes a job in a library devoted to 'Psychical Research', where he meets Liz Gold, a young woman of Jewish origin. The two are attracted to each other and sleep together. A little way into their courtship Liz and Leamas have a conversation that reveals her secret.

'You've got me wrong,' she said, 'all wrong. I don't believe in God.'
'Then what do you believe in?'
'History.'
He looked at her in astonishment for a moment, then laughed.
'Oh Liz . . . oh no. You're not a bloody Communist?'

Liz is not just a rank-and-file member, but the Secretary of the Bayswater South branch of the Communist Party of Great Britain (a fictional jurisdiction which, in reality, would consist mostly of Hyde Park). The Communist Party that Le Carré presents, through Liz, is one composed of well-meaning dupes, bores, sexual misfits and traitors. Not very much like the Parliament Hill Fields branch at all, with its earnest lawyers and health workers. The fictional branch's treasurer, George Hanby, 'was a pompous, dirty-minded little man, always leering at her and trying to touch her'. She only became secretary because someone called Mulligan had proposed her election, thinking 'she'd sleep with him if he got her made secretary', while 'the others had voted for her because they liked her, and because she could type. Because she'd do the work and not try to make them go canvassing at weekends.'

More people are hymn-singers than door-knockers. I certainly remember comrades who disliked taking part in the evangelising and who, like Liz Gold, might have preferred simply to attend meetings and lectures. Activism is a difficult way of life, and the Party was quite small. In October 1963 my mother lamented in her diary: 'Monday. Branch committee in the evening. There seems so much to do, no-one to do it. No Lit last week, it's terrible.'

But the *Daily Worker* did not sell itself. Or rather, though some *Workers* were sold at newsagents' and some were delivered to the homes of supporters, it was considered a necessary aspect of Party activity to sell them on the street. The idea – which seemed natural to me as a child – was that a presence could spark a conversation, a conversation a sale, a sale a contact, a contact (in time) a conversion. So as Jehovah's Witnesses or Mormons would go door to door with the good news, Communists would stand on street corners selling it. Branch members had their rota for *Worker* sales, they sold in pairs, and Lavender's turn seemed to come up once a fortnight.

She fulfilled her duty in all weathers. 'Gaitskell dead. Usual hoo-ha,' she wrote on 18 January 1963. 'Went with Wally through snow and ice to sell dailies. Sam home very late.' And on Friday 8 February, 'Sold Workers with Elsie. Freezing! But sold.'

'Hoo-ha', incidentally, was how Lavender described those moments when the capitalist press and the BBC decided that a death or birth or other event was of sufficient importance to require special treatment of the 'nation mourns' or 'country celebrates' kind. It was my mother's way of noting her refusal to be co-opted into an emotion she – and many others – did not feel. She was selective, of course. The acclamation for Gagarin was not a hoo-ha at all, but in 1965 when Winston Churchill died, that was a very big hoo-ha indeed.

Thinking back on it now, Lavender and the elegant Elsie Gollan must have seemed an odd pair to call 'Daaiiillyy Wor-ker! Dai-ly paper of the Left!' in their distinctly middle-class accents outside Kentish Town tube, blue-nosed on a chilly morning. At that time the area was solidly working class, with large council estates and rows of terraces subdivided into accommodation for poorer families. If she ever felt the incongruity of her situation, my mother never expressed it in my hearing.

The daily paper of the Left had not finished with Lavender for that weekend. On Sunday afternoon, a thousand Communists and sympathisers came together in the Royal Albert Hall – just across the park from Le Carré's Bayswater South – for the annual *Daily Worker* rally. General Secretary Gollan made a big speech attacking the Tory government, after which the legendary East End Communist, Solly Kaye, wound up with a vigorous call for money for the cause. The Red Army choir – like Welsh male singers in uniform – was not able to be present as planned, due – Lavender told her diary – to a ban imposed by the Foreign Office.

My mother was 'as usual' one of the voluntary stewards. She wore a red armband, took the tickets, pointed people to their seats, and as comrade Kaye reached his exhortatory crescendo, passed the collection tins down the rows of seats. Three years later, aged eleven, I was a steward too, and was as proud of my armband as I was of the long-barrelled Wyatt Earp Buntline Special (provided with linseed to oil it) that I was given for my birthday the following year.

Another winter morning, a week in which Charles de Gaulle, President of France, said he would veto Britain's membership of the European Economic Community and – probably unnoticed by my mother – Charlie Watts joined the Rolling Stones, Lavender was out on yet another Party errand. 'Got up early, ploughed through snow with Elsie to give out leaflets re the closing of the line at Gospel Oak. Freezing.'

The line in question was known as the North London Line –
one of the very few rail links running east–west across the capital.
This was the era of Beeching and there was a belief that the
future belonged to the motor car and that local rail was somehow
obsolete, so there were constant plans to shut it down. The
campaign which the Parliament Hill comrades and others waged
was successful and despite several subsequent attempts to abolish
the service, it remained, and is – at the time of writing – so
popular that you can rarely find a seat on one of its sleek trains.
Today's commuters cannot know they should thank those chilled
Commie leafleters of a generation ago.

The business of producing leaflets was one every Party
activist understood. Sam worked out of a succession of Party
offices where somewhere, in an inky corner, on top of a
cupboard or a table, stood a duplicating machine. A stencil was
made, ink poured in and a handle turned to produce hundreds,
sometimes thousands, of single-page A4 or A5 leaflets. Next to
the machine was a large bin where the smeared casualties of
an imperfect process would pile up almost as fast as the mound
of good leaflets. Party members would then pick these up and
distribute them in high streets, outside stations and on housing
estates. All gone now. Roneo, Roneo, where now art thou,
Roneo?

At weekends, on a Saturday, Mum would sometimes go and
sell *Workers* or hand out leaflets at a regular outdoor 'speaker
pitch'. This would be a street corner or a bit of pavement deemed
particularly likely to attract a small crowd to listen to someone
sounding off for half an hour or so about greedy landlords or
monopoly capitalism. The performance would take place from
the second step of a three-step stepladder, with a placard propped
up against it. The speaker would use a loudhailer to address
passers-by in a strangely altered, crackly voice – three-quarters
human, and one-quarter Dalek. Good pitches were occasionally
contested by various political groups. In May 1963 Lavender turned
up to sell *Daily Workers* at the usual place in Camden Town 'only

to find that the West London Young Socialists had pinched our pitch!' Such acts of geographical and political encroachment were a matter for some irritation. Why couldn't these rivals stick to their own pitches?

Advancing the Party's case through getting the message out was one half of a member's duty. The other half was the relentless business of raising the money to do it. The Labour Party famously had trade unions to contribute directly to their coffers, and the Conservatives got a lot of money from wealthy donors. For smaller parties, allowing for the occasional bequest from that unlikely person, the rich Communist (and excepting the small amount of cash that came secretly from Russia), it was down to the members. Jock Nicholson, the railway worker who stood as the Party candidate in St Pancras North for over twenty years, wrote in his autobiography that his ingenious wife Bridget used to charge to take visitors on 'Marx and Engels' walks round parts of North London where the hirsute revolutionaries had lived and worked. Otherwise, members provided money through Party dues, collections at Party events and choosing (as Lavender did all through her life) to cut the Party in on a share of any windfall.

Since standing on the street shaking a collection box was unlikely to make money for the Communist Party, the best way of raising cash was to sell things. Post-war austerity cast its shadow well into the '60s. American-style cornucopia was yet to arrive in Britain even though it was six years since Britons had discovered from their Prime Minister that most of them had never had it so good. And things were not cheap. Almost any product, except cigarettes and spirits, cost more as a proportion of a normal income than it does now. People had less and could afford less.

Several times in 1963 my mother mentions being part of a team that would take over a couple of classrooms or the assembly hall of an Edwardian primary school (to be had at

the cost of the caretaker's overtime), put out five or six trestle
tables and a table where someone would collect a nominal
entrance fee, and sell jumble. The jumble sale ('rummage sale'
or 'flea market' in America) was the easiest fundraising operation to organise. Jumble being stuff you didn't want but that
someone might buy.

Comrades were not generally wealthy and there was a good
chance that if they or the people they collected from didn't want
something, no one else would want it either. (There were two
exceptions: clothes that the children had grown out of before
the garments had given up the ghost, and clothes belonging to
people who had very recently done just that. Dead people left a
lot of good knitwear.) Sometimes such sales disappointed even
my mother's low expectations. 'Jumble sale,' reads one entry for
1963. 'Not really enough jumble.' But I can also remember the
almost glorious randomness of what would appear on those
tables – collections of incomplete jigsaws, old and often broken
toys and souvenirs from various holidays, usually in what were
known as 'the socialist countries', and my amazement at the
things that people would buy. Cast-off knickers. Pairs of patent
leather shoes.

While jumble sales were a drab if sometimes blitzily cheerful
way of taking money from the poor (while helping them out),
Daily Worker bazaars were shinier affairs, organised well in
advance, taking place in grander buildings such as town halls at
Christmas or in springtime. Everything at a bazaar was new and
nothing belonged to anyone just deceased.

On 25 February 1963 my mother told her diary that after
having spent the afternoon lobbying 'at the House of Commons
with teachers on the local government bill', and there being no
branch committee meeting that night, she 'started on toys for
bazaar'.

When I first read this entry a year or so ago I was puzzled.
Then – a flash of memory – I remembered the sitting-room table
that sat in the bay window, covered in scraps of brightly coloured

felt. My mother would make one kind of 'toy' – little, soft mice. She'd take three pieces of green or red material, sew them together leaving an opening, and then stuff her creation with cotton wool and close it up. On to the very roughly musine object she would sew little eyes, thread whiskers, front legs and, finally, a black tail. She could make ten or so of these while watching *Play for Today* and when she had enough she would hand them over, as a donation, to the bazaar organisers. These mice must have been bought by someone – Lord knows who – otherwise she wouldn't have continued to make them.

Despite their scarlet tablecloths and aura of newness, I wasn't as interested in bazaars as in jumble sales. Greyish arbitrariness was replaced by brash predictability as every year the same things appeared on the bazaar stalls – things that weren't of much interest. For the adults there were prints, posters, records and books, mostly cheaply imported from behind the Iron Curtain. And then there were the things made by Party members, invariably women: mostly cakes and pincushions. Besides my mother's handiwork, the toys too were imported from Eastern Europe and Russia, were made of wood and were folksy. There were lacquered pop guns, strange oversized egg cups in which you were supposed to catch a wooden ball attached by a string, pecky hens stuck to one side of a table tennis bat, that would dip and raise their heads as the bat was moved around. These were wholesome artefacts, of the sort favoured by modern Steiner parents looking for more 'natural' toys for their offspring than the usual guns, cars and plastic dolls. For the same reason they were despised by us children.

More money was raised from members and their families through Party socials. We held dozens of these at our house. Comrades paid on the door and often brought the bottle that they would pay to drink. Others had friendship or acquaintanceship, but a Party member had comradeship: a common purpose, a shared view of the world, a mutual understanding. The French origin of the word (which of course they probably didn't know), originating in the Latin *camera* – room – meant people who shared a sleeping room. It evokes a warm, companionable chamber in a Renaissance inn, with the cold outside and human association inside. The wind howls, the comrades debate, tell stories, mend their hose and snore.

Other less lucrative duties filled any available space. On 24 February Lavender spent her Sunday meeting 'new recruits' to the Party, most of whom, she wrote (without apparent irony), were 'overworked working mothers'. In the afternoon she 'called on Rothsteins with lit.', which meant climbing the hill behind our house to deliver a tract or two to the veteran Communists who lived there. My father wouldn't have been available to look after me and my brother Owen, who came along two years after me, since he was at a weekend Party school from which he returned that evening 'whacked'. That Tuesday my mother wrote: 'Sam home late. He has not one free evening this week.'

Wednesday was a day for meetings, which 'began very badly with harsh words about money. Went to work in tears. Sam off to Oxford for the night speaking to students. Went to hear James Aldridge on Bulgaria. A fascinating talk.' Better still was the evening in November 1963 (a week before the assassination of President Kennedy) when Lavender went to listen to Party member Margot Heinemann lecture on 'the modern novel'.

Heinemann was a celebrated party veteran, beautiful and brilliant, with a sad and romantic past. At Cambridge in the mid 1930s with, among others, the historian Eric Hobsbawm, she had fallen in love with the young poet, John Cornford. It was to her that Cornford sent the famous poem 'Heart of the Heartless World' shortly before he was killed while fighting for the Republicans in Spain. Very few Party homes, right up to the '60s, would not have had this poem somewhere in the house.

Heart of the heartless world,
Dear heart, the thought of you
Is the pain at my side,
The shadow that chills my view.

The wind rises in the evening,
Reminds that autumn is near.
I am afraid to lose you,
I am afraid of my fear . . .

After the war Heinemann, also a poet as well as being a teacher, had raised a daughter with the Communist scientist J. D. Bernal and was often seen at Party events, elegant and quiet. When she did speak, though, she clearly had a didactic gift. 'I never enjoyed a lecture more,' wrote my mother.

Perhaps the most visible and public thing Party members did to show their affiliation and beliefs was to attend demonstrations, or as we said at home, 'to go on a march'. Many Party branches had their own banners, some rather scrappy things with the lettering hanging off, others magnificent constructions with shiny wooden poles that you could take apart for carrying, and gold letters on a scarlet background. The Parliament Hill Fields banner was a middling one, but the comrades were proud of it and enjoyed taking turns to carry it. Occasionally there would be a panic when there was a march coming up and no one could remember who had taken the banner home after the last one. Hadn't Pete and Elvira had it on the No To German Rearmament march last Sunday? Or was it Ken Herbert who'd decided that the branch should be represented on the lobby of Parliament in support of striking dockers?

Hefting the banner was hard on the shoulders, especially when there was a wind. If you were marching into the gale the poles pushed back and dug painfully into the carrying comrade's scapular notch. If the tempest blew from behind then the shoulder was strained forward as the comrade attempted to stop the banner blowing away and landing on top of the Islington comrades or whoever were walking along in front.

So for those who weren't quite up to banner deployment, or who had already taken their turn at one end of the standard or were still awaiting it, there were placards to wave. Placardry was also a minor (if less spectacular) art. For some marches – not most – the Party would have produced the placards itself and they were straight from the placardeers, fresh blonde sticks emerging from behind well-printed posters, with a Party-approved slogan on each one: Fair Rents for Tenants, Homes Not Bombs, Support the Railmen. You'd first encounter them stacked in the Party offices or in the Party van, poles up, waiting to be unloaded.

Though a spanking new printed placard smelled and felt good, even as a boy I preferred the home-made ones. Often these were recycled affairs with darkened wood and a new bit of paper pasted or stapled over the old one, kept in a cupboard under the stairs or a cellar and then brought out and re-inscribed in crayon or newfangled 'magic marker' with the bearer's own slogan. These were both more unreliable and more heartfelt than the Party ones, sometimes misspelled, often almost philosophical in tone. Ban the Bomb marches were the best for these self-created placards, which might just consist of a large question mark or an extended question such as 'Which is to be banned, the bomb or the human race?'

The march itself had its pleasant rituals for a child. The toddlers were wheeled along in pushchairs, carried on their dads' shoulders, or given little flags to wave. The street was suddenly not for cars, but given over to the stroll-bunch-shuffle-stop-space-stroll again cadence of a city centre demonstration. People chatted, the occasional bystander waved or shouted 'Go home to Russia!' (an insult which, given my grandparents' origins, I initially thought was remarkably and worryingly insightful) and then we would leave before the end, take a short cut, and have a lemonade at the Lyons Corner House near Trafalgar Square, where our marches would often finish up in a series of amplified speeches from the plinth above Nelson's lions.

There would be chanting – essentially shouting in the streets – which seemed almost transgressive in early '60s Britain, and was therefore delightful. These yells would take the form of simple repetitions of a phrase or rhyme; the most effective in my childhood marching years addressed the war in Vietnam and was imported from America. 'Hey, hey, LBJ, how many kids did you kill today?' was a spectacularly successful distillation of observation, anger and pleading. I remember not liking so much the call-and-response chanting when someone with a loud voice or a loudhailer would give a first line or word. Even as a ten-year-old I thought the collective answering made us sound like sheep, reacting together to a shepherd's prodding.

Best was when there was music – a guitar or two, and a protest song, which quickened the tempo of the demonstration. If the trade unions were involved in an official way there might even be a marching brass band from a Yorkshire mining village.

Marches differed in tone and mood. In 1962, aged seven, I remember us driving my older sister Sabrina to the beginning of the annual Easter march organised by the Campaign for Nuclear Disarmament, which was forming up on a tree-lined road near the Nuclear Weapons Research Centre at Aldermaston in deepest Berkshire. That mood was one of excitement because the range of people was so different and somehow less restricted and more optimistic than the usual demonstration, despite the terrifying theme of the impending nuclear holocaust. Sabrina and the others marched the forty-five miles back into London over four days from Good Friday to Easter Monday and I imagine that no one who was there has forgotten it.

Every year, on the first Sunday in May the Party would hold its own May Day march in which the emphasis was on working-class unity and the Party itself. We'd start at the Embankment and end up in Hyde Park for speeches, sandwiches and schmoozing with the comrades, and in my memory the sun always shone. In 1964 the Sunday was 3 May and my mother took us all along, with my three-month-old brother Ben in his pram, noting in her diary that 'Sabrina looked lovely with the Young Communist League banner'.

There were solidarity rallies for Greek Communists, there were meetings of the Young Communist League for Sabrina, there were Party day schools in small halls and there were Party weekend schools in trade union country houses and in a rather odd collection of green-painted huts in the Kent countryside called 'Coppice Camp'. I was too young to go inside the huts when lectures were going on, but the historian Raphael Samuel told the story of a comrade called Ernest Keeling attending a session on elementary Marxism given by a grizzled Scottish Party veteran. 'What,' demanded the older man, 'happens to the state under communism, Comrade Keeling?' 'It, er, flows away?' ventured the nervous neophyte. 'It wither.r.r.r.rs away, Comrade Keeling, wither.r.r.r.rs away!'

Learning or marching, leafleting or jumbling, there was never not something for a member of the Party to do. There was never not an action that had to be undertaken for the sake of the movement. A pause was unimaginable. No vacuum was unfilled. Life was to be fitted in around the unceasing demands of the struggle.

My siblings and I lived in hourly intimacy with Lavender's activism, but since he was hardly ever at home, or if he was he was working on one of his books, Sam's Communist life was perceived in glimpses, rendering it almost exotic. His Party world was different: it was his job; his career, in fact. He was a Party full-timer.

Every so often, because Lavender was ill, having a baby or away on a visit to relatives, Sam would find himself, inescapably, with a child or two to look after for a few hours at a weekend. So he would take Owen and me along with him to whichever Party office he was working in and park us with books and drawing paper for a few hours while he held meetings somewhere else in the building, or made phone calls.

The first office I remember was William Rust House, the headquarters of the London District Committee of the Party and of the Party's newspaper. This was in a five-storey office block on the Farringdon Road, a street running from King's Cross to Blackfriars that had been carved through notorious slums in Victorian times along the line of the Fleet river. Instead of the river, now underground, were railway lines. My memory of looking out of Sam's office window furnishes these lines with steam trains chugging down the cut. But I'm not sure that can be true. Just as it wasn't true – as I also recollected – that the building was an old and rather decrepit place. In fact it had been converted out of a bombed-out brush-and-sponge factory by the architect Erno Goldfinger only a decade or so before. But

austerity, tobacco and busy, careless men had turned it into a
rather smelly and untidy place, even in the mind of an untidy boy.

A place, though, with its own musty romance. In my father's
office a bronze-coloured bust of Lenin on the mantelpiece was
the only decoration. But on the floor-to-wall bookshelves, below
the rows of Soviet-printed volumes of the Marxist classics, were
dozens of bound copies of the illustrated magazines produced in
Britain during the First and Second World Wars. For hours I'd
examine the cutaway diagrams of the impregnable Maginot Line –
which the Germans would obviously never breach – the photographs of effete-looking Indian maharajas who were endorsing
the imperial war effort, or the artists' impressions of the Royal
Artillery at the Marne. Then, since no one actually cared about
these books, I would deface them by placing a piece of carbon
paper and a sheet of A4 underneath a chosen illustration and
drawing round it with a pencil.

This pleasurable minor vandalism went on while my father
was Area Organiser for North and Central London. But in the
autumn of 1963 he was promoted to being District Secretary
in South Essex. South Essex, taking in the north-east suburbs
of London and the new towns between the Thames and
Southend, was a strategically and psychologically important
region for the Party. It was a centre of the new proletarians,
the tens of thousands of skilled workers at the huge Ford plant
in Dagenham, at the electronics giant, Plessey, and the satellite
engineering and components works around them, and who
lived in the terraced houses of Barking or on the new estates
in Harlow, Basildon and Benfleet. If the Party was to have a
future as the sharp working-class prow of a large socialist coalition (violent revolution having been given up, in effect, during
the war) then South Essex was one of the places where it had
to succeed.

It was a longer journey from home to the Party offices in
Essex. Sometimes we would drive up past the white-stoned art
deco magnificence of Walthamstow Town Hall into

the low-rise bustle of Ilford. A migrant town where many lower-middle-class Jews had come to live after leaving the East End (my Uncle Joe among them), Ilford had the smell of spark plugs, oily rags and petrol about it. On a roof in Ley Street, where the party had its shopfront premises, the pioneer John Logie Baird had once worked on his early televisions. It was a coming place where you might almost feel on your skin the warmth of the white heat of technological revolution, as Harold Wilson was to call it.

As you know, Sam Aaronovitch is leaving Central London to become the District Secretary of South Essex.

We think that comrades will want to drink his health and wish him good luck.

So we invite you and all friends to a

FAREWELL PARTY

SATURDAY, JUNE 29th.

from 8 p.m.

at 2 Dartmouth Park Avenue, Dartmouth Park Hill, N.W.5.

(nearest tube: Tufnell Park)

Refreshments available but by all means bring a bottle.

Sam's time here, as I observed it when I wasn't playing with plastic soldiers among the placards and duplicating machines, was a round of leaflet and report writing and meetings with men with cockney accents. Out of the office there were visits to Party recruits in tiny semis in the new towns, and motorcades involving driving around Barking or Basildon in a placarded Party car with a public address system on the roof, telling the shoppers about peace and socialism, the vices of monopoly capitalism and the horrors of racialism (for some reason the Party always called it 'racialism' not 'racism', which I think was originally an Americanism).

This was Sam's routine, his normality. And, in dramatic terms, it was banal enough despite the giant size of the great international cause. Yet sometimes there were episodes of vivid political theatricality in which Sam played a proper part. Such as the Great St Pancras Rent Strike of 1960.

My memory of this event is composed of sounds and images. Of the serious hubbub of men and women coming into and out of our house with leaflets, placards, banners, loudhailers and excited faces. Of taking the bus down to Kentish Town with Lavender or Sabrina, walking to a block of terraced flats and looking up and seeing a barricade and barbed wire on the top floor. Of policemen standing on the street looking at us as we looked at them. Of Sam, in shirtsleeves, on a stepladder, a loudhailer in his hands, regaling a small crowd of passers-by in a compelling voice. Of conversations about a Don and Edie Cook, and how their kids were getting on, given all the strife. And, perhaps more than anything else, being told by my mother how our neighbours on our middle-class road were angry with us because of what our renegade family was doing.

What happened was this. Since the 1930s most homes built in Britain had been built for rent and most of those were council owned. It followed that a very large section of the working class lived in such homes and that the rents they paid

were a big part of their expenditure. So the conditions of the
flats and the size of the rents were of great interest to the
Party. For years it had helped organise tenants' associations on
the larger estates, and had linked these associations with
others – also involving Party members – in other parts of the
country.

In 1959, unusually in its long Labour history, St Pancras Borough
Council was run by the Conservatives, and in July of that year
the councillors approved rent increases in excess of those recommended by the recent Rent Act. It must have been easy to infer
a class motive to the action – the wealthy of the borough imposing
extra burdens on the workers – and in the following weeks a
United Tenants Association was set up, bringing together twenty-
four local associations, with the London Party (and Sam) playing
a big part in its establishment. There was a committee for each
large block of flats and regular public meetings of the tenants
themselves. Demonstrations involving council workers and local
railwaymen (Euston, St Pancras and King's Cross stations were
all in the borough) were held and tenants barracked councillors
inside the Town Hall. Individual councillors were targeted and
their houses were visited by groups of women and their phone
numbers rung at all times of the day and night. It was this which
made us very unpopular locally, since the Conservative chair of
the Housing Committee, Councillor Prior – a gingery balding
man who looked like the vicar in *Dad's Army* – lived with his
family no more than forty yards down the road from us and it
is hard to believe that Lavender did not permit herself the occasional appearance outside the Priors' alongside the comrade
tenants.

In January 1960 the UTA organised the rent strike by St
Pancras tenants, and the council quickly responded by posting
nearly eighty notices to quit. By May these cases were about
to come up in court and it was decided by the UTA that most
of the threatened rent strikers should pay their rents, leaving
a core of militants who would resist whatever action the

authorities took and around whose resistance a campaign could be built. They would, in effect, be martyrs. The ones chosen were a former paratrooper and Party member, Don Cook, and another Kentish Town tenant, Arthur Rowe. Cook's wife Edie was not consulted. Years later she told an interviewer, 'One day he just said: "We're not paying our rent this week", and that was how it started . . . I supported him because I knew by the reaction of people around us that he was doing the right thing.'

Through the summer the legal process ground on towards its inevitable conclusion: forcible eviction of Cook and Rowe by the council bailiffs, aided by the Metropolitan Police. By the beginning of September the flats in the Kentish Town blocks were barricaded and hundreds of tenants had begun a renewed rent strike. It would have been around this time that I was first taken down there to see what was going on.

The Rent Office, where tenants went to make payment in cash, was empty. At Cook's block, Kennistoun House, banners draped from balconies read 'No Evictions', and an effigy of our neighbour, Councillor Prior, was hanging in the courtyard. The barricade at Cook's flat was supplemented by a piano and a pile of old furniture. Now effectively locked in, Cook and a few comrades were supplied with food sent by washing line and, in these days long before mobile phones, a ship's bell was installed on the balcony of a neighbour's flat to warn of the approach of the authorities.

On 21 September Cook sent a dramatic note across the washing line to be conveyed to the Party HQ in King Street. It was intended for publication:

I write this from my barricaded top-floor council flat at Kennistoun House, St Pancras, where we are reaching the climax of a long struggle against rising rents. As we await the bailiffs in the fourth week of this siege, many hundreds of council tenants are now on full rent strike . . . A rocket

stands mounted, ready to fire an alert which will bring
hundreds of neighbours rushing to the defences within
minutes from the blocks of council houses and private
dwelling houses whose roofs I am looking down.

The next morning at 6.45 the rocket went off, the bell rang, and
the tenants came out in their pyjamas to find the police had
cordoned off the approach and that the bailiffs were embarked
on the eviction. Leighton Road was soon filled with demonstrators and bystanders, unable to help the beleaguered rent strikers.
There were scuffles and arrests, but by noon Cook and Rowe and
the others were out. The bailiffs had smashed their way into the
flats, surreally taken tea with their opponents and then seen them
off the premises.

That evening there was a march from Kennistoun House
through Camden Town to St Pancras Town Hall. By the time
the marchers got to Euston Road they had been joined by railwaymen and by militant builders from the huge Shell building
site on the South Bank. One estimate put the numbers of
demonstrators at 16,000, a large number for an essentially local
dispute.

In Euston Road there was a big fight after some of the demonstrators tried to get through a police cordon and into the Town
Hall. The police, unable or unwilling to discriminate between
the militants and the bulk of the demonstrators, laid about both
with equal, gory dispatch. The reporter for the *Daily Express* was
obviously taken aback by what happened. 'It was a nightmare
of confusion of flying fists and boots,' he wrote. 'Unconscious
men, blood streaming from their faces, were dragged across the
streets.'

The now homeless Don Cook was defiant. 'The barricades of
St Pancras have only just begun,' he said in a statement. 'We will
continue to fight and justice must prevail.' Ewan MacColl and
Peggy Seeger, the balladeers for progressive causes, wrote a song.
It began:

As true a story I'll relate
HEY HO! COOK AND ROWE!
How the landlord told Don Cook one night,
HEY HO! COOK AND ROWE!
Oh, you must answer questions nine
HEY HO! COOK AND ROWE!
To see if your flat is yours or mine
HEY HO! COOK AND ROWE!

And ended in a prediction as confident as Don Cook's:

O, now I've lost my board and bed,
I'll barricade the streets instead.
So all you tenants, settle in,
Keep up the fight, you're bound to win.

The rent strike had been exhausting and hope for victory resided in the Conservatives being defeated in the next local election. But eighteen months later when Labour regained power in St Pancras, the new council discovered, after taking legal advice, that they actually hadn't the power to reduce the rents set by their predecessors. So the rents remained high and the tenants paid them. The battle had been heroic, the language had been glorious but the defeat had been total. In deep retrospect I think that the Party realised (though could not admit) that too high a price had been paid for too little gain.

The week after the evictions cinemagoers throughout Britain watched, between the B and the A movies, the Battle of St Pancras as reported by Pathé News. The title of the sequence was *Eviction Battle On!* To dramatic music the plummy but authoritative voice of the newsreader declaimed over scenes of scuffles between police and demonstrators, 'It was as though the social clock had been put back 100 years', before more modestly announcing that 'there has been nothing in London on this scale since the Hunger March thirty years ago.'

Half a century later, on the British Pathé website I found myself looking at events of September 1960 and the scenes outside the Town Hall. At 2 minutes 30 in, on the evening street where a battle is taking place, a demonstrator is about to be arrested by two determined-looking policemen. But a much calmer man in a light jacket and wearing glasses appears behind him and attempts to lead him away from trouble and to the side of the road. That second man is Sam.

5

Family Party

'The theatrical profession,' said Mr Vincent Crummles. 'I am in
the theatrical profession myself, my wife is in the theatrical
profession, my children are in the theatrical profession. I had a
dog that lived and died in it from a puppy.'

Charles Dickens, *Nicholas Nickleby*

You belonged to it, you met your wife in it, you brought your
children up in it. It was a great fraternity, a bit like the Catholic
Church, only secular and up-to-date.

Peter Cadogan, veteran Communist Party activist

How can I give an idea of the complete otherness of the world-
view that I was brought up with? The facts of existence, the
assumptions about how the globe turned that we imbibed were
not the same as – and often the opposite of – what everyone else
deemed normal. Perhaps there are children of very devout
Muslims or Evangelicals who will read this and nod along. Our
world had a parallel history, a separate culture and argot, its own
music, a distinct cosmology. Even where the mental furniture was
the same as everyone else's, it was often put in a completely
different place.

While the Party did connect us with other Communists, our
existence deep in its bosom sometimes isolated us from the
un-Communist world. Almost every relative I had (that I knew

about) was in the Party, with the ironical exception of my Uncle Joe, who never talked politics in my hearing and who was, apparently, an 'observant' Jew, whatever that was. So those that weren't members were dead, mad, or – as in the case of my maternal grandfather, Wyndham – unmet.

There were things that other people did that we didn't do. We didn't believe in God, pray, go to church, stand up for the Queen in the cinema when they played the national anthem (which in any case, wasn't our anthem, our anthem being the Internationale). We didn't moan about strikes, because we liked them, and we would complain about South African oranges in the local greengrocer's when most people had no conception of food being political.

But sometimes it just meant missing out. My best friend at primary school, Michael, who lived just up the hill and was my constant companion, was in the Cub Scouts. So at weekends and some evenings he would dress up in a green jumper and grey shorts, put on a rather fetching-looking cap, and 'go to Cubs'. There he would be involved in something intriguing called 'activities', at the end of which he'd emerge with a new badge to sew on his jumper, or a dangly bit of cord or ribbon.

Every month or so Michael's Cub troop would go to St Anne's church, salute the flag and say special prayers for the Queen, the soul of Baden-Powell, Akela and Baloo or whatever their adult officers were called. I could have gone along to the left-wing variant of the Scouts, the Woodcraft Folk, who also dressed in green and rather anachronistically played a game called British Bulldog, but they weren't so local and I had no close friends who were Folkies.

Most weekends my brother Owen and I did attend Sunday School, though. Socialist Sunday School. Though it wasn't denominational when it had been set up in the nineteenth century, by the time we attended it was almost entirely run by Party members. At St Pancras SSS much of the time was taken up with writing and rehearsing plays with a suitably socialist or anti-fascist theme for the London Socialist Sunday School play competition which took place annually in the utterly romantic if shabby Party-linked Unity Theatre near Mornington Crescent. (I remember playing a Little John outlaw figure one year, and a Nazi general the next.) Our biggest rivals were the children of Marylebone SSS, who were coached by the actress wife of one of Britain's leading thespians, and whose plays, frankly, were amazingly professional.

Other children read comics, mostly the *Beano* and the *Dandy*. We didn't. Not because they were ideologically incorrect – most things were, and policing the whole of life would have been impossible. Nor even because they were expensive, though they weren't cheap. The problem was that the best-known comics publisher, D. C. Thomson, in far-off Dundee, was non-union. In an industry characterised by the strength of its union organisa-tion, D. C. Thomson stood out as a 'scab' outfit so its products were boycotted by almost everyone on the organised Left. Fortunately, for a while – until I decapitated his wife's rose bush with a tennis ball – the newsagent who lived next door would bring over his unsold comics and we could luxuriate in the rare experience of reading what all the other kids read.

Walt Disney movies – despite the fact that he was apparently a bad man (anti-union, anti-black, anti-Communist) – were not forbidden. But Lavender's movie tastes, even in the company of her children, were singular. All her adult life she was a real arthouse movie buff, a subscriber (despite the expense) to the British Film Institute's magazine *Sight and Sound* and a regular at the National Film Theatre on the South Bank. When we were lucky we saw a silent Buster Keaton comedy at the Academy on Oxford Street, but more often we watched something like the Russian version of *Hamlet*, black-and-white, shown without subtitles but accompanied by a man reading along in rough time with the dialogue, and tubed into the ear by a rudimentary headphone. This one man – it seemed always to be the same man – would be the voice of everyone from the Ghost to Ophelia.

This is the kind of thing, of course, that stands you in good stead in the long run. But I really wanted to sit and be amazed by the great historical Hollywood epics that involved spectacle and fighting. At the age of seven, I begged to be taken to see *The*

Alamo, starring John Wayne and Richard Widmark. I was too young to go by myself, and Lavender had no desire to see it. A few years later, we did get to see John Ford's last Western, *Cheyenne Autumn*, partly because it was on the side of the Red Indians (Native American not being a phrase in use at the time).

Naturally, discussions at school concerning films and music tended to pass me by. When I was ten or eleven my mother suddenly became worried about this. With characteristic caprice she decided that I should go and see some of the many Elvis Presley and Cliff Richard movies that were on release. She didn't intend to take me herself, but for several weeks she badgered me about how *Viva Las Vegas* or *Swingers' Paradise* might connect me with other children. There was absolutely nothing in the way she'd brought me up, in our family's range of interests or in my own intellectual history to suggest that Elvis or Cliff would hold any allure for me. They didn't. I thought they were absurd. I didn't go.

Sam had no interest in sports or popular culture or any of the usual working man's hobbies and pastimes. We didn't go fishing, my father didn't play football in the park with us and we never watched any sport on television. For a while he took Owen and me to the Robert Mayer Youth Concerts at the Royal Festival Hall, but after two or three concerts he was disappointed by our lack of appreciation for classical music, and we stopped going.

Our otherness hadn't mattered too much at primary school. While aptitude for football or fighting still remained the prerequisite for great popularity among the boys, the teachers were keen on thinking and learning. When I was eleven the boys I was friendliest with applied for the local grammar schools and the head of the school, despite being a left-wing Labour Party member, told my parents that he thought I could get a scholarship to Westminster.

They didn't tell me about this conversation until years later and they didn't put me down for Westminster. Or even for the nearby grammar school, right next to the girls' comprehensive school that Sabrina had attended. Instead, they set their sights on one of the newish North London comprehensives, sparkling and technocratic (in their imagination, at least). They had heard great things from Party teachers about Holloway County, a 1,200-pupil school in Islington. It was a place that was nearly two miles' walk from home, and they in no way culturally prepared me to be educated with the sons of the sons of toil.

Other Party families managed not to be quite so faithful to the idea of comprehensive education. So, for example, Communist teachers (including A. L. Morton) taught at ultra-progressive private schools, like A. S. Neill's Summerhill and Dartington Hall where the children ran free in the countryside and were not forced to take exams. The historian Eric Hobsbawm and his wife sent their children to local grammar schools. But my mother's projected stoicism meant that, in her mind, I was certain to cope.

But if I was isolated at eleven, so too were most Party members. The Cold War meant that many ordinary people, relatively unversed in politics, had a crude and unshakeable notion of Communists. There were still such things as employment blacklists. Communists could be vetted out of the Civil Service, even where the work had no possible relationship to national security. Some trade unions operated a bar on Party members being officials. The BBC had an intelligence officer who cast his eye over all job applicants to ensure that no Communists got in.

Legend and rumour held that there were informants inside the Party (though no one knew who they were), and that bugging devices were probably being used to monitor communications. Both assertions were later vindicated. In 1975 builders at the Party HQ in Covent Garden discovered a black box full of wires inside the conference room. Now on display at the People's History Museum in Manchester, the bug had been placed there by MI5, with the help of Johnny Gollan's long-time personal assistant, a woman called Julia Pirie. For the two decades she worked in King Street, she was an MI5 agent whose reports and photocopied documents would – according to later accounts – be passed to her handlers during cricket matches at the Oval. (She must have made other arrangements during the winter.) In the 1970s, when the Troubles in Northern Ireland eclipsed all other domestic security concerns, she was pulled out of Party surveillance to help forestall Provisional IRA attacks. Right up until her death in 2008 she continued to receive a pension from the Communist Party pension fund, though the Party itself was no more.

To me, though I knew this kind of surveillance was supposed to be happening, it made no sense. I couldn't think of anything that Sam and Lavender did that warranted such scrutiny. Everything – the marches, the speaking, the meetings, arguing, the strikes, the rallies – was out in the open. We were our kind of normal in the plainest view possible. How much more normal could you be?

The Party and Communism gave us a place to be on almost every question, no matter when and no matter where. 'Which side are you on, boys?' a striking Kentucky miner's wife in the early 1930s had written. The American folk and protest singer, Pete Seeger, a man of extraordinary energy and good humour, sang it on one of our relatively few records. An anti-strike-breaking song, it asked fellow miners to decide whether they stood with the heroic workers or the hated bosses, because 'they say in Harlan County, there are no neutrals there. So which side are you on, boys, which side are you on?'

Even in relatively progressive schools in London the history that was taught was as kingy and queeny as any modern Tory could possibly want. Julius Caesar gave way to Hengist and Horsa, Alfred fought the Danes, William the Conqueror built castles and cathedrals. The Lionheart went crusading, leaving Prince John to be bad at home, Edward I was the Hammer of the Scots, Henry V the vanquisher of the French, Elizabeth of the Spanish and the Catholics. Charles got his head cut off, Bonnie Prince Charlie was defeated, there was an Industrial Revolution, Victoria reigned for many years and was much loved, and most of the land surface of the globe came to be coloured pink. This essential structure of British history (though it included no Scottish or Welsh history from before 1600 and 1300 respectively) was supplemented by magazines, comic books, TV programmes and children's literature.

But the British Communists had their own history, easily as valid as the frankly propagandistic national history that everyone else learned in primary school. By the age of eleven I could tell you which side I was on even if I was rarely sure how I had arrived at any particular conclusion. I was for the Greeks and against the Persians because the Persians were historically backward, as was proved by the fact that their huge armies couldn't defeat the democratic Greeks' small ones. Spartacus was good, and the Romans were bad. For all their aqueducts and mosaics the Romans were suppressors of national liberation movements, such as the Iceni led by Boadicea. Harold was better than William the Conqueror because the Normans were feudal, hated commoners and – after their regrettable victory at Hastings – put up motte-and-bailey castles to help suppress popular feeling. Subsequent rebels such as Hereward the Wake, Ivanhoe and Robin Hood, insofar as they existed, were to be admired. Wat Tyler was a hero, Richard II was treacherous, Elizabeth I was on the right side of history, Philip of Spain on the wrong. The English Civil War? Roundheads, no question. The American Civil War? The Union for ever. In some battles, such as Waterloo and Agincourt, there was no inner compass, so I was free to be patriotic and back the victorious underdogs.

Much of this alternative story was captured in an attractive book entitled *A People's History of England*, written by the historian A. L. Morton and published by the Left Book Club. From the title the reader knew immediately that a distinction was being made between this account and those which were not about the people, but about the rulers, the elites, the tycoons.

When it was first published in 1938 the *People's History* was reviewed in the Party-linked journal, *Labour Monthly*, by a young historian, Christopher Hill. Hill, who was to become one of the country's greatest writers about its own past, distinguished Morton's work from that of other 'innumerable popularisers, purveying historical pornography'. This was because Morton was one of the few using the correct tools of historical analysis. 'Much of the detail unearthed of late years makes nonsense of old Whig interpretations, and is forcing Marxist conclusions on unwilling historians,' argued Hill, adding, with the certainty of the era, 'The future of historical writing is with the Marxist.'

There were, of course, monstrous exceptions to the rule that history was made by peoples and movements and not by individuals. But at least a clear alternative to post-1066 historiography had developed, based on class and popular struggle. ('Struggle' inciden- tally is, like 'comrade', a word that almost always locates its user on the Left. Otherwise it is only really religious people who deploy it, in their case to describe their battles with various demons.)

So various rights under Anglo-Saxon rule are abolished under feudalism. The lord owns the serf and the land. What was once legitimate hunting becomes poaching. Over time the peasants push back, especially after the Black Death made labour scarce, and the result is the Peasants' Revolt.

Meanwhile the growth of trade and the tending of wool- producing sheep on the country's pastures green lead to the beginning of a fully fledged mercantile class. This class rises in wealth and seeks political influence. It supports the monarch in centralising state power and curbing the barons, and it seeks new religious forms more appropriate to its individualistic approach to wealth. The result of this alliance is the Reformation and the reign of Elizabeth.

But the alliance cannot hold. The new capitalist class, with the support of ordinary people, seeks to get rid of the monarch's absolute power. Of course, once it manages this – through the English Civil War – it betrays various popular tribunes (Diggers, Levellers, Ranters and so on). Now though, partly because of technological advance, we are on the edge of the Industrial

Revolution. The first popular reactions against the new form of capitalism take the form of machine-breaking and rick-burning. It is the age of Ned Ludd and Captain Swing. As labour becomes geographically concentrated it turns into a proletariat and seeks rights for itself – rights which the capitalist class resists. This battle becomes the true story of modern Britain. From the Tolpuddle Martyrs and the early unions, through the co-operatives and practical utopians like Robert Owen, to the New Unionism of the 1890s, workers organise to resist immiseration. They organise too to gain political power first through the Chartist movement and then through the foundation of the Labour Party.

Advances are uneven. They are suppressed through state violence, bought off – at the expense of colonised peoples – with the spoils of Empire, seduced by the propaganda of the bourgeoisie and sold out by their very own leaders. The results are the General Strike, the appeasement of Hitler, the abandonment of the Spanish Republic and a disastrous enmity with the Soviet Union. Pockets of heroic working-class militancy, in places like Clydeside and the Rhondda, show, however, that the working class is never totally defeated.

Whether or not a committed British Communist had ever read a word by Morton, she would nevertheless have been able to recount a historiography like the one above. And she might just as easily have encountered it in non-didactic form in a play by a Party playwright, or a book by a Party-oriented children's writer. Geoffrey Trease's historical novels were to be found in every Party member's library. His first, *Bows Against the Barons*, has as its hero a peasant boy who falls in with Robin Hood and fights against serfdom. In *Cue for Treason* two boy actors thwart a plot against Elizabeth I and encounter the consequences of social policies such as the enclosures. The hero of *Thunder of Valmy* battles foreign attempts to turn back the gains of the French Revolution (an event otherwise represented in popular fiction only by *The Scarlet Pimpernel* and *A Tale of Two Cities*). I never read either *Black Night,*

Red Morning or *Comrades for the Charter*, but their titles suggest both their content and orientation.

The greatest carrier of the political message was not speeches or pamphlets or books. It was music. Emotion and ideology took fastest wing in song. The Party, knowing this well, always had good musicians and great tunes. Topic Records, which produced both folk and protest music, often used performers who were in, or close to, the Party. This music surfed on the wave of what became known as the second British Folk Revival, usually dated to around 1945. (The first had happened in the early years of the century.) Folk clubs opened all over the country. Old songs were revived and new ones, in a folk idiom, were written. Songs of struggle, of the battles against poverty and racism, were exchanged across the Atlantic.

The performers I knew best were the ones who had sung of Cook and Rowe: the grumpy, gravel-voiced old songster Ewan MacColl and the younger American woman, Peggy Seeger, whose half-brother was Pete Seeger. MacColl was both a revolutionary and a famous cultural figure in Britain. He had collaborated in a celebrated series of radio documentaries for the BBC using his own songs to depict the lives of miners, fishermen and travelling people, so his fame extended far beyond the Party. In 1949 he wrote 'Dirty Old Town', the classic of love in an industrial landscape, and composed for Peggy Seeger (over the phone, apparently) 'The First Time Ever I Saw Your Face'.

MacColl's overtly political songs could be savage. This one – which has always stuck in my mind because of its bitter sarcasm concerning the claims of the free world – was written in the late 1950s after an African American had received a brutal sentence for a minor felony:

> *In Alabama 1958*
> *The cost of human life is very low*

A man that's black is trampled down
Just like they were a thousand years ago

But these are more enlightened days
No room for all these savage ways
Leave and let them go
Now every man may walk his road in peace
For all are free!

In America itself, in the period after the decline of Woody Guthrie and before the emergence of Bob Dylan, Pete Seeger plucked a banjo for the cause. Seeger had been singing 'If I Had a Hammer' for years, but the song that best encapsulates his leftism is his version of 'Banks of Marble', written by Les Rice. It took the form of a tour of America's toilers:

I saw the weary miner
Scrubbing coal dust from his back
I heard his children cryin'
Got no coal to heat the shack

But the banks are made of marble
With a guard at every door
And the vaults are stuffed with silver
That the miner sweated for.

You don't really need to understand Marx's theory of surplus value to get the point of that lyric. So a significant amount of what I knew about the world as a schoolboy came straight out of songs.

Take the Labour Party, the most powerful working-class political organisation, but with an establishment orientation on its right. I intuited some of the contradiction, but what gave that intuition force was Leon Rosselson's parody of 'The Red Flag' (the rousing song performed at every Labour Party conference) released by Topic. It was called 'The Battle Hymn of the New Socialist Party' and ended like this:

We will not cease from mental fight
Till every wrong is righted,
And all men are equal quite,
And all our leaders knighted.
For we are sure if we persist
To make the New Year's Honours list.
Then every loyal Labour peer
Will sing The Red Flag once a Year.

Songs provided a bestiary of landlords, exploiters, racists and warmongers. Like Paddy Ryan's man who waters the workers' beer:

I am the man, the very fat man,
That waters the workers' beer . . .
And what do I care if it makes them ill,
If it makes them terribly queer
I've a car, a yacht, and an aeroplane,
And I waters the workers' beer.

Or, that other villain, the greedy landlord:

Please open your hearts and your purses
To a man who is misunderstood
He gets all the kicks and the curses
Though he wishes you nothing but good . . .
So pity the downtrodden landlord
And his back that is burdened and bent
Respect his grey hairs, don't ask for repairs
And don't be behind with the rent.

That was obviously supposed to be funny. One strand of song, however, was terrifying for a child. There were plenty of cartoons and illustrations of that horrific image, the mushroom cloud. The songs were somehow more graphic. Here is the first verse of the anthem for the Campaign for Nuclear Disarmament:

> *Don't you hear the H-bombs' thunder*
> *Echo like the crack of doom?*
> *While they rend the skies asunder*
> *Fall-out makes the earth a tomb;*
> *Do you want your homes to tumble,*
> *Rise in smoke towards the sky?*
> *Will you let your cities crumble,*
> *Will you see your children die?*

I was the children and I didn't think I wanted to die. On another record was the lullaby 'Crow on the Cradle', written by Sydney Carter who also wrote 'Lord of the Dance'. Its words were less a call to action than a prediction of personal annihilation. Your parents are rocking you to sleep with one hand, it warned, and reaching for a shovel to dig your grave with the other.

I don't know if any study has been done on the psychological effect of the Cold War on its children or if my parents ever discussed the emotional impact of songs dealing with nuclear war, but it's hard to believe that this annihilating pessimism – albeit in warning form – did us much good. Fortunately we had Civil Rights to sing and be happy about, because the music of the black struggle was as bright as that of nuclear disarmament was bleak. 'We Shall Overcome' may be sung at a dirgey tempo, but it is self-evidently optimistic. It isn't 'We May Overcome' or 'We'll Do Our Best to Overcome'. Overcoming is coming.

As performed by Pete Seeger almost all the songs of the Civil Rights movement were joyous; celebratory, even. One of his favourites, 'If You Miss Me at the Back of the Bus', starts where Rosa Parks started and gradually takes the narrator, a black

American in a segregation state, via a swimming pool and a
college, up to the courthouse to vote:

> If you miss me from the back of the bus,
> If you can't find me back there.
> Come on up to the front of the bus,
> I'll be sittin' right there.

No one, though, had political songs like the Irish had political
songs. In the days before the Northern Ireland Troubles began
in 1968–9 there was, for left-wing Brits, a glorious simplicity to
the struggle. Ireland had been oppressed for 800 years, its
struggle for freedom marked by the Rebellion of 1798, the
Easter Rising of 1916 and the subsequent turmoil. We were on
the side of the Irish. That was why we possessed an LP of *Irish
Rebel Songs*, performed by a man called Enoch Kent, who
sounded like the voice of a Bessemer converter. One song on
the album concerned the fate of Roddy McCorley, a participant
in 1798, who was caught and hanged at the Bridge of Toome
in 1800.

> O see the fleet-foot host of men,
> who march with faces drawn,
> From farmstead and from fishers' cot,
> along the banks of Bann;
> They come with vengeance in their eyes.
> Too late! Too late are they,
> For young Roddy McCorley goes to die
> on the bridge of Toome today.

The Scottish songs were best, though. There were beautiful
love songs, naughty songs involving sexual metaphors, historical
songs of battles and heroes. My favourite involved that terrific
Scottish capacity for mockery. One of our records had a song

written by a man called John McEvoy after the famous incident on Christmas Day 1950 when four Scottish students broke into Westminster Abbey and stole the Stone of Scone, which had been used for the coronation of the Kings of Scotland until pillaged by Edward I.

Sung to the tune of 'The Soldier and the Sailor', it began like this:

> Oh the Dean o' Westminster wis a powerful man,
> He held a' the strings o' the state in his hand.
> But with a' this great business it flustered him nane,
> Till some rogues ran away wi' his wee ma-gic stane.

And it ended thus:

> So if ever ye come on a stane wi' a ring
> Jist sit yersel' doon and appoint yersel King
> Fur there's nane wud be able to challenge yir claim
> That ye'd croont yersel King on the Destiny Stane.

In 1996, in a suitably pompous ceremony, the Wee Magic Stane was returned to Scotland, where it sits in Edinburgh Castle, waiting for the moment when it will be taken back to Westminster Abbey for a new monarch's coronation. In this way I had discovered a little about the relationship between Scotland and England and between pomp and circumstance.

Some bits of learning, especially about sex, were much more accidental. In those unimaginable days before the Internet – those sepia days of libraries and cuttings – if you were a ten-year-old wanting to know about rude things, you'd have to look them up in books. Something like *Lady Chatterley's Lover* was obviously wicked, but it included incomprehensible activities involving the flora of Nottinghamshire and a lot of swearing that, it seemed to me, adults would be unlikely to indulge in, given how firmly they suppressed even words like 'bloody' when used by their children.

Judging by title alone the most promising book on my parents' bedroom shelves was *The Second Sex* by someone called Simone de Beauvoir. It even had quite a racy cover. What was inside, however, was not a series of accounts of the act itself, shorn – that being the proper word – of plant life. Instead I was introduced to a critique of Freud's concept of penis envy (the appendage de Beauvoir described as 'this weak rod of flesh') long before I came across the concept itself.

This was not exactly titillating, especially the bit about fear of castration, but it was intriguing. It told me first that even highly educated men were keen to underestimate women, and second that some women were not content to be underestimated. One sentence stayed with me, from a section rejecting the psychologist Alfred Adler's notions of women's desire for power. 'When a little girl climbs trees,' wrote de Beauvoir, 'it is, according to Adler, just to show her equality with boys; it does not occur to him that she likes to climb trees.'

My mother, partly imprisoned by her era and by the traditional Communist idea that class was the most important distinction, was nevertheless digging around on feminism's borders. The book was hers, not Sam's. In part this was due to a contradiction inherent in the Party's status as a form of insurgency against the prevailing order, yet also as the custodian of an eternal truth and defender of 'real existing socialism'.

The ethos of Communism in the post-revolutionary period in those countries where it had come to power was essentially puritanical. School anatomy textbooks in Russia, for example, would omit the reproductive system, reducing their imagined human beings to empty-groined Kens and Barbies. As the *Communist Review* had once put it, 'The Communist Marxist-Leninist standpoint is that of Monogamy!'

But the British Party's origins lay as much in feminism as in temperance, and it had attracted support from rebels and outcasts in the Arts and Crafts Movement, whose arenas of rebellion against the bourgeoisie were sexual and personal as well as ideological. They defined themselves against the conventional, identifying more with Engels's denunciation of the family, and with free-love Communists such as Alexandra Kollontai, rather than the over-stern and distinctly anti-sex (though otherwise entirely correct) patriarch, Vladimir Ilich.

This tension led to 'contradictions' – a marvellous word which often permitted incompatible opinions and actions to be tolerated. Women Party members showed no inclination to become baby machines for the movement, and one possible reason for this was that a higher proportion of Party women than Party men seemed to have been educated. My impression is that the meeting of poor boy and middle-class girl that was represented by Sam and Lavender was not so uncommon. Rebellious young women met political young men and the result, at least for a time, was that Lenin was banished from the bedroom.

Not long before he died I went to interview a former Party member called Kim James at his home in Northamptonshire. James had joined the Party during the war (as many did), served in the Royal Tank Regiment, had married a French woman he'd met in Paris and then become an artist and art teacher. I was trying to talk about the politics of Stalinism. James, however, went off on a different tack.

'It was a feast of sex, the Party!' he beamed. 'You've no idea! We were hippies before it was even thought of. I never screwed around so much in my life. The Party was full of charming, charming women in leading positions.' James then reeled off a list of names. 'Noreen Branson, Barbara Niven, Betty Matthews – I was in love with Betty Matthews.' One by one he named the sedate if sometimes twinkling matrons of British Communism that I'd known in my boyhood.

A decade or so earlier, for the first and only time, I met
Sam's first wife, Bertha. She now lived in Israel, was over on
what might be her last visit, and was tying up the loosest of
ends. It was a strange conversation to have in any circumstances, since I had never even met his second wife, and was
born long after Sam and Bertha split up. The thing she told
me that stuck in my mind was what happened to her after
Sam went up to Glasgow during the war. She remained behind
in the East End, but they were still married. From time to time
a comrade from Scotland, in London on Party business, would
arrive to stay with her, at Sam's suggestion. And it was not
uncommon, she said, for such a lodger to expect to share more
than a roof. The implication was that this form of *droit de
camarade* was regarded by some Party members as a normal
thing. The other implication was that Sam knew about it and
approved. But it was wartime, and perhaps different rules
applied.

Well, not everyone had fun. Perhaps the saddest discussion I
ever had about my father with a stranger was with a man called
Peter Brinson, who died in 1995. I met Brinson when he was
director of the UK branch of the Calouste Gulbenkian Foundation,
which funded many art and youth projects, and I was President
of the National Union of Students.

As so often happened (and still does) Brinson told me that he
had known Sam. He had been a young tank commander with
Monty at Alamein, and had joined the Party on demobilisation.
But his interest was in dance and in bringing dance to the masses.
Specifically he was an expert on ballet – writing and choreo-
graphing dances and films. In the mid '60s he formed a group
from the Royal Ballet called Ballet for All and toured the country
bringing high culture to the workers. Back in the 1950s he had
met Sam when he was Secretary of the Party's Cultural
Committee and had, like others, admired his thirst for art; he
had even loved him a little for his charm and political leadership.
But Brinson was gay, and when it came to homosexuality the

Communist Party was no more progressive than the society it planned to revolutionise. Instead of embracing Brinson, Sam rejected him, did not allow him near the centre of the Party's cultural life, making it clear that he thought homosexuality both a sickness and a liability. Thirty years later Brinson could still recall the sense of rejection that he had felt. Actually, I think he still felt it.

On race, however, the Party was stalwart. The Conservative and Labour Parties were equally concerned not to lose support among the white majority in the electorate and in 1968, shortly before Enoch Powell's 'Rivers of Blood' speech – and with bipartisan support – Labour brought in the Commonwealth Immigrants Act which, in effect, curbed non-white migration into Britain. The Party argued that this was racist legislation, which Labour staunchly denied.

In 1998, when the Cabinet papers for the period were released, it became clear that the Labour denial was untruthful. Among the papers was a memorandum from the sponsoring Home Secretary, James Callaghan, written a few weeks after the Bill was passed. In the memo Callaghan dealt with the argument that migration was not a great problem because as many people were going out as were coming in. 'This view,' he wrote, 'overlooks the important point that emigration is largely by white persons from nearly every corner of the United Kingdom, while immigration and settlement are largely by coloured persons into a relatively small number of concentrated areas. The exchange thus aggravates rather than alleviates the problem.' In other words, it was almost entirely a matter of race.

The Communist Party's opposition to racism often counted against it among the very people it sought to attract. Even before the dockers and meat porters famously marched in support of Enoch Powell, there had been eruptions of anti-immigrant anger among various groups of workers, not least among transport workers in our part of North London. The formal arguments were the usual ones – wages and conditions being undercut by newcomers. And the informally expressed prejudices were the usual ones as well.

I knew all about this almost before I ever met someone who was black. I remember Sam coming home after a speakers' session at the docks where the subject of immigration had come up. He'd been talking about how racism divided the working class and a few of the dockers had decided they wanted to divide him. Then two large West Indians had materialised, one on either side of him, and his would-be assailants had backed off.

We were on the side of black people. We were on their side in Britain, in the colonies (one of my earliest memories is of my parents' outrage at the execution of Patrice Lumumba in the Congo), on their side in the Southern states of America and on their side in South Africa. Nor was the Party a Johnny-come-lately to these struggles. It had been involved all along, the whole painful way, when other parties had considered the matters unimportant or had taken the other path.

For Sam such an affinity came naturally. He too was from a despised race and had been working alongside black people since he was a teenager. For Lavender, however, overcoming her upbringing was far more difficult. The books of her childhood were the books of Empire, with their naïve and warlike natives, if they weren't stories of white women who had brought compassion, God and washing to the heathens. So while she entirely embraced the fight against racism, and committed herself to the side of the blacks, she never quite lost the habit of patronising people of other nations and races. We had the Little Black Sambo books at home, she would still make decisions through 'eeny, meeny, miny, moe, catch a nigger by the toe' and, if she wanted to discombobulate her children, would turn pure Mrs Jellyby and threaten to adopt 'a little black baby'. It would never have occurred to her that a little black baby might not have wanted to be adopted into our peculiar family.

I rarely came across outright racism as a boy. There were strange sexual and scatological jokes in the playground about a couple called Rastus and Liza, just as there were miser jokes about Scots and Jews. But I didn't really understand them and I'm not sure their tellers did either. But when I was ten an Australian boy came to spend a year at the school. And he loathed black people, from the 'Abos' of his own country to anyone looking remotely dark in my country. They were stupid, smelly, disgusting and inferior. I used to listen to him with amazement, wondering where this hatred came from, especially since his parents were academics. But he was a good drawer, had loads of toys and was in his own way charismatic, so I let it go. Besides, my best friend liked him and I understood that it would be unwise to force a choice between us.

Once this slightly enhanced sensibility led me into trouble. A girl in our school – a Greek Cypriot with very dark hair and very white skin on which the fine hairs on her upper lip made a downy moustache – was ostracised by some of the girls, who said that she smelled. One day she stayed at home and the supply teacher, who lived near us, had a history of *froideur* with Lavender and who didn't approve of our politics, led a class discussion of the problem. We were asked why this bullying was going on and I said that I thought she was being picked upon because 'she is different'.

The teacher decided to interpret analysis as justification. She loomed over me. 'I am astonished,' she told me, 'that you, coming from your background, should say such a thing!' – and sent me out of the class. Things like this seem to have happened most of my life.

Sam had parallel struggles – the political and the personal. It was not enough for him to be a super-activist, he had also to be expert in something. He believed that economic behaviour determined human behaviour and class relationships and since those were the most important relationships of all he turned himself into an economist: a Marxist economist. In the small spare room next to mine and Owen's bedroom he created a study where he kept his growing number of economics books, which he read in such spare time as he had, making notes in the margins and then writing up his notes. And then, for small amounts of money, he wrote books for the Party publishing house, Lawrence & Wishart, typing them up badly and slowly on an old machine. In 1955 he published a book called *Monopoly*, in 1961 *The Ruling Class* and in 1964, perhaps to help people going through the process he had just gone through, a primer called *Economics for Trade Unionists*. All of them were well received on the political Left, but he found researching and writing them at the same time as working long hours for the Party and bringing up a young family quite exhausting.

So the father I knew was often exhausted. When he was at home he was either preoccupied, busy in his study or on the edge of anger. It was not uncommon for him to lose his temper when, after bedtime (we were put to bed early), we made too much noise and disturbed his writing. He would suddenly come in and thump us, mostly ineffectually, through the bedclothes. We would have a much better time with him on the weekend drives to his office or to meetings, when we got a chance to see the man that the outside world saw.

That world, insofar as I encountered it, adored him. Of course, not many people are going to write to a journalist and tell him what a swine they thought his dead father was. But even allowing for that, all the various letters and emails over the years have said essentially the same thing: Sam was charming, inspiring, a great teacher, a wonderful public speaker, a brilliant man. So he must have been.

But by the 1960s he was a man whose brilliance had been contained in too small a vessel. He knew that had he been better educated, or born into the proletariat proper, he would have advanced much further and more quickly, not least in the Party itself.

So he wrote books and he reached out. Strangely, he became a proponent of a dialogue between Christians and Marxists. The ultra-militant atheism of Communism had been left behind somewhere in the 1940s, and as part of the constant fight for a 'popular front' or a 'broad progressive alliance' against first fascism and then monopoly capitalism, religious people were now seen as possible allies.

In May 1967 the *Catholic Herald* reported a meeting of 200 people in the unlikely location of the Cauliflower pub in Ilford to discuss a rapprochement. Sam organised this event, at which the Bishop of Barking and the Party theorist James Klugmann were the main speakers. 'The five worst words in my dictionary are that "You can't change human nature",' said Klugmann, 'and it's up to Communists and Christians to do so.' Sam summed up, but the account of what he said is rushed and garbled.

Forty years later an elderly man wrote to me and described how he had been a 'radical young vicar from Dagenham' called to the bedside of the dying mother of a parishioner. It had soon become clear to him that the old lady was both a Communist and an atheist, and that a conventional church funeral would not really satisfy the needs of the moment. So when she died he wrote to the South Essex Party requesting advice on what he should do. Sam wrote back and between them they concocted a service involving readings on justice from the Book of Isaiah: 'Learn to do well; seek judgment, relieve the oppressed, judge the fatherless, plead for the widow.'

Sam also did his best to break through to some of the more celebrated progressives of the period. I remember him being excited about a correspondence he was having with the famous Oxford sociologist, Professor A. H. Halsey. Halsey was a regular broadcaster on the BBC, an advisor to the Labour Party and himself a Christian socialist. He persuaded Halsey to address a meeting together with him, set a date, sent out invitations, informed that part of the press that he knew anything about. And, of course, was let down when Halsey pulled out at short notice. He reached out and was spurned.

Sam's political life contained not only disappointments but also irritations. One of our then neighbours, a man called Dick who had lived four doors (or, more properly, four garden gates) down, contacted me when I was working at the *Guardian* to recall that he used to see Sam quite often occupying the speaker's pitch outside Kentish Town station, and would stop to heckle, something which he imagined to be in the spirit of political interaction, but which coming from a close neighbour must have been disheartening if not unpleasant. This habit might explain why my mother, though she liked Dick's wife (who was called, if you will believe it, Jane), was never complimentary about her husband.

Dick's letter explained to me that he was aware of my mother's dislike, and had created a strange birthday and Christmas ritual of 'Lavender's present' in which he would 'wrap up a box of matches or a penny pencil, hang it on the tree and say it was from Lavender'. When he left his wife and children and started again with another woman, he told me, he had carried on this tradition, 'perpetuating in my new family the name of a woman none of them have ever met'. It says something about this man that he obviously thought I would enjoy this anecdote.

Lavender herself was less ecumenical than my father. Like him she lacked education, and like him sought to 'improve' herself through evening classes in (at various times) Russian, Italian and psychology. But she never felt confident enough with politics to step outside the limits she understood the Party to have set. Within them she would occasionally, as she put it, set someone 'straight' about Russia or Communism or racism, usually at a party. But she wasn't about to start a dialogue with any vicar.

She didn't limit her straightening out to the animate. It was entirely typical of her relationship to the world that a diary entry for one Thursday in March 1963 reads: '80th anniversary of Marx's death. Went to Marx's grave. Highgate Boys School [a public school] had laid mucky old wreath. Removed it.' Probably dozens of other Marxists had been up there that day and seen the various tributes, but only Lavender felt compelled to do away with the one that had come from the wrong people. This very discreet form of civil disobedience suited her entirely.

My mother prized fidelity above all. If you had committed to something or somebody then it was almost a moral duty to defend them and stand by them until death or a Party Congress changed the situation. It made social transactions as a child quite difficult. You weren't allowed to fall out with your friends, change your mind about who might come to a birthday party, or – later – break up with a girlfriend. She was disapproving when I grew my hair long in the late hippie era and even more disapproving when, a few years later, I cut it short again. I had, in a sense, let my own hair down. On a grander scale she was even cross with the Party when in 1966, without a vote, it changed the name of the *Daily Worker* to the *Morning Star*.

Lavender's concept of loyalty led her to adopt a strange habit, which was that she would usually criticise you to your face and defend you behind your back. In discussing a dispute she would take anyone's side but that of the person she was talking to. So if, perhaps, one of her sons had been punched by another boy at school, she would invent a difficult home life for the assailant and detect a punch-attracting character flaw in her own progeny. If a bad-tempered bus conductor hadn't let you on to a not particularly crowded bus and made you walk home and be late for tea, well that was the conductor's job and she was probably a good trade unionist. It was maddening and made me feel that my own mother was never really on my side. Only much later did I realise that, when I was criticised by teachers or relatives, she would defend me in turn with partisan vigour. I think the only thing that such a perverse trait had going for it was that it allowed my mother to watch other people's reactions to her provocations.

Overwhelmingly her greatest loyalty was to Sam. When he was away she moped – pined, almost – and counted the long Party hours until he was back. She was not a woman who had married a man in order to have children, but one who had had children to keep the man. In that way she was like Zoë Heller's anti-heroine Audrey Litvinoff in *The Believers*. She was committed to the struggle, but above all committed to her man. As for her children, as Heller put it, 'she was still in some shock regarding the servility of motherhood – the sheer thankless drudgery of it'. She had no real model of parenthood, and it is easy to see her substituting Sam for the missing father who had deserted her and her sisters. In the end, like Audrey, she judged people and children by whether they were a threat or an enhancement to her marriage.

And here, if anybody could have seen it, was the fault line in their marriage. Sam was a natural radical, a striver, a restless changer of his own circumstances, intensely outwardly focused and, in his own way, ambitious. My mother, meanwhile, strove above all to retain and build up what she had. In that sense Lavender was a natural conservative, sensitive to threats to the established order of her home, marriage and surroundings.

These tendencies, so centrifugal in nature, could become reconciled in one place above all. The Party amalgamated the radical and the conservative, the idea of massive, transformative change with the existence of a clear hierarchy of decision and the demand for loyalty.

A couple of years ago I found a wonderful example of how this apparent contradiction resolved itself in Sam and Lavender's relationship. My mother had found and kept a letter that she had sent to my father in the period before I was born, when she was twenty-nine. I find her writing here so poignant, so funny and so revealing that I am quoting it at length.

Again, Sam was away from home on Party duties for a few days, but seems to have given Lavender some homework to do regarding what Communists called 'the balance of class forces' and the circumstances in which an alliance of the British people might come together to topple monopoly capitalism. So, after the love-you/miss-yous, Lavender wrote, as if getting down to business:

> Now to your exercise. I should imagine that those sections of the people you mention could be united against the monopolists for various reasons. The technicians and scientists would be frustrated by the halt in technical development,

hence their revolt, the petty traders and producers would be ruined, since they have no vast reserves of capital and could not compete with the monopoly capitalists, so their only resource would be to unite with the working class, large numbers of whom would be unemployed. Presented with the socialist picture where 'the sky's the limit' where technical development and expansion is concerned etc what else could they do?

I have no idea whether Lavender was relying for her answers upon books, remembered conversations or had put the issue before some of her own friends. Whichever it was, she knew how to end her answer with a beguiling political naïvety:

I expect this is the most complete example of muddled thinking you've ever come across, and I see now I've left out the managers. I don't really see where they come in at all, I shall leave that for you to tell me.

Perhaps Sam, on his return, taught my mother the correct position of the managing classes on the British road to socialism. She, in return, certainly had things she wanted to teach him. In Lavender the genteel and the rebellious contended, just as in the Party the puritanical and the bohemian battled one another. But there was no escaping the fact that aspects of her behaviour, such as her table manners, had been formed among the provincial *haute bourgeoisie* of the 1930s. My father's table manners, however, had been based on nothing other than the need to eat and drink what you had been given before someone else took it away. And in this one respect he repelled her, eating with his mouth open, talking with his mouth full and deploying whichever item of cutlery came to hand first.

There is a story in John Aubrey's *Brief Lives*, concerning Sir Walter Raleigh and his son. They were sitting next to each other at dinner, when the young man started to recount how, that day, he had met a London whore and suggested that they transact some business. No way, she had replied, for she had had sex with his father just half an hour earlier. An astonished and humiliated Sir Walter responded to this massive impertinence by giving his son what my dad always called 'a clip round the ear'. The son in turn smacked the face of the man on his other side, saying 'Box about, it will come to my father anon!'

So my mother, not wanting continually to confront my father with his solecisms, instead persistently and sometimes physically corrected those of her children. He couldn't be shouted at for holding a knife in the wrong hand, but we could, and he would surely get the message. Which, eventually, he did.

I have met Catholics, lapsed and practising, whose childhood experience seems to have been very similar. Some retained an affection and a connection with the faith often beyond any residual belief in God. Their social and familial existence had been defined by their Catholicism, both in their prayer and their partying. Talking to them, I realised they were scarcely aware themselves of how they had been affected by the simple fact of having been raised in the Church of Rome. But something said or implied would tell an ideological Henry Higgins about their past.

Our politics were not the product of overt indoctrination but of imbibing, over the years, all the tenets and preoccupations – spoken and unspoken, conscious and unconscious – of the Party. It wasn't 'do as I say', it was 'do what seems natural'. My mother, however, always had a keen sense of everyone's obligations and kept a gimlet eye on whether my siblings and I attended meetings and even 'socials'. She would take against some of our friends if she thought they were discouraging us from our duties. But this was mostly a pursed lip and slight beetling of the brows.

By the time I was born, a third of the membership of the Party still had parents who were Communists. By the late 1970s these 'red diaper babies', as they are known in America, included the deputy editor of the *Morning Star*, the editor of the theoretical

magazine *Marxism Today*, the editor of the Party's weekly news-
letter, the full-time student organiser and the Secretary and the
National Organiser of the Young Communist League.

Some Party kids felt, long afterwards, that they had suffered as
a result of their parents' commitment. In 1997 *Children of the
Revolution* was published in which British Communist offspring
told their stories. Co-edited by Gillian Slovo, the book was summarised by its publishers as relating an essentially negative narrative.
It explored, they said, 'how being communist made many children
feel isolated from their school mates, and how they were often
made to feel secondary to political activity'. Among those interviewed were the *Guardian* journalist Martin Kettle, whose father
Arnold Kettle was a leading Party academic; the comedian Alexei
Sayle, the children's writer Michael Rosen and the Scots poet,
Jackie Kay.

Kay and Rosen had both enjoyed their parents' radicalism, but
Kettle in particular felt that his Party upbringing had been bad
for him. He felt 'very, very deeply' that it had been 'stifling'. There
was, for example, the puritanism of socialist self-denial. 'You felt,'
he said, that 'it was wrong to be too concerned about yourself.'
What he was talking about was a Party variant on the 'how can
you leave that on your plate when children are starving in Africa?'
guilt trip. Why should you complain about your own circumstances when people were dying for the cause from the Congo
to Alabama? Then there was the phenomenon of the lover of
humanity in the abstract, who in real life loathed people.

And for the children of particularly active parents there was
the problem of Jellybyism. Readers of Dickens's *Bleak House* will
recall how Ada and Richard, the wards in the endless Jarndyce
legal case, are taken to overnight lodgings in London with a Mrs
Jellyby. When they arrive at the Jellyby residence they find a child
outside with its head stuck between the railings, and inside a
house in total disorder, other children in a rather grimy and
neglected state and the lady of the house herself dictating phil-
anthropic letters to Caddy, her oldest daughter. Mrs Jellyby clearly

cares more for the children of the natives of Borrioboola-Gha than she does for her own children, or indeed for herself.

Certainly we were poor. By the time I was born Sam had been on a Party full-timer's pay for a decade. This was supposed to be set at the average worker's wage, but had slipped over the years. By the mid 1950s it was something like half of what a coal miner earned. George Guy, a worker in the sheet metal industry who went on to become a trade union leader, turned down a big Party job because 'on the party wage I'd find it difficult to adjust my standard of living'. My mother supplemented Sam's earnings with part-time clerical work at a doctor's surgery in Kentish Town. Every now and then her guardian in Worcestershire, now very elderly, would send a small cash sum, or she would get an ironic dividend from a small number of shares that he had bought for her.

This situation was paradoxical. We lived in a semi-detached house in a North London suburb called the Holly Lodge Estate, which my mother had been given. The rooms were full of books collected by both Sam and Lavender. But we had no money. The difficulties faced by my mother in bringing up a family surface regularly in her diaries. In July 1957 she wrote to my father – away at a Party school – that she had made one loaf of bread last four days. This was for a family of four.

In the cold winter of 1960 money for coal ran out and Lavender recorded sitting in the living room in her dead aunt's fur coat. On one of our grim camping holidays in Devon, when I was just nine, she wrote, we 'were very short of money, so not much to eat'. It wasn't until we pitched up at my aunt's farm a few miles away that any of us 'growing children' ate as much as we felt we needed.

I remember this feeling of shortage, of lack of plenitude, very well. Most of the other children in my class at primary school had money for sweets at break-time, but I didn't. My best friends got two or three times as much pocket money as me. We dressed in cast-off clothes and our house was shabby. One friend came round to tea and then reported back to classmates that we 'sat around on orange boxes'. I was always asking for things that the other kids had but that my parents couldn't afford and I can see now that Sam – who worked a sixteen-hour day and most weekends – hated this constant complaining. To him, in one famous phrase used when I was in my early teens, I was 'mean and grasping'.

This relative poverty had other consequences. As Lavender noted one autumn, when I was diagnosed with pneumonia, 'David v. poorly all day. Didn't go to work. 15 shillings down drain!!' Since there was absolutely no chance of affording any childcare, the onset of more marginal illnesses (like chickenpox or measles) could not be regarded as a reason for taking a day off school. It would simply cost too much. Several times I was sent home from school having arrived with one disease or another, a high temperature, or a cough that you could hear at 100 yards.

Lavender's most Jellybyesque quality was that, despite our poverty, if she got a windfall from her shares, she would give a large part of it to one of the myriad 'fighting funds' that the Party, the *Daily Worker* or various international campaigns were continually running. Among her papers after her death I found a letter from John Gollan, written at a time when we were absolutely on our uppers, thanking her for her 'incredibly generous contribution' but wondering whether she could afford it. He knew well, through Elsie, that she couldn't. My guess would be that shares in BP or some other multinational had just paid off, and that her conscience (and, possibly, her sense of mischief) required that the money be ploughed back into destroying the power of organisations like BP.

So there we were: books, elevated discussion, decent house, no money. Anthony Trollope would have recognised us without any difficulty. On account of Lavender's country upbringing of ponies and pets, we were never without a dog, though our dogs – male and female – were not neutered, often escaped from the garden and became notorious in the neighbourhood either for being on heat or for siring multitudes of puppies. We also maintained, at any given time, at least a couple of gerbils, hamsters (our cat, a great eater of hamsters, was not replaced when she died), rats or budgerigars.

We would have been short of money even if we hadn't maintained a minor menagerie. But some of our hardship was offset by the peculiar nature of what would doubtless now be called 'the Communist community'. There was always, for example, a 'Party builder' who would do jobs more cheaply for comrades than for other people. (Not necessarily better, however, as Lavender discovered when the task of shoring up the collapsing garden shed led, mysteriously, to the destruction of her beloved honeysuckle.) There was a Party carpenter, a Party accountant, a Party plumber, (as we have seen) a Party dentist and several Party doctors. There were Party babysitters, and employer Party people might give preference when finding part-time work to employee Party people. There were even Party hotels, campsites and guest houses scattered around the country, sometimes even in places that one might want to visit. One year, when I was five, we got a free holiday to Bulgaria, allocated to the families of Party officials. We travelled there and back by train. It was my first trip abroad, and I didn't make another for six years.

In the mid '60s Sabrina became the first member of our family – probably for several generations even on her mother's side – to go to university. She went to read biochemistry at Salford and found lodgings with a Party family, the Susses. Henry Suss was a clothing worker, a union official, and had taken part in the mass trespasses on Kinder Scout. He was also a lover of Shakespeare, and the Communist candidate for the seat of Swinton and Pendlebury.

Three or four years later, when Sam went up to study at Oxford he lodged with the Dunmans. Helen Muspratt Dunman was a professional photographer who had joined the Party in 1936 after visiting Russia to take photographs of life on the Volga. Her husband, Jack, also a Communist candidate, was an activist on behalf of agricultural workers and a friend of Wogan Philipps.

Party people, then, were our normality. The way they behaved, what they talked and argued about, seemed everyday to us. Unlike Martin Kettle, I find it hard to regret the eccentricities of a life on the far Left. For example, one of the very earliest entries in Lavender's diaries, written in the second week of January 1963, tells of her first experience of what was soon to become known as the Sino-Soviet split. 'Startling statement in the *Daily Worker* on Communist International Unity,' she wrote: 'Tobins all of a twitter.'

Or two years later when a comrade who was an architect dropped by to give free advice about some refurbishing. 'Colin came to look at the kitchen and stayed and stayed [i.e. overstayed, in Lavender's view] to discuss political economy, surplus value etc. He and Sam disagreed over socialist planning.' Someone comes to look at the appliances and ends up arguing about the socialist state's capacity to match supply and demand. This seems to me not a poor heritage, but an oddly rich one.

6

Going Back to Russia

Long live our Soviet motherland,
Built by the people's mighty hand.
Long live our people, united and free.
Strong in our friendship tried by fire.
Long may our crimson flag inspire,
Shining in glory for all men to see.

The national anthem of the USSR

Above all there was Russia. The one thing that anyone else knew about Communists, and that Communists knew about themselves, was their affinity with the Union of Soviet Socialist Republics.

But first, Greece and other places . . . Lavender, for example, was far more concerned with Greece. And it was not just a passing whim, either. At some point in the '50s she had become acquainted with a woman called Betty Ambatielos. Betty had once been Betty Bartlett. In 1940, in Cardiff, she met Tony Ambatielos, the craggy-looking Secretary of the Greek Seamen's Union. When the Germans invaded his homeland a year later, Tony escaped to Britain and married Betty. On the liberation of Greece Mr and Mrs Ambatielos moved back.

What followed is a largely forgotten and bloody part of modern European history. For four years in Greece there was a civil war between the Left and the Communists on one side, and the monarchists and conservatives – backed by Britain – on the other. In 1947 Tony, a Communist, was arrested along with a number of other union leaders, tried and given a life sentence. Two years later – the Civil War over and lost – Betty decided that her campaign for his release would be more effective if waged from Britain. So she returned and became a central figure in the League for Democracy in Greece – whose pamphlets and posters were a recurrent feature of my childhood.

In 1963, Queen Frederica of Greece came on a visit to London, basing herself in Claridge's. Tony was still in prison and Betty – a woman with a determined jaw but a sudden sunrise of a smile – organised a twenty-four-hour vigil on the pavement outside, in which Lavender took part. Perhaps I did too.

It was as a result of this demonstration that one of the most celebrated scandals of the 1960s took place. On 11 July a plain-clothes detective sergeant called Harold Challenor arrested a pacifist artist called Donald Rooum. While arresting Rooum, Challenor said to his prisoner, 'You're fucking nicked, my beauty. Boo the Queen, would you?' and hit him on the head. Back at the police station Challenor then added a half-brick to the small pile of Rooum's possessions with the words, 'There you are, me old darling. Carrying an offensive weapon. You can get two years for that.' In that era courts generally accepted police evidence as beyond contradiction, but Rooum had the rare foresight to get his jacket forensically tested, and when no trace of brick dust was found, Challenor's account collapsed. And so did some of the popular assumptions of post-war Britain.

Whether or not I stood outside Claridge's, certainly in April that year I had been present in a large hall in London – a theatre, I think – when Manolis Glezos, a Greek Communist hero, was welcomed to London on his release from prison. Glezos, a wonderfully handsome man with a dashing moustache, had risked death in 1941 by pulling down the swastika flying over the Acropolis and putting a Greek flag in its place.

Nearly half a century later the broadcaster John Humphrys went to Athens to cover the Greek economic crisis for the BBC radio programme, *Today*. While there he interviewed an elderly man who was campaigning against the austerity measures being implemented by the beleaguered government. It was Glezos and I was suddenly back in that hall.

Tony Ambatielos was released in 1964, re-imprisoned by the Colonels in 1967, released again in 1974, and with every turn we celebrated or campaigned according to the latest news. The year 1968 found me, aged thirteen, collecting money for Greek political prisoners like Tony outside cinemas showing the Costa-Gavras film, Z, the lightly fictionalised account of the murder five years earlier of a leftist Greek politician, Grigoris Lambrakis. Thunderously scored by the Greek socialist composer, Mikis Theodorakis, whose music was a backdrop to my early adolescence, the film unspooled the progression from unpunished murder to the infliction of justice on a series of right-wing army officers.

In 1975, a year after the Turkish invasion of Cyprus had led to the fall of the Colonels, I hitch-hiked to democratic Greece, taking with me a gift from Lavender for a Greek woman called Vasiliki, the wife of a formerly imprisoned trade unionist, with whom she'd been corresponding for years and to whom she had been sending small sums of money. Vasiliki's small flat was in a working-class area of Athens, and when I arrived, out of the blue, she was mortified that she had nothing to give me in return. Rather desperately she picked up a knick-knack – a Giacometti-thin ancient Greek on a chariot – from her mantelpiece and insisted that I take it. Vasiliki couldn't have known how much it was valued: my mother kept it in the bathroom (where she necessarily saw it several times a day) until she died.

Solidarity was a constantly used word. It meant 'on the side of', and we were often in solidarity with people that no one else seemed to care about. As others began to holiday in Spain, we would not (actually we couldn't have afforded it) because of our solidarity with the workers oppressed by Francoism. Where even some Labour people seemed to be either relaxed or fatalistic about apartheid in South Africa, we were in a state of constant active solidarity with the 'liberation movement', in this case the African National Congress. When Conservatives would invoke the connection with our 'kith and kin' in Rhodesia, we saw only blacks living second-class lives in their own country. Admittedly the North Koreans, with their ferocious implacability, were a little baffling even then. At Collet's bookshop you could buy their posters, invariably depicting determined-looking soldiers bayoneting imperialism or capitalism. The term 'peace-loving' didn't seem to apply.

Like being Jewish, or Catholic in the era of the Latin mass, the Party gave you instant communion all over the world, even with the many places where it was banned. Party members from around the globe would turn up at events, rallies and socials. One snowy Christmas in the early '60s we visited the home of a female Vietnamese diplomat, Lin Qui, for drinks. A French Communist couple appeared at our door and stayed for a week. An urbane and elegant professor from the Italian Communist Party came round for dinner in a green jacket and charmed us all, his lines and features so well defined that he resembled a character in a Tintin book. But mostly – apart from some Communist-run towns and regions in Europe – this was a communion with powerlessness, and gave us a slightly hunted feeling.

The peculiar exception to our association with persecution was the People's Republic of Bulgaria. Between birth and the age of thirteen I travelled abroad three times, and two of those visits were to this small Balkan socialist state of around six million souls. I think we went to Bulgaria the first time because Aunt Gill, Lavender's younger sister, was there, and Sam got a subsidised holiday through the Party-linked travel agency, Progressive Tours.

Gillian's path to Communism began with the East European dancing that, believe it or not, used to happen on summer weekends in London's Hyde Park. After taking part in some Balkan twirling – dressed up very fetchingly in authentic folk costume – she found herself invited to receptions at the embassy of the young People's Republic, and went to Bulgaria in the late '50s to work as a teacher. As a child I liked her; she had a crinkly smile and an attractive smoky voice. She still does.

I was young enough to be missing my two front teeth but I still recall images of our family's endless train journey through Europe with its Austrias and Yugoslavias, an exciting (though to my mother, terrifying) plane ride in a rickety Ilyushin from the capital Sofia to the Black Sea coast, and then two weeks in the extraordinary, almost inexplicable sunshine of the Golden Sands resort. We ate goat's milk yoghurt and drank some kind of cold peppermint concoction.

The second time, I went on my own. I was just twelve and acquaintances we had made on our first visit had offered to put me up for a month, as by the early '60s Aunt Gill was back in England, suffering from a complicated past. The plan was to stay for a week or so in their flat in Sofia, then drive through the mountains to the coast, returning via the spa town Velingrad. With some money pinned inside my jacket like Emil in *Emil and the Detectives*, I got on the boat-train at Victoria and for three days chugged eastward, changing trains in Munich and Belgrade. I arrived safely in a station with no platforms and you can imagine how many times my children have had to hear that story of my cross-continental precocity.

I was met by my hostess, Leda Mileva. I picked up during my visit, without quite understanding it, that Leda was socialist aristocracy. Her father, Geo Milev, was a martyred national poet. Severely wounded in the First World War, he had set up a modernist magazine in Sofia. In the early 1920s there had been the sorts of clash between socialists and reactionaries that happened in many European countries, ending in a military coup.

After one massacre Milev had written the poem 'September', which included these lines about the ambitions of the workers and peasants:

> From the boundlessly high
> Bridge of the sky
> With levers and ropes
> We'll bring down heaven,
> The land of our hopes,
> Down
> To the sorrowing
> Blood-soaked earth.

A year later, after more violence, Milev was abducted by men in uniform, and murdered, his body not being found until thirty years later; his daughter, Leda, was just five. By the time I met her at Sofia station she was herself a published poet, a writer of books for children and the deputy director of Bulgarian Television. Her husband, Nikolai, was also a writer and translator. They had two children, the younger of whom, Boyan, was a spectacularly handsome, dark-haired, tanned, almond-eyed sixteen-year-old.

It was 1966. Socialist Bulgaria was anxious to assure its citizens – especially its younger citizens – that their lives were not just as good as, but better than, those of capitalist Westerners. The Bulgarian film industry had run out of patriotic themes and was engaged in making a series of derivative youth movies in which young people went to the beach, sang songs and fell in love. One female star of these films was a beautiful girl called Milena – a willowy Sophia Loren – and Milena was Boyan's girlfriend.

One evening Boyan and Milena took me to meet their buddies in a park in Sofia. As if we were actually in such a movie, Boyan picked up a guitar and played us the number one pop hit in Bulgaria that July – V.A.C.A.T.I.O.N., a sunny bit of pre-Beatles bubble gum Americana.

To someone whose idol was Bob Dylan, reheated Connie Francis was something of an anachronism. But her invocation by these Balkan teens suggested an innocent quality, as though the Bulgarians were somehow younger than we were in the West.

That sense of innocence did not last. Later that evening Boyan gave me a raunchy account, delivered in slow English and punctuated by a smacking of his lips, of what he and Milena got up to when no one else was around. I was in the early throes of a confused puberty and the heat and Boyan's lubricious confessions combined to create a disturbing summer. Years later, wondering about Boyan's very un-Stalinist sex life, I discovered that his father, Nikolai, was one of Eastern Europe's foremost translators of the poetry of Allen Ginsberg.

Leda and Nikolai were part of the Bulgarian Party elite. Their lifestyle was not opulent, but they were a great deal better off than we were and moved through their society far more easily. I sensed (rather than knew) that though they too were Communists they were on the winning side whereas we were on the margins. Bulgarian public architecture, for example, was punctuated by newish plaques and memorials to Communist and patriotic martyrs – often women – who had died in the fight for socialism and against fascism. The statues back in Britain were almost always of someone else's heroes: a monarch, a colonial general, a triple-barrelled viceroy. The ruling class's heroes.

In Varna we stayed in the Writers' Rest Home, a modern, airy block beside the Black Sea, provided by the Culture Ministry for the vacationing of the nation's poets and novelists. Writers from other 'socialist countries' stayed there too and I made an East German pen friend called Sabine. Sabine was a pretty blonde girl of about fourteen, but though I was one year too old not to notice her attractiveness, I was two years too young to do anything about it. She lived in East Berlin and we wrote to each other for a couple of years; now I wonder what the Stasi made of our correspondence.

I also shook hands with Todor Zhivkov, the squat, suited visiting leader of the Bulgarian Communist Party – and thus the country's most powerful man – watched England win the World Cup on a television in the lounge, and suffered the most embarrassing episode of projectile diarrhoea of my life. Fortunately none of these episodes overlapped.

Being a model-making boy of my time, I was more interested in cars than politics. Bulgaria was on the land route between Germany and Turkey and Turkish *Gastarbeiter* would drive their Mercedes, Opels and BMWs from Bavaria to the Bosphorus, to show their families what they had achieved. There were too the various marques of the East European car industries, set up to show the citizens of the socialist world that they could also be consumers. So, for the first time, I saw tinny Trabants, squat Wartburgs, efficient-looking Skodas, iffy Yugos and the Russian Moskvich. The Milevs drove a Volga, a ponderous but comfortable Soviet car, not unlike a Morris Oxford.

On a Bulgarian mountainside on a stopover during the return drive from the Black Sea, the family and I fell to discussing whether British involvement in Cyprus was 'as bad' as what the Americans were doing in Vietnam. The Bulgarians insisted that it was and I felt simultaneously slightly indignant and rather got at. After all, British Communists, with no MPs and complete lack of influence on government, could hardly be held responsible for colonial policy. Also, there just weren't the bombs and gunships in Cyprus that television and the *Daily Worker* showed that there were in Vietnam. It is only now that I realise, writing this, first that I was feeling a little patriotic and homesick and second that I was probably being punished in a tiny way for the fact that it was England, and not Bulgaria, that had just won the World Cup. Or possibly, after nearly a month of their precocious but gawky and awkward guest, even my very generous Bulgarian hosts had had enough.

★

I didn't go to Russia, even though, imaginatively, I spent my boyhood there. Lavender and Sam each visited once. Dad went to Moscow in the late summer of 1962. A note in the Party's archives shows that he attended a conference on 'The Contemporary Problems of Capitalism' where the main speech was given by a comrade Arzumnyan. However enlightening the conference, all I remember from the time was his delighted story of how he had been given a free health check in a sparkling new clinic and how Soviet doctors, concerned about long-term after-effects of his rheumatic fever, had put him up in a Party sanatorium for a few days. Critics could say what they liked about the Russians, but was this not socialism in action?

Lavender travelled there the following year on a Russian cruise ship, which docked at Copenhagen and then at Leningrad. To her (though the circumstances of her trip were, as you will see, emotionally complicated), this was something like a pilgrimage – not to Lourdes perhaps, but certainly to Jerusalem. Standing in for the Stations of the Cross were the stations of the Revolution – the cruiser *Aurora*, whose fore gun fired the blank that marked the beginning of the October Revolution of 1917; the Winter Palace which was stormed by the Bolsheviks who evicted the capitalist ministers of the Provisional Government; the Smolny Institute, where Lenin had his headquarters.

Apart from those two, short physical encounters, Russia was a place of the mind, supplemented by images from films, books and newspapers. Where these were too obviously propagandistic, even as a child I regarded them as a form of boring fairy story, as in the case of the cheerful tractors-and-clinics newspaper, *Soviet Weekly*, published under the auspices of the embassy and distributed to those comrades who wanted it as part of the 'lit' round. They were there to sell a message and so they didn't really count.

But there were plenty of authentic sources of Russian information and images. The men of the Red Army choirs who came to London to sing 'Song of the Steppes' and 'It's a Long Way to

Tipperary' were real (and obviously jovial) fellows who would no more invade a country than sing a deliberate bum note. How could these basses and tenors with their broad faces, high cheekbones and throaty melodies be anyone's enemy? Except, of course, enemies of the warmongers in the Pentagon and the monopolist profiteers, who wanted both to have an annihilating war on Russia and also to make huge amounts of money.

Each year too, we would watch, on television or in the cinema newsreels, the May Day broadcast from Moscow. On his platform on Lenin's Tomb we saw the smiley Mr K (and later the homburged Laurel and Hardy of Messrs Kosygin and Brezhnev) taking the salute as his great country paraded in front of him.

Much of the parade consisted of ordinary-looking citizens carrying flowers and banners and from whose ranks well-rehearsed moppets in folk dress would emerge, running skip-skip up the steps of the Mausoleum to present bouquets to the Party's leaders. But what the news broadcasts tended to concentrate on was the mobile weaponry that clunked its way past the members of the Politburo. First came the high-stepping troops in perfect formation, then the armoured cars, followed by the tanks and the self-propelled guns. Slightly more disconcerting was the display of trailer-mounted surface-to-air missiles (the famous SAMs), and then the nuclear rockets. This habit of trundling ICBMs past the saluting leadership, against the backdrop of banners reading MIR (PEACE), seemed odd to me even then. But I supposed I was glad that Russia had such missiles to protect itself against the Cold Warriors.

If the missiles were strange, I was more used to the iconography of May Day in Moscow. We too had images of Marx, Engels and Lenin in triptych. Nor was it any great surprise to see big posters of the current Soviet leaders being held aloft. But now I see what should have been apparent. We did, after all, have a large book of Russian paintings, many of which were done by the *fin-de-siècle* realist, Ilya Repin. I adored Repin's detailed depictions of Russian historical and contemporary scenes. There was the one of the seventeenth-century Cossacks sitting down, al fresco, cackling and guffawing, to compose an insulting letter to the Sultan. And another of Ivan the Terrible cradling the body of his son, whom he had just killed in a mad rage.

My favourite was *Easter Procession in Kursk Province*. It shows the rich and poor of old Russia, the beggar girl, the peasants, the fat priests, the brutal-looking policeman on his horse, accompanying the golden banners and great, gilt reliquary as they are carried by monks along a dusty, earth road. The May Day Parade was a direct successor to Repin's procession, not just psychologically (which I couldn't see at the time) but visually too (which maybe I could have, but didn't). One was supposed to belong to the old world that had been left behind and the other to the infinitely better new world that replaced it.

Russia was an innately sympathetic place because it was a Motherland, not – like Germany – a Fatherland. Fatherlands were authoritarian, militaristic and stern. Motherlands were heavy and sad – like Stalin's moustache – with love for the people. Mother Russia was a fertility goddess whose *chernozem* (black soil) produced steppes full of golden wheat. In one or two old Soviet books that we had in our house there were pictures of Stalin – Uncle Joe – standing in that wheat.

Russia was ours and I gloried in her achievements and identified with her heroes. Lev Yashin was the world's finest goalkeeper, the MiG-15 was a versatile jet fighter, the T-34 the best tank in the Second World War, Russia produced more manganese (whatever that was) even than America, the trans-Siberian was the longest railway, which it needed to be because the USSR had the world's greatest land mass, and from the shores of the Baltic to the Sea of Japan a myriad peoples called themselves Soviet citizens.

But how did it get to be what it was? Which, whatever it was, was not what was taught in British schools or written about in British newspapers. I accreted, as a child and an adolescent, a version of the history of Russia and of the Soviet Union as believed by British Communists. This tale was central to the capacity of Party members to understand the world and it went like this:

For centuries Russia was a vast and backward country ruled by tsars and their stupid and brutal underlings. It was the land of the serf and the knout. In the towns and cities there were clusters of wonderful artists, poets, playwrights, musicians and novelists. But in the countryside there was an impoverished, illiterate, superstitious and oppressed mass of peasantry. By the turn of the twentieth century, though there were pockets of industrialisation, and a growing proletariat, Russia was still almost the least likely country in Europe to experience a working-class revolution.

Even so, its intellectual classes did spawn a number of idealists who fought against Tsarism. There were the anarchists Mikhail Bakunin and Pyotr Kropotkin, and a young man called Aleksandr Ulyanov, born in Nizhni Novgorod, who became part of an unsuccessful plot to assassinate Tsar Alexander III, was captured and hanged in May 1887. His young brother Vladimir was to become the man known as Lenin.

My pictorial image of life under Tsarism came from watching, at the age of about seven, the first of the trilogy of films based on the writer Maxim Gorky's autobiography. Made in the late 1930s by Mark Donskoy, the film opens with a shot of a team of barge-haulers: a line of men of all ages, tattered, exhausted and straining along the river shore, pulling an enormous barge. If the picture is familiar it is because it is taken directly from another Repin painting, *Barge Haulers on the Volga*. And there is no inaccuracy here, Repin's work dates from 1873, when Gorky was a small boy, growing up (like Ulyanov) in the Volga-side city of Nizhni Novgorod (later to be renamed after Gorky even before his death and later still to revert to its original name).

More vivid even than these public tableaux are the scenes from within the boy's family, many of whose adult members are drunk, stupidly religious, sentimental or violent. His grandfather is a bully, his father dies early, his uncles are spendthrift, his mother tragic. Only his grandmother, a warm but fearful woman, can give him the love he needs. Eventually the young Gorky, a personification of the young Russia, leaves home and sets out across the steppe, for a new life.

The next scene is a snowy day in St Petersburg in January 1905. The Russian Empire has just been humiliated by the Japanese in the Far East. Thousands of soldiers and sailors have died and billions of roubles have been spent. Now ordinary workers at local factories have come together to march on the Tsar's Winter Palace to present a petition about their many grievances. They carry long, thin banners and are led by a black-clad young priest called Father Gapon. But as they approach the city centre the crowd is met by a line of soldiers with bayonets fixed. Someone gives the order to fire and dozens fall to the ground, their blood crimson in the snow. This day becomes known as Bloody Sunday and is the rehearsal for the revolution of 1917.

That same summer there is an incident in the southern port city of Odessa that is another harbinger of the end of Tsarism. Sailors aboard a battleship named after Count Potemkin, Catherine the Great's minister, mutiny over their terrible conditions and cruel treatment. Their action is welcomed by the ordinary citizens of Odessa, who head towards the docks to welcome the mutineers. The citizens gather on the famous Odessa steps – the great staircase from the city to the port.

Here, as depicted in Eisenstein's *Battleship Potemkin*, in one of the most famous scenes in cinematic history, they are shot down by white-clad troops who advance mercilessly down the steps. A boy is trampled to death. A mother is hit by bullets and as she dies she knocks the pram carrying her child, which careers down the steps. A woman in pince-nez is slashed across the face by the sabre of a Cossack. It never occurred to me, as it probably didn't to most others watching the film, that this scene was fictional. It was black and white, it was a silent movie, and I took it to be documentary.

Meanwhile in garrets and lodgings in various European cities exiled Russian revolutionaries – small in number but huge in ideas – were meeting and organising to bring about the downfall of this almost visibly rotten system. They took on pseudonyms or stirring *noms de guerre*. Lev Bronstein became Trotsky, a Georgian, Iosif Vissarionovich Dzhugashvili, metamorphosed into the man of steel, or Stalin.

But towering intellectually over all was the man of iron, Vladimir Ilich Ulyanov – Lenin. After leaving Russia he went from place to place – London, Geneva, Munich – on the way setting up the Russian Social Democratic Labour Party (RSDLP) and its newspaper *Iskra* (*The Spark*), writing definitive pamphlets on the nature of the coming revolution, polemicising against those who opposed him and – when necessary – splitting from those he regarded as insufficiently revolutionary and adamantine. If Marx was the theoretician, the philosopher of the Revolution, Lenin was its uncompromising organising genius.

When the RSDLP split, the largest faction, the Bolsheviks (from the Russian for 'majority') went with Lenin. The others, the Mensheviks, who were more timid, were on the other side. When the Revolution did finally come it was Lenin who was vindicated.

The event that turned peasant Russia into the vanguard of the world proletarian revolution – something that no Marxist should have expected – was the First World War. The Tsar marched his troops against the eastern flank of Germany and the northern flank of Austria. The Russian troops were brave and stoical (as Russians are) but fought without proper equipment, under corrupt officers, in the cold and damp of the East Prussian lake district. They were defeated, thrown out of Poland, and then pushed back to a line that more or less stabilised for two years, at enormous cost.

By early 1917 the war was bankrupting the Empire and mutinies were breaking out in many units of the army. The message of the Bolsheviks and other Left groups was carried to the front line by soldier agitators – bread, peace and land! In February 1917 the Tsar was forced to abdicate and was replaced by a Provisional Government, led by a centrist called Alexander Kerensky. The Government refused to end the war and so the killing of worker by worker continued. Lenin, from Germany, almost alone called for another revolution under the slogan All Power to the Soviets (the workers' and soldiers' councils that were being set up). In April 1917 the Germans sent Lenin back to Russia in a sealed train. He arrived at the Finland station in Petrograd (formerly St Petersburg) late on the night of 16 April. And, despite the fact that those around him doubted the chance of success, he set about organising a second – Workers' and Peasants' – revolution.

In October 1917, over the famous ten days, the Revolution took place, beginning in Petrograd. The Winter Palace was stormed, Kerensky was chased out and a new government was set up, based on the soviets. A new era in the history of mankind had begun.

So there they are, Lenin and the Bolsheviks, presiding over the first workers' state. They have a broken-down, impoverished country to run and a war to conclude. First they make peace with Germany on the disadvantageous terms of the Treaty of Brest-Litovsk, then begin the business of building socialism.

At first all is optimism. There is an explosion of artistic activity and innovation as the world is reinvented. The Soviets are also the missionaries for a new way of life the world over. In 1919 the Communist International (the Comintern) is established in the new capital, Moscow, the aim being to help revolution to spread to other countries. But this is where the capitalist world intervenes and sets in train a pattern that will cause the revolution to become distorted. A cartel of White Russian generals – Kolchak, Denikin, Yudenich and Wrangel – take up arms in various parts of the new country, assisted by foreign powers. There is a brutal civil war, which lasts the best part of three years. British troops land in

Archangel, Japanese troops in Vladivostok, Greeks in the Crimea, the French in Odessa. A Czech legion made up of former soldiers of the Austro-Hungarian Empire commandeers the Trans-Siberian Railway. One by one these threats are defeated by the Red Army and its romantic armoured trains.

In the middle of this brutality the Tsar and his family are shot near Ekaterinburg, which was an unpleasant thing to happen but which I understood to be a consequence of Allied meddling. In any case, with so many deaths of ordinary workers and peasants, why would anyone of good faith want to single out Nicholas II's death as more deserving of attention? They wouldn't.

Now, at last, the Soviet state can exist properly. It takes over the industries and the land and begins the business of planning to meet need, rather than to satisfy greed. A huge backward country has to become a modern nation in a fraction of the time that it took Britain or even America. And in a place with no history of democracy or liberalism, and facing enemies at every step. No wonder that Lenin and his comrades often find themselves having to be more autocratic than one might wish. But, comrade, you cannot make an omelette without breaking eggs. To think otherwise is to be utopian, unserious.

Then Lenin died, far too early, and the Soviet Union lost its greatest mind. The man who took over (osmotically, I must have supposed, since I never found out quite *how* he became leader) was Stalin, who was a man for the hard, terrible times that were the 1920s and '30s.

Stalin, unlike the flamboyant and slightly theatrical Trotsky, was a pragmatist. He saw that revolution had not spread to the rest of the industrial world, as was once hoped and that socialism had, if necessary, to be built in the USSR alone. So he embarked on a breakneck industrialisation designed to enable the Soviet Union to compete with the capitalist powers, while remaining true to the spirit of Lenin. Through a succession of Five-Year Plans Russia forced itself into the twentieth century. New cities were built by the Urals, new canals joined mighty rivers, vast new

factories appeared where once there were only fields. Iron production, steel production, coal production, manganese production,
all doubled, trebled, quintupled and propelled Russia into the
league of great nations. Collective farms, created out of the
smallholdings of an inefficient peasantry or the great estates of
absentee landlords, used mechanisation, available for the first
time, to grow more food than ever before. Hunger, famine, illit-
eracy became things of the past. Doctors were trained, hospitals
and clinics opened, every child went to school. In Moscow a
beautiful Metro system, with marble halls and elegant sculptures,
symbolised the ascent of Soviet man. If there was a word to
describe the Soviet worker, the Soviet mother, the Soviet airman,
it was 'heroic'.

But a heavy price was paid for these successes. Stalin was
seduced by the Cult of Personality, and began to believe what he
was told by ruthless and fawning courtiers. He became inflexible
and impossible to criticise. Eventually he was persuaded by men
such as the security chiefs Yagoda, Yezhov and Beria that there
were myriad plots against him and that those responsible had to
be rooted out. Stalin gradually mutated from valued colleague of
Lenin to dictator. As a tragic result many brave, good old
Bolsheviks were tried and shot or sent to the gulags for nothing.
Later they were rehabilitated. It was a terrible error.

The great service Stalin had performed, however, was to build
up the Soviet Union's capacity to win an inevitable war against
fascism. It was obvious from the moment of Hitler's coming to
power in 1933 that he would eventually attack the Soviet Union
and seek to destroy it. And it became clear too that the capitalist
powers of Europe, notably France and Britain, would be content
to allow that attack to take place.

When Francisco Franco's Fascist legions landed on the Spanish
mainland and the Civil War began, the democracies placed an
arms embargo on the combatants, starving the legitimate
Republican government of supplies. Hitler and Mussolini had no
such inhibitions and German and Italian airmen piloted bombing

raids over Republican cities. In April 1937 they attacked the Basque town of Guernica, and the resulting carnage became the subject of Picasso's magnificent painting. Lavender bought a print of that painting in the early '60s and it hung, uncheerfully, on the sitting-room wall.

Only the Soviet Union and the heroic International Brigades rendered assistance to the doomed Republic. And in 1938, as Hitler threatened Czechoslovakia, the Soviet Union stood ready to join with Britain and France in the country's defence. But Chamberlain and the French preferred to allow the Nazis to dismember the central European democracy, shepherding Germany towards the east and a confrontation with the workers' state.

That's why Stalin signs the infamous pact with Hitler, comrade. The West isn't prepared to help in an armed battle against fascism, and the Soviet Union must buy time to build up its air force, its tank force, its artillery, to equip its divisions and set up its armaments factories. It's a horrible thing to have to do, but the very existence of the USSR is under threat. Who wouldn't do the same, in the same position? Who wouldn't form a buffer zone on its threatened borders? Who wouldn't annex the strategically important but otherwise insignificant Baltic states, little slices of Rumania, a bit of right-wing-ruled Finland that gave access to Leningrad and (since the Nazis were there anyway) the eastern part of Poland? Dreadful necessities in dreadful times, made necessary by the actions of the Western powers.

As Germany was diverted for a short time by the phoney war and then the Blitzkrieg, Russia rearmed, preparing for the day when Hitler would unleash the new Knights of the Teutonic Order into the Soviet lands. On 22 June 1941 Operation Barbarossa began, and in a moment the Soviet Union became Britain's ally, the Soviet peoples became gallant defenders of their homeland and Stalin became Uncle Joe. Brave British seamen gave their lives taking equipment across the ocean to our Russian allies, steaming icy seas while being hunted by U-boat wolf packs.

At first the Nazis triumphed and believed, in their arrogance, that they would be in Moscow by the end of the year. But Stalin refused to flee or to panic, despite stupendous losses in the early days. Marshal Zhukov returned from the east and, as winter came on, counterattacked and pushed the Germans back from the gates of Moscow.

Still the Nazis came on and as they did they slaughtered and destroyed. They hanged partisans, shot whole villages, killed all the Jews and burned the land. On and on until they reached the great Volga at a place called Stalingrad. This, not Alamein or D-Day, was the turning point of the war. Here the German army was fed into a meat-grinder and ground. The Red Army counter-attacked, and then for two years – sometimes quickly, sometimes slowly – rolled westward, taking huge casualties but inexorably defeating fascism. The Russians threw the Nazis out of the Soviet Union and then out of Poland, Hungary, Austria, Czechoslovakia, liberating city after city. Until, at last, in 1945, Tommy shook hands with Ivan on the banks of the Elbe. Drank toasts with Ivan. Imagined a future with Ivan, free from war and hatred.

But hardly had the war ended when the West once again began to cast the Soviet Union as its enemy. Stalin wanted only to rebuild a country, a continent, ravaged and laid waste by war. But America had emerged from the conflagration hugely strengthened and determined to stamp its system on the rest of the world. Whereas Russia had suffered from war, the United States had profited from it. The generals, bankers and armaments manufacturers in the latter could afford to contemplate another one. So the speeches about the Iron Curtain and the Cold War began. Given their recent history, what else would the Russians become, other than paranoid? McCarthyism seemingly ruled America and – its mirror image – Communism governed Eastern Europe, ushering in progressive social systems, but oppressive political ones. The Bomb loomed over all.

The West remained belligerent but after Stalin died things became better in Russia. Mr K took over. And although the Soviet

Union and its allies were forced to act in Hungary in 1956 when the old Fascists took advantage of some popular discontent and launched a counter-revolution, the momentum around the world (look at China! look at Cuba!) was towards socialism and towards socialism's exemplar, the mighty Union of Soviet Socialist Republics.

This narrative was believed by my parents, their friends and many on the British Left and then handed down to me. It seemed to explain everything and was essential to the business of being and remaining a Communist. It was coherent, some of it was true, and a lot of it was tru-ish. It rounded off the sharp corners of Soviet history, making that system's virtues its own but attributing its vices to others or to pitiless circumstance. 'Terrible mistakes,' we were told, 'were made.'

Having once been made, though, the mistakes could be made again. In 1963, on her visit to Russia, Lavender looked around her with not untempered hope. 'I feel Russia's people will survive the pressures, the Puritanism and bureaucracy; the savage times of the Stalin era which must have split them apart,' she told her diary. She wasn't stupid and she could see that it still wasn't paradise. Seven years earlier Khrushchev's 'secret speech' to the 20th Congress of the CPSU revealed that most of the 'lies' that were told about Stalin in the West, lies that they had spent years rebutting, had in fact been truths. The result was a slightly wary supportiveness. Things had been bad when she'd thought they were good, but they were getting better now. Still, she couldn't quite trust in the way she had when she was younger.

She'd heard the song, sung derisively at Party members on demonstrations by disobliging and infantile Trotskyists, to the tune of 'Clementine':

> *Oh my Stalin, Oh my Stalin,*
> *Oh my Stalin Party Line*
> *First he changed it, then rearranged it*
> *Oh my Stalin Party Line!*

The song didn't discourage everybody. There were people in the Party, and some outside, who refused to allow themselves even my mother's level of mild questioning. I can recall from early on the different emphases given to the words 'anti-Soviet' by different comrades. Most of them used the term to cover what they thought of as the Cold War propaganda in the 'bourgeois press'. These sinks of prejudice would always depict the Russians as living a uniformly grim existence in a totalitarian state, such as that described in George Orwell's *Nineteen Eighty-Four*.

But other comrades regarded any criticism whatsoever as 'anti-Soviet'. If anyone harked back to Stalin's crimes or worried about the stories of how dissent was treated in Russia or winced at the crudeness of Moscow's censorship of the arts and political discussion, they too were branded 'anti-Soviet' by the militant pro-Sovietists. These rather over-zealous defenders of the world's first workers' state were, I discovered, known as 'tankies'. They were good comrades but, perhaps, a little old-fashioned. I was far too young then to realise that the term 'anti-Soviet' connoted anyone more critical of the Soviet Union than the speaker was.

In the meantime, the new world of Castros and Nkrumahs looked at Russia and saw its sputniks and Gagarins, its kindergartens and sanatoria, its mighty fleets and armies. It might perceive that Russian democracy, with its factory councils and local soviets, was different to the once-every-four-years democracy of the West, but it was no less valid for all that. Russia, for all its faults, was what Japan was in the '80s and what South Korea is now. The tide was still in.

PART II

AND I'LL CRY IF
I WANT TO

7

Floreat Domus

Tranquil consciousness of effortless superiority

H. H. Asquith on Balliol College students

In April 1966 Sam and Lavender went to the Morrises' for drinks. Probably in Muswell Hill. Max Morris was a poor Glaswegian Jew made good, slightly older than Sam, and a headmaster at a secondary school in Brent in north-west London. He was also a member both of the National Union of Teachers and the Communist Party's executive committees, and therefore something of a *ganze macher* in the movement.

Max was stocky, pugilistic, funny and had an un-Communist liking for loud jackets and louder jumpers. His wife Margaret, a history lecturer and writer (she wrote a popular history of the General Strike of 1926), was tall, fair-haired, good-tempered and, even to my juvenile eye, very beautiful in a Garboish way. They were among my parents' most interesting friends. They were also, now that I think about it, much wealthier than us, with Sam on his Party worker's pittance of a salary and Lavender doing what part-time clerical work her children's illnesses would allow. Consequently the Morrises had a certain allure, managing as they did to fail to combine political rectitude with genteel poverty.

The significance of the encounter was not obvious to Lavender at the time, though it soon would be. She recorded the occasion in her diary in around twenty words: 'Margaret Morris very drunk. Max highly indiscreet about Sam's prospects. Said powers-that-be think Sam is too ambitious.'

'Sam's prospects' clearly meant his ability to advance within the Party hierarchy. The 'powers-that-be', accessible to Max in his capacity as a leading national cadre, were the eight or nine members of the Political Committee, the central politburo of the Party. What my dad was being told was that the ruling elite of the organisation he had devoted his life to considered him flawed in such a way as to preclude his further advancement. The subterranean accusation of excessive 'ambition' would have been a difficult one to refute, since it was never to be made directly. It was as likely to mean 'too clever by half' (this was the Communist Party of Great Britain, after all) as it was to refer to a desire for purely personal gain. And what must have been particularly galling to him, as it was to Lavender, was that the judgement appeared to be shared by his old colleague, the General Secretary John Gollan – husband of *her* very close friend and colleague, Elsie.

A few months later, the job of London District Secretary, the top regional post in the Party, became vacant. For three years, as South Essex DS, Sam had been driving out to Ilford, Dagenham or Harlow every weekday morning and most weekends, and then back again. He had been a success in the job, recruiting Party activists in factories and on estates. And he'd enhanced his reputation with his book *Economics for Trade Unionists*. So Sam now thought that he had a very good chance of getting the upward move he wanted and deserved – and that Lavender, desperate to see more of him, longed for.

A twelve-year-old solipsist, I knew little about it and it's probable that Sam's application for the new post was being prepared and discussed while I was swimming with Boyan in the Black Sea. Some three weeks after my return from Sofia my dad got news from one of the less exalted Party functionaries of the decision made by the London District Committee. As Lavender recorded it: 'Tony Winslow was on the phone to say that Frank Stanley was new London District Secretary – Sam got only 3 votes. We were both so despondent we hardly spoke to each other all evening . . .' Then she added, 'Retired to bed feeling so fed up I wanted to tear up my party card.'

A child experiences moments like this, not through knowing exactly what chemicals have been added to or subtracted from the sea in which he swims, but as changes of water temperature and ocean colour. Now the water is warm and now, suddenly, it is icy. Nothing the swimmer can do will change anything; he simply learns what to try to avoid.

I say this because though I don't recall precisely what happened the next day something must have, as Lavender 'woke up at 5.15 am absolutely despairing, feeling that it's me and my four children that hold Sam back from advancement'. While this black mood did not quite betoken a *Jude the Obscure* moment, with all of us hanging by ropes in a closet and a note reading 'Done because we are too menny', it wouldn't have made for a happy day either. Indeed, Lavender went into work later on, where she found 'Elsie full of jolly frivolity. Not her fault but I wanted to kick her in the teeth.' My mother rounded off 19 September with 'took three Valium when I went to bed, so tired from lack of sleep – and I'm no help to Sam.'

Frank Stanley, the new London District Secretary, was a shop steward for the Amalgamated Engineering Union in London – a union where the Party was very strong. The railway worker and Party candidate Jock Nicholson later wrote in a memoir that he was sure the new man 'did not have anything like the same political acumen as Sam. The factory proletariat had been elevated above the political thinker.' But Jock didn't know about the Max Morris indiscretion. Frank Stanley wasn't positively appointed. Sam Aaronovitch, the ambitious, restless, self-taught intellectual, was negatively dis-appointed.

And that was that, eventually. Sam's rise through the Party to which he had given everything was over. My dad had believed for years (had been told for years) that he was a charismatic and brilliant political figure on Britain's far Left. People who had known him would say it to me a decade after his death. He despaired for a while ('just three votes' out of the thirty or so members of the District Committee), probably lost his temper more easily with us than he had before (his and my relationship at this time was horrible and not without physical violence), then decided to make his mark in something else.

The something else was academia. He had taught himself economics, so he decided to become, heading for his forty-seventh birthday, an economist. To have any chance of earning a living at it, he had to go to college, but his CV, though full of exotic politicana, boasted not a single qualification. And if Party workers were poor, students with large families were poorer still. Yet if he could find someone to take him because of, rather than despite, his age and his highly unconventional background, and if he and his family could manage for three or so years on more or less nothing, then with his Stakhanovite capacity for work, who knew what he might achieve?

Lavender was surely distraught when he first mentioned it to her. My mother's idea of loyalty was that you should never leave anything and that you owed it to whomever or whatever you were with, to stay with them. Given what had happened to her as a girl this was not surprising. In her mind, despite her card-tearing fantasy, the Party was family and working for it was working for the family. Besides, a Party wife was what she was and what she knew how to be. Sam's hardening resolve to shake the foundations of our lives would not have recommended itself to her.

Sam began to delve. The period when membership of the Party was practically a disqualification from any job in the public realm was slowly coming to an end. There were Party members and sympathisers scattered among the universities and colleges, many of whom he already knew from previous Party incarnations. And planning had just begun for a new Open University, as education-alists were talking excitedly about encouraging the recruitment of 'mature' students – those hundreds of thousands of clever Britons who had missed out on higher education because of war, or class or lack of ambition.

As Sam looked, the world began to open up for him. It was almost tangible, this lifting of his horizon, this new life born from a moment of despondency, as he would come home and talk about people he'd spoken to – many not even Party members – at Birkbeck College or Leeds University. In the end, the doors that were flung widish for Sam were the great, heavy, wooden double ones set in the mid-Victorian gatehouse of Balliol College, Oxford.

This surprising invasion of the establishment's very heartland had something to do with the fact that the Master of Balliol since the year before was the great historian of the English Revolution, Christopher Hill, and Hill and Sam were well known to each other.

For over twenty years Hill had himself been a member of the Party, and a leading member at that. He had joined as a post-graduate in the Oxford of the '30s (had it been Cambridge, he might have ended his days in a vodka-bottle-strewn flat in Moscow), and as the defining conflagration of his own time approached he had begun to write about the English Civil War. After serving in the Intelligence Corps, he sought work in various universities, where he discovered that his political affiliation was a major barrier to the advancement that his talent would otherwise have commanded.

In the late 1940s and early '50s Hill had been part of the remark-able batch of intellectuals, including Eric Hobsbawm, E. P. Thompson, George Rudé and Victor Kiernan, who made up the Communist Party Historians Group. At the height of their intel-lectual activism the organisation came under the aegis of the Cultural Committee of the Party of which Sam was the secretary. They produced a periodical – *Past and Present* – which was easily the most interesting of the Party publications that found their way into our house, taking dusty purchase on a shelf. And though Christopher Hill had left the Party in the wake of Hungary and subsequent discussions about 'inner-party democracy' (there wasn't very much) his had not been a departure of bitter public renunciation. I knew this because his post-Party books, like *Puritanism and Revolution* and *The Century of Revolution*, also took up shelf space.

Christopher Hill could not have decided on his own to allow the unqualified and middle-aged Sam into Balliol, when many a gilded youth had been turned away. There were admissions committees and economics dons who had to agree too. This was, after all, the college that had nurtured the last but one Conservative Prime Minister, Harold Macmillan, and the man who was expected to be the next, Edward Heath. It was the college that was still proud to repeat another Prime Minister Herbert Asquith's terminal smuggery that Balliol men possessed the 'tranquil consciousness of effortless superiority'. Whatever else Sam possessed it was never a sense that anything whatsoever was gained without effort.

But it was now the '60s. Glass was replacing stone. And the radicalish tutors of Balliol came up with a way to ensure that Sam would not rob a brilliant eighteen-year-old of his place in

the intellectual sun. Instead of accepting my dad as an undergraduate, they took him, a man who had not so much as a CSE
on his record, as a student for a doctorate in economics, an Oxford
DPhil. If he did the work and his thesis passed muster, Sam would
become Dr Aaronovitch.

It was an astonishing thing to happen. I'm astonished by it now.
Not that it was as simple as just turning up in October 1967 and
asking where to find his supervisor. A condition of his entry was
to show an understanding of statistics. As Sam had last opened a
maths book in the early 1930s, he set to work in any spare moment
in the months before he left Party work to learn what he could
about how to read numbers. It was agonising.

Meanwhile Sam's resignation announcement caused a flurry
among the local comrades. Rose, the Party dentist, upbraided
Lavender so badly on Sam's letting down of the movement – and
offended my mother so much – that we switched to a non-
progressive dental practice up the hill. There we discovered that
some practitioners actually used a local anaesthetic before they
did fillings, and that the usual way of dealing with pain was not
to rest the patient's head on your bosom and say 'Now, be a big
boy and it won't hurt.'

Rose was – openly at least – in a small minority, though
support for Sam was still cloaked in the language of revolutionary rectitude. My mother's best friend wrote to her with
the consolation that 'if Sam succeeds in doing what he wants,
it's possible that he could be of even greater service to the
movement than he is now'. Old Hugo Rathbone, the former
Labour Monthly man from two roads away, batted away an otherwise unstated worry. 'Sam won't be the first or only one to be
exposed to bourgeois economics,' Hugo said, 'and if he can't
withstand the pressure, who can, I should like to know.' Others,
the implication seemed to be, had been seduced away from the
movement. The capitalist world was full of traps for the unwary,
many of them honeyed.

In Whit week of 1967, at the Derbyshire Miners' Holiday Centre in Skegness, the Young Communist League held its 26th Congress, with the swinging title 'The Trend is with Communism'. Sam was to speak, and the whole family went up. The sun shone occasionally and there was crazy golf to play when it did. One evening (I was two months away from thirteen) there was a concert and disco featuring a band that some enterprising comrade had booked ages before. It was the Kinks, and I was there, at the back of a dark hall, when they played their new song, 'Waterloo Sunset'.

A few weeks later I was at another event at which famous musicians performed. This was Sam's leaving party from South Essex and from Party full-time work. It was held in Walthamstow Town Hall and Ewan MacColl and Peggy Seeger, also friends of Sam's from his Cultural Secretary days, sang for a couple of hundred people. It was, if you like, Walthamstow Sunset.

Then Sam left for Oxford, where he would spend half the year for the next three years. He made plenty of new friends and one of the younger ones, when Sam was dying thirty years later, would ask me, 'How is the old Bolshevik?' In the group photo for 1968, taken in the Balliol quad, the much older Sam is in the front row, suited and legs splayed, among the geeks and golden boys. The late Christopher Hitchens, the well-wisher, makes a face from row three.

Though Sam had stopped toiling full time for the Party, after all those years of loudhailer street-corner rallies, those decades of placardeering, the endless work weekends in drab Party offices, neither he nor his family had deserted it. He served on its Economic Committee, addressed Party events, spoke at Party schools, and Lavender was still active in the Party branch. My sister was a member and would later be a Communist Party local candidate. My brother-in-law and Owen and I would all become Party members. But the intensity had departed, the stifling, almost inexplicable married intimacy with the organisation had gone. Our times had changed.

*

In the late summer of 1968, in parallel universes, the Beatles released the single 'Hey Jude', the Democrats prepared for their Convention in Chicago, the Aaronovitch family went on their first non-Bulgarian foreign holiday, to the Italian seaside town of Sestri Levante, and the Soviet Union invaded its ally, Czechoslovakia. With Johnny and Elsie Gollan on a walking holiday in Scotland, the first British Communist to learn that the troops of the Warsaw Pact had crossed the border was Bert Ramelson, the veteran Industrial Organiser.

Ramelson was a Party legend, leading a life of considerable adventure even by the standards of those turbulent times. His was a face we often saw at Party gatherings and his name was on articles for the *Daily Worker* and various pamphlets. After a childhood spent in the Ukraine and in Canada, Ramelson volunteered in the Spanish Civil War and during the Second World War became a tank commander in North Africa for the British. After the Germans took Tobruk, Ramelson ended up in an internment camp near Ancona on the Adriatic coast. There, he helped organise a mass breakout of two thousand prisoners as soon as the Allies landed in Sicily. Though most were recaptured, a small group, including Ramelson, trekked 400 miles southwards before meeting up with the Allies' advancing troops.

When the war was over Ramelson settled in Leeds and became an area organiser for the Yorkshire District of the Party. For twenty years, like Sam, he toiled away in the service of Communism. In 1965 he moved to London and became the National Industrial Organiser of the Party, a very big job in an organisation that sought to be in the vanguard of the industrial working class. He soon become infamous – in what Party people called either the 'bourgeois' or the 'capitalist' press – for his role in the seamen's strike. So much so that the Prime Minister, Harold Wilson, named Ramelson as one of the ringleaders of the dispute during a debate in the House of Commons.

In effect, Ramelson was number two in the Party, and the man to go to if the General Secretary was away or incapacitated, both

of which Gollan was, being up a distant Trossach. That's why
Ramelson's phone rang shortly after 3 a.m. on 21 August 1968 and
why he was driven across the river to the Soviet Embassy in
Kensington Palace Gardens.

He was met by Ambassador Joseph Smirnovsky – a man that
Pathé newsreels show to have been thin-faced, jug-eared and
nervous looking. In a memoir, Reuben Falber, the Assistant
General Secretary of the Party at the time, recalled that this business of receiving 'messages' from the Soviet leadership – a process
presumably replicated in many other countries in the world – was
a peculiar one. After a Party official was called to the embassy, a
letter would be produced and then read out loud by a Soviet
diplomat, who would then put the letter away. At no stage would
it be handed over, even for a moment.

So it was this time. Smirnovsky's message from Moscow was
that leaders of the Czech Communist Party had requested that
the Soviet Union and its allies in the Warsaw Pact 'assist' in
resisting an imperialist-backed attempt to overthrow socialism.
In other words, the Russians were invading Czechoslovakia.
Ramelson asked Smirnovsky for the names of the Czech leaders
who had requested such drastic assistance. There were five, he
was told, but their names could not be divulged, to which
Ramelson tartly informed Smirnovsky that the British Party could
not, in Falber's words, 'accept so blatant an intrusion into the
affairs of a fraternal party and another socialist country'. Then
he left.

I was having far too unhappy and angry an adolescence to take
in the details or the nuances of what was going on. But the sweep
of it was this: in January 1968 the old, dour leader of the
Czechoslovak Communist Party, Novotny, had been replaced by
a shiny-skinned man with a beak nose and a perpetual smile,
called Alexander Dubček. Within a few months it became apparent
that the new leadership was determined on a course of liberalisa-
tion. First there was an opening up of the press and a new freedom
to print critical stories and articles. Then there was a repudiation

of the mistakes of the immediate past. And finally a new party programme was published which, almost unbelievably for Eastern Europe, said that 'socialist state power cannot be monopolised by a single political party or a coalition of parties'. In other words, there should be real political competition in Czechoslovakia, which would entail the possibility of the Communist Party being voted out of office. The courts would be independent and the security services would no longer be used to harass dissenters. The phrase that began to be used, hopefully at first and then more confidently, was 'communism with a human face'.

Communism with a human face was a wonderful thing to be able to put against the assertion that the United States was the true champion of world freedom. Communism with Stalin's face had a selling problem, even in the era of Vietnam. Most British Communists and many other socialists looked at what was going on in Prague that spring and saw the beginnings of a new post-post-war world. I saw that. What I didn't see were the signs that the Russians weren't enjoying the Prague Spring. Nor did I notice the Party's nervousness in fully embracing what was happening.

In 1956, as we have seen, the Party bought the Soviet line about fascist counter-revolution and lost nearly one-third of its membership, including many of its intellectuals, after it supported the suppression of the Hungarian Uprising. Even more than that, de-Stalinisation under Khrushchev made Communists question, if ever so gently, the many, many things they believed about Russia. The Party programme, called *The British Road to Socialism* (available from any good lit secretary near you, price two shillings and sixpence) was predicated on the idea of a specifically Anglo and democratic transition to Enlightenment. This omelette would be made with a local recipe and, if possible, without breaking eggs. It did not require Party members to accept all that Moscow said.

Instances of open disagreement were few, but the first occurred in 1964 when Khrushchev was himself deposed and replaced by the duumvirate of Alexei Kosygin and Leonid Brezhnev. The Soviet explanation was that Mr K was suffering 'ill-health'. The British Party openly doubted that.

A second emerged during the trial in 1965–6 of the Soviet writers Andrei Sinyavsky and Yuli Daniel. Both men, encouraged by de-Stalinisation, imagined that they could get away with writing things that were highly critical of Soviet society. And both men found out that, once more, the wheel had turned. The British Party, while warning of the dangers of everyone being too hostile to Russia, nevertheless regretted that artists were being subjected to 'administrative measures', when an open political debate would be better and (it was implied) more effective in countering such negative ideas.

According to Reuben Falber, at the end of the Party's Executive Committee meeting in May 1968, it was left to the always outspoken Max Morris to ask, under Any Other Business, 'when are we going to discuss Czechoslovakia? It is being discussed everywhere except in the place where, above all, it should be discussed, this Executive!' So, discussed it was – at the next meeting in July. But by then Falber himself was being called over from time to time to Kensington Palace Gardens to be read letters of concern by a dour diplomat, a Mr Biryukov, outlining Moscow's worries about 'anti-Soviet' attitudes in Czechoslovakia, forces 'hostile to socialism', a Czech Party leadership 'in danger of losing its grip on the situation'. Falber would then tell Mr Biryukov that the British Party did not share these concerns and return to his office in Covent Garden.

By the time the Executive Committee was discussing Czechoslovakia, the Party's inner leadership was alarmed enough to send John Gollan on a mission to Paris and Rome to talk to the leaders of the French and Italian CPs. Was there anything they could do to stop the disaster of an invasion? These two parties were the largest in the West, with memberships in the several hundreds of thousands and significant parliamentary representation. Both had recently sent senior figures to Moscow and both had got the distinct impression that the Russians were losing their patience and were no longer listening.

As summer deepened, so the intoxicating lily pollen of freedom wafted through Czechoslovakia and threatened to be carried beyond. For each wanton manifestation of liberty, there was a push-back in *Pravda* or some other journal which, uncoded, meant 'watch it, you're going too far'. In the first week of August there was a moment's respite when a smiling, unbelievably young-looking Brezhnev kissed the cheeks of his Czech host on the sunny open platform of Bratislava train station. The leaders made a declaration of determination to solve problems, while respecting 'sovereignty and territorial inviolability'. Less than three weeks later Soviet tanks squeaked and trundled into Prague and – as in Oscar Wilde's 'Selfish Giant' – spring turned, overnight, to winter.

By 9 a.m. an emergency meeting of the Political Committee was held in King Street. The seven members present agreed, unanimously, to a statement condemning the Soviet action. They did not, however, call it an 'invasion', preferring the term 'intervention' because they didn't want to use a word that would be more likely to increase pro-Soviet opposition within the Party.

Had he got the London District job Sam would have been at that meeting. Instead, like the Gollans, he was on holiday. On that day we set out by coach on the long drive from Sestri Levante to Florence. Our guide, a dapper, balding man with long, dark sideburns, had taken us to the top of the Campanile di Giotto and it was there, as we caught our breath, that he told us that the Russians had invaded Czechoslovakia. He was probably a Christian Democrat, because he obviously thought the whole thing rather droll and in any case typical of Communists. We were appalled.

Once, in 2012, when I was appearing on a television programme with a maverick far-Left MP, George Galloway, he accused me

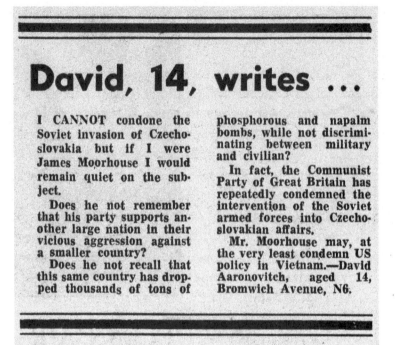

David, 14, writes ...

I CANNOT condone the Soviet invasion of Czechoslovakia but if I were James Moorhouse I would remain quiet on the subject.

Does he not remember that his party supports another large nation in their vicious aggression against a smaller country?

Does he not recall that this same country has dropped thousands of tons of phosphorous and napalm bombs, while not discriminating between military and civilian?

In fact, the Communist Party of Great Britain has repeatedly condemned the intervention of the Soviet armed forces into Czechoslovakian affairs.

Mr. Moorhouse may, at the very least condemn US policy in Vietnam.—David Aaronovitch, aged 14, Bromwich Avenue, N6.

of 'loving Stalin'. Stalin had died before I was born, of course, but his point, I suppose, was that I must have been a supporter of Russian military intimidation. If I had had time, and had anyone been interested, I would have drawn a picture of that hot moment overlooking Florence, and how it was for me. I see the guide, I see Brunelleschi's dome over his shoulder and I can recall exactly how I felt. I was sad, disappointed and disillusioned at an age almost too early for illusions. I knew what the Russians had done was wrong as surely as I knew what the Americans were doing in Vietnam was wrong. In the coach back to the Ligurian coast Sam and Lavender were angry with each other. My mother's first response – piqued as she was by the way that the information had been presented by 'that horrid little man' – was loyal defiance. The Russians had liberated Czechoslovakia in 1945, she said, so they were entitled to prevent it from falling into the hands of anti-socialist forces in 1968. Sam, however, saw it the way I did.

Though Lavender soon changed her mind, the invasion opened up a split in the Party that was to last for the next two decades. On the one side there were the 'tankies', the diehard pro-Soviet loyalists who hated the increasingly independent position the leadership began to adopt. In the middle was the mass of party members who would, in the end, go with what the leadership advised. And on the other side was a younger and intellectually vigorous group of Party members, often second generation and not infrequently arrogant, who were arguing for more 'communism with a human face'.

The same thing happened throughout the wider world of Communist parties. Parties became 'hard-line' or 'revisionist'. The US Communist Party, one of the smallest, joined the South African Communist Party in loyalty to Russia, putting such international heroes as Angela Davis and Joe Slovo on the other side. The West German, Israeli, Chilean and Portuguese parties joined them, as did the Cypriot party, AKEL, which had many members in Britain. In opposition were the Italian, French, Swedish, Dutch and (clandestine) Spanish parties. Fidel Castro managed to say that such interventions were always wrong, but in this case necessary. The pro-Chinese Albanians pulled out of the Warsaw Pact and Yugoslavia's Tito condemned the intervention.

That veteran member of Sam and Lavender's branch, Andrew Rothstein, when he wasn't perambulating in his homburg, wrote articles for the semi-party magazine, *Labour Monthly*. One, penned as the crisis approached, was headlined 'Czechoslovakia, the Soviet Union and the Cold War Ghouls'. It began, 'It is time to look at the genuine problems with a little balance and understanding' and ended up 'balancing' right over towards supporting the Soviet Union in whatever it felt it had to do. Andrew was by no means alone. Falber writes of John Gollan coming back from a meeting in Hackney where there were a number of Jewish members, having faced a dusty reception for the leadership line. Gollan apparently said to Falber without irony, 'I suppose a Jew who stayed in the party after the 1956 revelations will put up with almost anything the Soviet Union does.' 'Needless to say,' Falber continues, 'I thanked him for the compliment.'

Meanwhile the impossible happened. At the Young Communist League Congress that year in Scarborough, when the fraternal delegates from the Soviet Union were announced, they were booed. From then on, although loyalists and tankies could co-operate within the Party, there was always an undermining suspicion between them. More important, perhaps, it was an end to certainty. We were out there sailing our tiny boat, alone, in sometimes hostile but (what was worse) more often apathetic sea.

8

How We Got to Be Last

The people, united, will never be defeated!

Common 1970s slogan

We took sunset for another dawn. The Soviet Union had let us down (or, if you were of a more traditional cast of mind, we had let it down), but nevertheless, throughout the world there were struggles going on and being won. Working-class power and Marxist strategies for economic transformation might have motivated Sam in the later 1960s and '70s, but for me and most of my generation, activist politics was the seemingly simple and emotionally immediate matter of stopping bad things from happening. And in my teens the first of those bad things was the war in the South East Asian country of Vietnam.

On Sunday 17 March 1968, aged thirteen, I got a Northern Line train and took myself down to Trafalgar Square for a demonstration against the war. Usually there would have been Party people to go with, but Sam, Lavender and the comrades were not there. This was not a unity march, but a gathering called by the Vietnam Solidarity Committee, which (believe it or not) had been set up by groups further to the left. The Party supported the British Council for Peace in Vietnam, which called simply for peace. The VSC called instead for victory to the Vietcong. So there was no Johnny Gollan on the platform beneath Nelson, but instead the sexy, if fey, figures of Vanessa Redgrave, looking like a Delacroix incarnation of the late '60s, 'Actress Playing Liberty Leading the People', and the General Marius of 68, student leader Tariq Ali.

I have no idea what was agreed with the police, but I do know that we weren't supposed to link arms, break into a run chanting 'Ho, Ho, Ho Chi Minh!' (Ho Chi Minh, or 'Uncle Ho' was the revolutionary North Vietnamese leader), brush aside a police cordon at Oxford Circus and end up, in our thousands, chaotically and joyfully racing towards the American embassy in Grosvenor Square. It was one of the most exciting moments of my life, before or since. Those thousands! We could do such things! 'Ho, Ho, Ho Chi Minh! We shall fight, we shall win! London, Paris and Berlin!'

But once we were in the square it became more frightening than exhilarating. In front of the modern, rectangular building topped with its US eagle was a line of mostly scared policemen. The demonstrators now were divided between those who wanted to get into the embassy (and then what?), those who just wanted to shout for a bit, and those who had no idea what would happen next. It was believed that US marines stood ready with machine guns.

What followed was known almost immediately afterwards as the Battle of Grosvenor Square. I wasn't at the front where the horses went in and where the more militant marchers and the police fought it out. And I wasn't at the back where I could slink away. So, like the tide around me, I ebbed and flowed, caught fast among the bodies. Ahead of me what reporters would call 'missiles' were thrown policewards – placard sticks, banner poles, a lump of earth excavated from the lawn in the square. Intermittently, to a great roar, a policeman's helmet would whizz into the air. I remember worrying that one of them might contain the policeman's head.

After an hour or more of this the crowd thinned a little, enough for me to edge backwards, and then home. The talk among the departing demonstrators was all of police brutality. People had been whacked over the heads with truncheons, ridden down by horses and kicked with regulation, iron-shod police boots. But the next day the papers were full of an image of a policeman, bent, his face contorted as a desert-booted demonstrator kicked him in the face.

In 2008 the *Guardian* published a photograph of a group of young demonstrators at the battle line in 1968. Several readers recognised their younger selves and were interviewed about their memories. Some had seen Mick Jagger on the route, others recalled the horses, one person had fainted, they all talked of their surprise at police violence, none mentioned violence against the police. All believed it had been an important day in the formation of their political views.

I wonder how they would have felt – what we would have done – had they known what had happened the previous day in a small village 100 miles south of Da Nang. A hamlet (wrongly named as My Lai) was believed to be a Vietcong base and troops given the job of destroying it were told that anyone around on that day and at that time was to be treated as an enemy combatant. The result was a massacre of up to 400 civilians, including many women trying to shield their small children. The pictures of the My Lai massacre, published in November 1969, were some of the worst of the whole war.

The casualties were not just Vietnamese but also, in our minds, us. People just a few years older than me who were crossing the US border into Canada to dodge the draft. It was 'Red' Rudi Dutschke, the charismatic leader of the Berlin students, who was shot and nearly killed by a lone would-be assassin less than four weeks after the Grosvenor Square battle. This was about all of us! Or, as the anti-war protestors outside the Democratic Convention in Chicago that summer shouted at the bayonet-armed National Guard, 'The whole world is watching!'

Two British cultural creations defined the moment. The director Lindsay Anderson made an allegorical film, *If*, set in a public school in the English countryside. The bolshy hero, played by Malcolm McDowell, is in a battle against the authorities, and especially against the sadistic prefects – a form of auxiliary police force of the uncaring school establishment – who enjoy beating those left in their charge.

At the end, in a sequence that has been described as surreal but that I took completely literally, the hero and his friends find a collection of automatic weapons in a storeroom. On Founder's Day they take to the chapel roof and as the school hierarchy, the masters, the head and the dolled-up parents, emerge after the service, the rebels gun them down. A firefight breaks out with members of the Combined Cadet Force, and the despairing head-master, calling for peace, is shot through the head by a girl member of the revolutionary forces. I didn't go to a public school, but many, many teenagers came back from that film harbouring fanta-sies of pedagogicide.

The second in 1969 was the vinyl 45 record of a one-hit group, Thunderclap Newman, playing that one hit, 'Something in the Air'. I received it as a present on my fifteenth birthday. The guitarist, Jimmy McCulloch, was also – amazingly – fifteen. And as if that associative pull was not enough, the Something of the song was Revolution. 'We've got to get together sooner or later,' the band sang on *Top of the Pops* to millions of listeners, 'because the Revolution's here. And you know it's right.' Other people are saying it, not just us! The whole world is watching!

But, in fact, the moment of successful generational revolt had already passed. The Presidential election of November 1968 brought into the White House not Bobby Kennedy – he was dead. It didn't bring Senator Eugene McCarthy, the great hope of the anti-war youth. It didn't even bring the man who defeated McCarthy for the Democratic nomination, Vice President Hubert Humphrey. It brought Richard Milhouse Nixon.

I wasn't patient enough to listen to Nixon's campaign promises of peace or old enough to understand what later became known as the 'Nixon in China' syndrome: that it would take a man of the Right to come to an accommodation with the Communist world. What I saw was the Nixon who extolled the virtues of the 'silent majority' over the 'campus bums', who invaded Cambodia in 1970, and on whose angry watch Allison Krause, nineteen, and three other unarmed student protestors were shot dead on an American campus – Kent State in Ohio – in May 1970 by the state National Guard.

Allison Krause was the one I remembered because of her dad, Arthur, weeping into his thick glasses as he asked the TV audience why this had happened. I have never and I suppose now will never forget his words, some spoken, some sobbed. 'She felt that our crossing into Cambodia was wrong. Is this dissent a crime? Is this a reason for killing her? Have we come to such a state in this country that a young girl has to be shot because she disagrees with the actions of her government?' Two weeks later Crosby, Stills, Nash and Young recorded 'Ohio': a whole generation would defy Nixon and his tin soldiers.

In the end Richard Nixon did begin the ending of the war. And even if the slaughter outlasted his disgraced presidency, the peace process he endorsed earned his Secretary of State, Henry Kissinger, a Nobel Peace Prize.

My personal politics were about outrage and excitement. I wasn't required to think about the practical politics of it – strategies for winning support, for changing things. The Party did all that, I knew, but I was 'getting it together'. And if I was by a long stretch the most political kid I knew, there were several of my friends who would now come on demos and turn up at rallies as well.

South Africa was our other great cause. And here we were not talking about some distant war whose progress it would be hard for us to affect. South Africa was a place where Britons travelled to, traded with, played sport against, and had family. It was also a place that had sent its dissident whites into exile and many of them had fetched up in North London, helping to organise against what we invariably called 'the apartheid regime'. Consequently you could find arguments as visceral and immediate going on about happenings in Jo'burg, Cape Town and Soweto as if they

concerned Exeter, Watford and Nottingham. It had something to
do with us.

Governments appeared to treat South Africa as an unfortunate
reality; deplorable, even. It is hard to recall now in these post-
Mandela days just how easy it was to find apologists for, or fatalists
about, apartheid. South Africa was a wealthy, ordered society
where our companies operated in comfort. Its (white) troops had
succoured the Allied cause in two world wars. It stood as a bulwark
against Soviet naval expansion in the southern hemisphere. If, for
argument's sake, pointed out the fatalists, the nation's black
majority, made up of different tribes with long histories of mutual
antagonism, took power, well what then? One only had to look
north to the Congo to see how easily civilisation could be
destroyed by savagery. No, blacks themselves would probably like
to see some small reforms, but other than that wanted nothing
more than a peaceful life, untroubled by the extremists of the
African National Congress.

It may seem unlikely to the reader that a teenager absorbed
the arguments around an issue like this, but I did. I listened to
Any Questions on the radio (I was going to write 'on the BBC' but
there was only the BBC) and engaged in debates with schoolmates
whose own views were – like mine, I suppose – mostly shaped
by parental utterances.

But what should we, could we, do about it? Since the nation
was in every way run by and for its minority whites, we would
boycott South Africa. We would campaign against its produce,
we would campaign against its whites-only cultural visits and we
would campaign against its whites-only sporting teams. This last
campaign – the sporting boycott – was made much easier by the
stupidity of apartheid itself. Racial classification was bound to
throw up cases that looked silly even to those who were prepared
to tolerate them. And though latent forms of racial prejudice
were widespread in the Britain of the late '60s and '70s, so too
were a liking for 'fairness' and a distrust of the bullying proclivities of petty officialdom.

These traits came together in the famous D'Oliveira case of 1968. Basil D'Oliveira was a South African cricketer who, to most Britons, looked like a chap with a nice suntan, but whose racial classification was 'coloured' – i.e. neither white nor black. To call a not-quite-spade a spade, he was mildly superior to a black but wildly inferior to a white. Unable to play cricket at the top level in South Africa, 'Dolly' left his homeland and came to Britain, where he turned out very successfully for Warwickshire.

Up until that point, it had been left to individual Britons – like the handsome batsman David Sheppard (later Bishop of Liverpool) – to refuse to play against the South African teams because of their practice of apartheid. But then, in 1968, with an England team due to tour South Africa and with an injury to a senior batsman, the MCC – the English cricketing authority – could no longer dodge the question. When it was announced that D'Oliveira had indeed been chosen to go on tour with England the South African government described the decision as political and, in effect, demanded his withdrawal. There was outrage in Britain on Dolly's behalf and the MCC had no choice but to cancel the trip.

Nevertheless, they still planned to bring the all-white South Africans over to tour England in 1970. To prevent this from happening a campaign was set up, led by a voluble Young Liberal exile from South Africa, Peter Hain, called Stop the Seventy Tour (STST).

But another South African sporting tour already loomed. The mighty Springbok rugby team was on its way. No sport, we were told, was more important to the rugged Afrikaans minority than rugby. It was also the sport of the less rugged British establishment. Disrupt the rugby tour and you could have a tangible effect upon white morale in South Africa, hearten the black majority, and show the way for future British policy.

That's why, in December 1969, I found myself attending my first ever Twickenham rugby match. (It wasn't to be my last. I took up the sport soon afterwards and played for two years with a marked lack of distinction, but with an enthusiasm that surprised me, for the school 2nd XV). But we were there to bury the game, not to watch it. Some of our several thousand managed to get on to the pitch, but my mind's eye holds the picture of a policeman leaning inwards over the low wall separating the pitch from the stand, the strands of long hair trailing from his black gloves testifying to his personal technique for dealing with the hairy protestors of the time. None of it was mine – that was my last year of short hair.

Cricket was much more vulnerable. After weedkiller was poured on the outfield at Worcester, the number of grounds that would be able to host the 1970 South African cricket tour was cut by over half. One of the BBC's leading and most loved cricket commentators, John Arlott, said he would refuse to cover the tour and other journalists agreed. Still the MCC refused to call off the South African tour to Britain. Almost incredibly the Warwickshire County selectors said that they would solve the conundrum by not picking any of their non-white players to play against the South Africans. The following day their main ground at Edgbaston was vandalised.

In the end the government and other Commonwealth states made the MCC's mind up for it. Eight African countries announced that they would boycott the forthcoming Commonwealth Games in Edinburgh if the tour went ahead. In April the Prime Minister, Harold Wilson, said that the forthcoming cricket tour was a 'big mistake' and in May the Home Secretary James Callaghan, in so many words, demanded that the MCC call it off. This the MCC now did with extremely bad grace. It was an enormous victory. The next South African cricket team to tour Britain over twenty years later travelled with the blessing of their new leader, Nelson Mandela.

You could win! In the thin, coastal Republic of Chile, in the autumn of 1970, Salvador Allende became the first democratically elected Marxist President. His Popular Unity coalition won

narrowly, but it won, and it was like Dubček all over again – a
real fusion of democracy and socialism. Everything was folk song
and poetry. *El pueblo unido jamás será vencido.*

Oceans away from Santiago and Valparaiso, in the most
domestic of settings, I was at last arrested. In 1971 the Conservative
government attempted to cobble together a deal with the rebel
white government in the former colony of Rhodesia. So a demonstration was called, which would pass in front of Rhodesia House
in the Strand (the former High Commission, but closed for two
years). That year we had a temporary *History Boys* form of solidarity in our Lower Sixth group at school and several of my
classmates were persuaded to come on the march. For all but two
or three of us it was the first bit of civic activism we'd ever been
involved in.

The demonstration was medium sized, perhaps five or six thousand, made up mostly of anti-apartheid activists. After speeches
in Trafalgar Square the march began. A few yards down the Strand,
it stopped to have a shout. There was some shoving against the
police line, and then arrests. Our group of schoolboys was standing
on the pavement opposite Rhodesia House when we saw a girl
being dragged by a policeman across the road by her hair.

When something like that happened, the demonstrator's code
was to threaten to write down the policemen's numbers in the
hope that they would stop doing the brutal thing they were doing.
So I shouted out, 'Take his number!' As I did, a black-gloved hand
fell heavily on my shoulder. In my statement later given to a
solicitor from a firm often used by Party people I said that 'I spun
around and saw a policeman standing in front of me,' so that
must be what happened. 'I told you to move on,' this middle-aged
and burly sergeant said. If he had, he'd spoken from behind me
and I hadn't heard. 'OK, I'll move on then,' I replied. 'Not soon
enough,' he said. Then he took my arm, bent it up behind my
back – not very painfully – and marched me to the police line,
which opened up for us, and to one of the green coaches parked
near St Martin-in-the-Fields church.

I was only seventeen but I'd seen this often before. Mostly guys in their twenties being led off by policemen, sometimes yelling and being roughed up a little, and then bundled into these paddy wagons. There was something slightly romantic about it, but also mildly embarrassing. A really clever demonstrator should know how to avoid arrest unless he or she's trying to get arrested. And I wasn't. I had failed my democraft exam.

In the green coach arrested demonstrators sat next to their arresting officers in a strange, almost intimate affinity. The act of the arrest meant a period of relaxation for the coppers, and the fulfilment of part of their notorisus arrest quotas. For the mostly middle-class arrestees there was nothing now to be gained from anger, or even from surliness. Once the police had you in their power it was probably just as well to try to mollify them, otherwise they might give you a punch or just keep you in the cells as long as possible. So desultory, amicable conversations were going on up and down the bus, including one between me and my captor, who was surprised and a little disappointed, I thought, to discover I was only seventeen.

When the coach was full we drove off, past homeward-bound demonstrators, some of whom stared at us, and over the river to the red-brick late – Edwardian hulk of Battersea police station. There, one by one, we were taken by our officers to the desk sergeant, sitting behind his large ledger. The charge was pronounced for the first time – in my case it was the rather petty sounding 'wilful obstruction of a police officer' – and I was asked if I had anything to say, which came out as 'I didn't do anything' (demonstrator lore was to say 'no comment', but that suddenly sounded a bit guilty and a little rude). The sergeant wrote it down word for word and I then signed beneath it.

Deprived of my door key and the small change in my pockets, I was put in a six-man cell with a couple of students and an energetic white-haired man in late middle age. Stuart Clink Hood – was ever a middle name more appropriate? – had been in prison before. During the war he had been captured in North Africa and held in a POW camp in northern Italy. After escaping, he joined the Tuscan partisans resisting the Germans, taking on the *nom de guerre* Carlino.

Despite returning from the war a man of the socialist Left, Hood was of such erudition and talent that he was taken on by the cagey BBC, and by 1960 was its controller of television programmes. Under his aegis, the fabled successes of *Z Cars* and *That Was The Week That Was* were made. He'd gone on to be a senior executive in independent television, then into freelance programme production and by the time I encountered him in that cell, he was a professor teaching film and television at the Royal College of Art. His obituary would later quote the radical Hood musing on his time among the partisans. 'If I go back to Tuscany, I ask myself, "Well, was it worth it? To establish all these holiday homes?" On the other hand, fascism lost.'

I obviously didn't know all that then. What I saw was an unusual and impressive type of demo-arrestee – a television producer who seemed both annoyed and amused at being in Battersea nick, and it made me feel a little bit less silly for having been frog-marched against my will into a police coach. In any case, we weren't there long. By early evening my flustered friends had contacted my parents to tell them what had happened, and at around seven my brother-in-law turned up to stand bail, fighting a small smile on his in-a-police-station face, and took me away.

My reason for telling this story of trivial riot is partly to contrast the reaction of my friends to my arrest, and that of my family. I was going to plead not guilty when it came to trial and the boys who had been with me on the demo now had to be deposed by my solicitor. It soon became clear that for some of them this had led to trouble at home. Why had they been on a demonstration at all? Would they now be marked down on some police file for future scrutiny?

For the Aaronovitches, however, it was a sort of Marxist bar mitzvah, a rite of revolutionary passage. Neither Sam nor Lavender actually took me aside and said 'I'm proud of you, son!' but I knew they were. In our line of living, getting arrested for something – obstruction, assault, fly-posting – was part of the business. I was there, I got nicked, the solicitors were called. Next time try to get out of the way.

On the day of the hearing in Lavender Hill Magistrates' Court, my friends arrived nervous and smart, ready to testify to their affidavits. I sat in the rather disappointingly un-Old-Baileyesque dock in front of the stipendiary magistrate. My policeman, who turned out to be from the Special Patrol Group (an elite demo-busting group of the Metropolitan Police), stood up and read out a version of our Strand encounter that tallied in no obvious way with what had actually happened. He'd asked me and a group of others to move on three times, he said, and three times I had denied him and rallied them.

Knowing what I knew about the forces of the state this casual perjury was unsurprising. This wasn't personal, the officer's testimony seemed to say, this was just business. He wasn't lying because he disliked me, but having arrested me for being – as far as he was concerned – in the wrong place, then his constabulary duties needed to be done. What managed to shock me, though, was when my sergeant told the court that my signed statement in the police station had actually been 'Yes, I admit to having obstructed this officer.' I think I may have gasped.

It was usually the case back in the early '70s that, where your account conflicted with that of the police, the magistrate would choose to believe the plod. But this magistrate didn't. Perhaps if my friends hadn't been there to testify he would have come down on the side of the sergeant, or maybe it was our innocence – but in long hindsight I now realise that the beak simply thought I was telling the truth, that the policeman probably wasn't, and that the cause of law and order didn't absolutely require me gaining a criminal record and a £20 fine. The case was dismissed, our application for costs was turned down, and I left court a street fighting man.

I could have been a druggie instead. Other people I knew were. Rebellious youth of that period smoked dope, dropped acid and – if they had money or were connected to the beau monde of actors and musicians in some way – snorted coke. This was never attractive to me, even though I sometimes took a toke or two of a joint. It seemed a frivolous, expensive and uninteresting way of being young. One evening I found myself on the benches outside the Freemasons Arms next to Hampstead Heath listening to two local drug dealers having a long argument about which of them – their supplies otherwise exhausted – should have the last Mandrax. These older guys enjoyed some cachet among my group of friends, who thought they were transgressive, but to me they were so pathetic and so essentially disengaged that they gave the drug culture a bad name.

My hero was not some pill-addled rock star, but Salvador Allende. In the late summer of 1973, at the end of my gap year, six of us crammed into an old Peugeot station wagon and drove to Scotland and the isles, ending up on the Hebridean island of Barra. By the time we got back to London in September, the news was of a military coup in Chile, that the avuncular Allende was dead having fought to the last in the Presidential palace and that the new military junta was rounding up the folk singers, the poets and the Communists. It was 11 September – the other 9/11.

The pictures were of book burnings and beatings, but perhaps the most terrible photograph was of the new ruler of Chile, Augusto Pinochet sitting truculent, grim and brilliantined in his uniform, his arms folded high, dark glasses hiding his eyes, and his little mouth turned down in fatal disapproval. This was a man of electrodes and disappearances; a not unfamiliar type.

Pablo Neruda, the Communist love poet of Chile, had written of such a man and such a time:

> The delicate dictator is talking
> with top hats, gold braid, and collars.
> The tiny palace gleams like a watch

and the rapid laughs with gloves on
cross the corridors at times
and join the dead voices
And the blue mouths freshly buried.

Neruda died in Santiago twelve days after the coup. The more conspiratorially minded had him as a victim of murder, the pragmatic knew he had been dying from cancer, the romantic blamed a broken heart. Ten days earlier I had joined a vigil outside the Chilean Embassy, which was still in the hands of the Allende – era ambassador, who at one point appeared, stricken-looking, at an upstairs window. Tariq Ali was there again, with his followers, anxious to instruct the mourning and suddenly stateless staff on where their dead boss had gone wrong. The Chilean workers should have been armed. 'Armed Road the Only Road!' chanted Tariq at the ambassador. I have never really forgiven him his heartless arrogance but, of course, he too was young.

That week, as left-wingers were being murdered in the football stadium in Santiago which had been turned into a prison camp, a column appeared in *The Times* written by a Chilean socialite and close friend of Prince Charles – the woman in fact who had introduced him to the young Camilla Shand. The coup, she explained, had been a regrettable necessity, but now things could get back to normal under General Pinochet. Forty years on I cannot help but curse this woman's name when I find it in the reports of a royal wedding or a royal funeral.

A month after the coup I was a student of history at Balliol College, Oxford, where I officially joined the Party and went seriously off the rails. I'd really only chosen Balliol because Sam had been there, its Master was still the fabled Marxist historian Christopher Hill, and I knew almost nothing about any other universities.

In fact I'd made a ridiculous mistake. The Modern History syllabus at Oxford was archaic, ending at 1914 and regarding all events after that as 'current affairs'. I liked my gentle dons in their towers and managed essays for them, but the lectures were a savage disappointment. A. J. P. Taylor delivered his at 9 a.m. so as to force the indolent out of bed, and his addresses were reputed to be – word for word – unchanged in two decades. Hugh Trevor-Roper demanded that students attend his efforts wearing gowns, so as – he said – to distinguish them from any townsman or woman trying to sneak in and tap his wisdom gratis. I went to see each of them just once.

My trunk with all my clothes was mislaid by British Rail and didn't arrive until several weeks into the first term, I had no money and the university – supposed seat of rationality – was profoundly irrational. There were no women in college and the male to female ratio in the whole university was something like eight to one. Payment for college meals had to be made in an odd scrip called battels, which was sold in books of tickets. Law students dressed up in tuxedos and pissed through the gates of Trinity College as their forebears had done for a hundred years. The place loved – still loves – its dressing up and ceremonies. I couldn't deal with the flummery. Matriculation Day found me in bed in my room surrounded by three young ladies who'd suddenly come to visit, when the Dean swept in, expelled them and demanded to know why I was not in the Sheldonian Theatre speaking Latin.

Yet everybody else acted as though this was in some way normal. And to make it all even more discombobulating, in the sad absence of any carnal adventure I discovered I had unwanted company downstairs. How these tiny bloodsuckers survived the cold that November I cannot think. I didn't tell anyone about my problem, but some graffiti in the Junior Common Room loo reassured me. 'Don't throw toothpicks in the toilet,' it read, 'Balliol crabs can pole-vault.'

As well as a haven for pubic lice, and possibly not unrelated, Balliol had become known as the college for Lefties. But the politics were archaic. The local Party student branch was run by a brilliant mathematician with a broad face like an affable North Korean despot and an ideology to match. His sidekick was an Ulsterman who liked to dress in a black greatcoat and stride around talking about the need for a *chistka*, the Russian for 'purge'. Both pictured themselves, I think, as heirs of the Cambridge Five and therefore committed to the defence of the USSR, a place they imagined was still leading the world in the fight against fascism.

They were well in with the area organiser (the nearby Cowley plant was one of the biggest car factories in the country and helped Oxford earn a Party full-timer), a man called John Tarver. His subsequent career illustrates what kind of comrade he was. In 1976 he left Britain to go and work in East Germany at Potsdam University. He married an East German woman and supplemented his income – it later turned out – by spying on foreign visitors for the Stasi, the East German secret police. On the night that the Berlin Wall effectively fell in 1989 Tarver was meeting his Stasi contact officer in a safe house in the city. 'I thought I would be doing something to defend the socialist system in which I deeply believed,' he told an interviewer later. I think my Oxford student branch comrades would have loved to do exactly the same thing.

But another kind of politics had now seduced me. There was a gigantic sit-in in the large Examination Schools Building on Oxford High Street. Hundreds, perhaps thousands, of students took some part. Friendships were sealed and babies were narrowly avoided in its dark sat-in corridors. For the first time we were 'militants'.

Five weeks into term, at a meeting in the occupied Examination Schools, I stood for the Student Union Executive on the Occupation slate, a grouping whose only policy was to occupy things. It was a completely bonkers strategy and arose from the fact that the various left-wing groups involved did not want to be outbid by any of the others in terms of militancy. With my comrades I set out fly-posting at night for the Occupation cause. Three people were needed for this: one to hold the poster, one to hold the paste bucket and brush, and the third to keep a lookout. My team was adept. In one night we vandalised almost every flat surface in central Oxford. It was a terrible thing to do. And since my name was on the poster it earned me an automatic fine from the University court. I appealed the fine and won, on the basis that they had no evidence that I had myself committed any offence. They didn't, but I had.

Much of my time was spent in the Balliol Junior Common Room, a place of fiery debate, long hair (mine was down almost to my waist by late '73) and late-night toast. It had its own legends, such as the incident a year earlier when the Prime Minister and Old Balliolian, Edward Heath (nicknamed, for snobbish reasons, 'Grocer'), visited his alma mater. The night before his arrival JCR members broke into the Senior Common Room and, in red paint, daubed what one Fellow later described as 'a distinctly disobliging message of greeting' on the walls. The message was 'Fuck Off Grocer', but the miscreants dropped a wallet at the scene of the crime and one student was rusticated for a term. This hero was still at the college when I arrived and sported a magnificent Marquess of Bath beard and hair combination. He became a Green councillor in Cambridge and – over forty years on – his grey beard is as bushy as his white hair is long. He looks like a rounded Gandalf.

There in the Balliol JCR I made friends with the Trotskyists, anarchists, Maoists, situationists and public school dilettantes who hung out there. From them I picked up the cause of the moment – the demand for a central Student Union in Oxford, to which I dedicated the rest of my short Oxford career. My days and nights were consumed by dramatic meetings full of speeches and pleas, demonstrations up and down the High and in and out of medieval alleys, and sit-ins or attempted sit-ins. Quite a large proportion of the undergraduate population at some point in the next few months, including an Anthony Blair from St John's College, took part in some way in the campaign. As we marched someone would shout questions and we shouted our replies: 'What do we want?' 'CSU!' 'When do we want it?' 'Now!' 'How do we get it?' 'Occupy!'

As things got more and more absurdly intense the wife of Hugh Trevor-Roper, Lady Alexandra, demonstrated a familiar misplaced loftiness when she told a *Daily Telegraph* reporter, apropos of the demonstrators (one of whom was the future Cabinet minister, Chris Huhne), 'I don't believe any of them come from this university, they were a very scruffy dirty lot. Some were on top of the roof shouting, they were all wearing dirty jerseys.' After that we added a new question and return to our chants. 'What do we wear?' 'Dirty jerseys!'

In the end, the authorities got their revenge. At the end of the first term (i.e. after seven weeks) undergraduates had to troop in gown and mortar board to the very same Examination Schools and sit three 'Preliminary' papers. One was on the work of Edward Gibbon and George Macaulay. The other two were about historians who did not write in English. The options included Alexis de Tocqueville in French, the Venerable Bede in Latin, and the Swiss historian Jakob Burckhardt in German. I had passed an O level in French three years earlier, had never studied Latin, and had been taught German for just one year.

My Prelim on Burckhardt was marked by my expulsion from the examination room for not wearing a white shirt under my jacket and gown. I was, technically, improperly unsubfuscular. But what possible sense did it make to order a student out from a history examination because his shirt was a horrid paisley-patterned blue rather than regulation white? I came back in the Christmas vacation to resit the exam and failed. At the end of the second term, despite being provided with a tutor, I failed it again. In my two-term struggle against Burckhardt, the dead Swiss won.

Back home in London that early spring I received a brusque and brutal letter saying that having twice failed I was 'no longer a member of the college and must cease residence forthwith'. The great campaign had been defeated (no CSU ever materialised). The emotion I felt was something like relief; the spire madness was over. What more could I fear?

In May I began applying to universities again and, that October, Sam drove me up to a gigantic hall of residence for students at the University of Manchester.

Manchester in the mid-'70s was depressed and shabby. But it was, unlike Oxford, a real city with a proper local culture and a big sense of itself. Here the Communist Party was a powerful local force in the trade unions and in city campaigns. It ran an office from a large Victorian house on the Hathersage Road, and its several full-timers were not Stalinist eccentrics with one galosh in the Lubyanka. The Party 'line' was a serious matter and political discussion had a practical quality entirely missing in Oxford. Foreign comrades from all over the world lived here and gave a sense of consequence and authority to the discussions of international politics. It was what I was used to.

In Manchester I encountered, properly and in full voice, what was called 'the women's movement'. It had obviously been there somewhere in Oxford, but there were so few women in the university that it hadn't seemed so important. In Manchester feminism was almost brash. There was a women's group at the university, another at the polytechnic, several in the city. The feminist badge with the fist inside the circle of a Venus symbol was a regular presence on banners at local political events.

Feminism was not an ideology like Marxism. There were no set texts, no Great Teachers and no incontrovertible truths. There was a cacophony, ranging all the way from a straightforward egalitarianism to a frightening male-rejection. In a society that still expected men to make the initial advances, the business of dating and finding lovers became almost impossibly complicated.

What was an acceptable suggestion and what wasn't? It became safer to let women tell you whether they were interested which, of course, they were reluctant to do. Worse still, some men I knew in Manchester were abandoned by girlfriends who, though heterosexual, decided to become what was known as 'political lesbians'. Or maybe that's just what they said.

The oestrogen was intoxicating. It may have been uncomfortable for young men, but there was something about feminism that I thought was magnificent. It was obviously a movement for 'liberation'. It was necessary because women were subjected to violence, coercion and sexual assault in countries that imagined themselves to be advanced. It was optimistic because it believed that liberation was possible. It was a movement of aspiration and if the moment had a pictorial representation it was the cover of the writer Sheila Rowbotham's book, *Women, Resistance and Revolution*, published in 1972 and showing a middle-aged, ordinary-looking woman throwing off her broken shackles.

Women also had the best demonstrations. In 1975 a Conservative MP tried one of many private member attempts of the period to limit the already limited abortion rights in England and Wales. The National Abortion Campaign was set up to combat this move, and its perambulations around the town were characterised by mini-carnivals of singing, drumming, dancing and ruderies. It was much more fun to be on a demo like this than on some dour and pessimistic march against the government's pay policy.

The anthem of the women's movement was a song by Peggy Seeger about a woman who just wanted to be an engineer and was thwarted at every turn until, in middle age, she was finally taken on by a cost-cutting boss. It ended on a note of defiant ambition:

> *I've been a sucker ever since I was a baby*
> *As a daughter, as a mother, as a lover, as a dear*
> *But I'll fight them as a woman, not a lady*
> *I'll fight them as an engineer!*

There may have been another, more personal reason why I liked feminism, but I didn't see it at the time. Women's liberation suggested the idea of the strong woman, or – at least – the un-dependent woman. The feminist wasn't pining for her husband or lover to come home and didn't build her fragile world around him, just as I did not want to be depended upon or built around. I tried exploring this once at a meeting of a group called Men Against Sexism, but the prevailing anxiety of those present in the polytechnic meeting room was whether or not they were gay and – whatever the answer to that was – whether they shouldn't sleep with other men anyway. I wasn't opposed to it in principle, but that particular group was composed of earnest chaps with beards who looked like the model for the man who had such serious illustrated coition in the pages of *The Joy of Sex*. Sex with them, whatever else it might have been like, did not sound as if it would be fun.

For two of my three years in Manchester I lived in a Party commune in a huge Victorian house near the road that ran south from the city centre to the suburb of Didsbury. The owners were a young Party academic at the university and his Party partner, a qualified general practitioner. They had two young children and had decided to operate their house as a collective in which they and four or five communards – chosen by them – would eat, cook, shop, clean and party together.

Comrade Professor A was – is – one of the most agreeable people I have ever known – intelligent, sensitive and unselfish. He is something of a theoretician and sat on the Party's economic committee. But the animating force in the house was his wife. Physically striking, comrade Doctor J was a feminist dynamo who dashed around Manchester speaking and organising and who also carried out early abortions for women who needed them, sometimes right there in the house. Or did I imagine that? She was also a woman of great and occasionally alarming enthusiasms.

The house was full of unintentional comedy. There was, for example, the argument over whether to put a lock on the main bathroom door. J was concerned that the children (then aged two and four), on encountering a barrier, would assume that anything relating to the body was somehow shameful, thereby perpetuating the alienation between the physical and intellectual selves that capitalism and patriarchy demanded. The fastidious house-comrade G – a postgraduate student of shy but obstinate temperament – was equally determined to be able to take a shit in peace. For myself, I simply had no great desire to walk in on others en commode, and certainly couldn't imagine cleaning my teeth while someone else was evacuating, which was – I knew – the kind of outcome J's policy was leading up to. In fact, had she won I suspect that she would have removed the entire door.

Twenty-five years later the Swedish director Lukas Moodysson's film *Together* – set in a Swedish commune in a not dissimilar house at exactly the same time – captured something of that Manchester collective. The commune's leader, Göran, is a gentle, conflict-averse idealist in a house full of less unselfish spirits. His girlfriend is cheerfully promiscuous, and the second couple in the house have split up because the girl has become a lesbian. Their son Tet, named after the offensive, plays a game with a friend in which they take turns to be General Pinochet and his left-wing victims. It all felt very familiar.

Our commune was distinguished in one very idiosyncratic way: we had all, at one time or another during our tenure, slept with J. Or rather, she had slept with us. J had a highly democratic attitude towards sex and the relationship between her and G was officially as open as a tram museum. On his side the openness was largely theoretical and intellectual, but on hers it was anything but: she was adept in uniting theory and practice. She would snog anyone she wanted to at a party, and she maintained a steady affair with a rugged revolutionary from a small splinter group – a man I knew only as 'Guy from Big Flame'.

So it was an unstated rule of membership of the commune for men and women that – be they ne'er so ill-favoured or inexperienced – J would appear one night in their bedrooms and exercise a revolutionary *droit de seigneuse*. My two turns came on successive early mornings a month or so into my stay. The door softly opened, J entered, dropped her dressing gown, slid into bed and had me. She had me one way one morning and another way the next. And all the while she was going on around me I understood how I was making up for centuries of women's oppression by being taken, willy nilly (and mostly, I suppose, willy), by one of Britain's leading feminists. It felt strange, but worse things could happen to a boy.

If the house and our bit of the Party was feminist, it was also resolutely anti-racist. That seems obvious today, but it was still an evolving view then. To be on the left of politics was not always and everywhere the same as being consistently opposed to racism. I had observed that myself in the late '60s.

In early April 1968 Martin Luther King was shot dead in
Memphis, Tennessee on the balcony of a motel. Just over two
weeks later in Birmingham, Great Britain, the Right Honourable
Enoch Powell MP, member of the Conservative Party's shadow
Cabinet and a former Secretary of State, made a speech that
tumbles down the decades, its sentiment echoed a thousand times,
its arguments made afresh every decade.

The apologists for Powell's oration – and there have been
many – have usually said that the most offensive passages of the
speech were not his words, but those contained in the conversations or letters of others. Powell, they have argued, was not a
racist – he admired Indians, for example – but someone who put
into words what many were feeling.

In fact Powell selected his sources carefully and approved their
sense. There was the 'middle-aged, quite ordinary working man
employed in one of our nationalised industries', who told Powell
that 'in this country in fifteen or twenty years' time the black man
will have the whip hand over the white man' and – in an irony missed
by both him and Powell – said he wouldn't be happy until his children were 'all settled overseas' as somewhere else's immigrants.

Or the letter-writer who told Powell the long story of a lone
old-aged pensioner living in a street which had supposedly turned
from all-white to all-black in just eight years. 'With growing fear
she saw one house after another taken over. The quiet street
became a place of noise and confusion.' Now she was a prisoner
in her own home. 'She is becoming afraid to go out. Windows
are broken. She finds excreta pushed through her letter box. When
she goes to the shops, she is followed by children, charming,
wide-grinning piccaninnies. They cannot speak English, but one
word they know. "Racialist," they chant.'

It was the native white English people, said Powell, who were
discriminated against, they who 'found their wives unable to obtain
hospital beds in childbirth, their children unable to obtain school
places', they who had not been consulted but now 'found themselves made strangers in their own country'.

I can still hear Powell's perorations in my mind's ear. There was a horrid avidity about the way, in his soft, Midlands purr, he pronounced his prophecy. 'We must be mad, literally mad, as a nation,' said Powell, 'to be permitting the annual inflow of some 50,000 dependants, who are for the most part the material of the future growth of the immigrant-descended population. It is like watching a nation busily engaged in heaping up its own funeral pyre.' And yet he didn't sound upset about it all, but excited.

The Party was strong in the London docks, but at that moment Powell was stronger. When the Conservative leader, Edward Heath, dismissed Powell from his front-bench post, hundreds of dockers marched on Westminster to demand his reinstatement. If there was one thing that the dock workers of London tended not to maintain an interest in, it was the composition of Conservative shadow cabinets. The slogan on some of the plac-ards, 'Back Britain not Black Britain' suggested the real motivation. A week after the speech 4,500 dockers were on strike.

I wasn't yet fourteen but I had no doubt what motivated the strikes and the speech. It was obvious from casual references to 'wogs', which at that time was the generic dismissive noun for any non-white person; obvious from the comments by a leading Fleet Street columnist Jean Rook on the BBC's *Any Questions* programme that she would 'loathe to live next door to a black man'; obvious from the jokes you heard at school about how blacks ate Kit-e-kat (a tinned cat food).

There was a disconcerting problem to be observed (or, in my case, slowly absorbed) in the Powell business. While *The Times* – the organ of the capitalist establishment, whose words would be read over breakfast by the genteel – condemned the Powell speech, some of those most class-conscious members of the proletariat we wished to put in power celebrated it. In the weeks that followed, black people were physically attacked or insulted by people invoking Powell. I might be on the side of the working class, but could I be sure that they were altogether on mine?

Battling racism became a major political theme in the troubled 1970s. An organisation called the National Front, a blending of populist Powellite racists with the leftovers of Mosleyite and overtly Nazi sects, rose just as the long post-war boom subsided. It won limited successes in elections, peaking in 1977 with 120,000 votes in the elections for the Greater London Council. Its marches were the antithesis of our feminist carnivals: ominous flag and drum fests borrowed from the sectarians of Northern Ireland.

So the young Left was galvanised into taking on the fascists. Nazi Germany would not be repeated here! Whether you were a Communist, a Trot or a free-floating anarcho-syndicalist, you could agree that racism and fascism were things to be fought and, if necessary, to be fought on the streets. They shall not pass!

This kind of fascist-confronting felt both necessary and exciting; sometimes too exciting since it involved the constant possibility of physical confrontation with the kind of people who were, at that time, giving football supporters a reputation for pointless, extreme violence. In the late summer of 1977, for example, at the scuzzy zenith of National Front power, I witnessed the closest thing to a proper riot that I ever saw in London. A National Front march against mugging ('85% of muggers are black, 85% of their victims are white!') was held in New Cross in South London, an area with a large Afro-Caribbean population. The older Left, including the Party, organised a broad-based counter-demonstration the route of which, as agreed with police, would not intersect the route of the National Front. There would be bishops, community groups singing songs, and even some Conservatives, who'd all head home, their peaceful point peacefully made, before the Front arrived.

This hardly seemed in keeping with the spirit of Cable Street 1936 (so reasoned many excited young Leftists), when – Sam among them – the Jewish inhabitants of the East End and their working-class allies forcibly prevented the fascists from marching. Far from not intersecting the route, they – legendarily – had blocked it, creating one of the most persistent folk legends in the history of the British Left.

As their predecessors had done, so would they do. In any case a third group had made up its collective mind that a bit of real violence might be appropriate here. Black kids in London were seriously fed up by the late '70s. They were more likely to be unemployed than their white contemporaries and their recreational habits were not understood by the authorities; particularly not by London's Metropolitan Police. The result was continuous friction between them and a law-keeping force many of whose members were given to casual expressions of bigotry when annoyed. And now a load of white thugs who hated blacks were going to come stomping through their streets guarded by the fuzz.

I was on my own that day and arrived at New Cross station in the mid-afternoon. Down both sides of the New Cross Road, where the Front would shortly arrive, the drab cafés and shops were lined with a thick coating of young lefties, some with banners – and with young bannerless black people.

When the Front hove into view, preceded by the sound of shouting, parabolas of bottles and sticks – first a few and then many more – arced and fell around the fascists and their police guards. From a building site adjacent to the road came bricks and smoke bombs. Within a few minutes a running three-way fight with head-kicking and blood developed in places where the police line had failed. In 1974 in less dangerous circumstances a student from Warwick had died during one of these confrontations. How no one died at the Battle of Lewisham, I have no idea, but over a hundred people were injured. The fighting between black boys and the police went on long after the National Front members (and I) had slunk off. It was a foretaste of urban riots to come.

Fortunately the Left managed to be a bit more politically inventive than its essentially thuggish opponents. A Trot group set up an umbrella organisation called the Anti-Nazi League, with well-designed natty little placards and logos. And popular musicians, whose appeal went far beyond what political people could muster, came together in a campaign called Rock Against Racism. You could express your opposition to Nazis by attending a concert with some of your favourite bands! How cool was that?

But when it came to the Party I don't think we had any idea that up was actually down. The Cold War seemed to be almost at an end in the era of what was called détente. Russia no longer needed any defending by us. Right-wing dictatorships had fallen in Portugal, in Spain, in Lavender's beloved (but never seen) Greece. The Vietnam war ended. A Democrat entered the White House, Mozambique and Angola became free and independent, turning the screw on the white supremacists of South Africa.

And a new form of Communism emerged, first as an intellectual tendency and then as a guiding force – a Communism in the snazzy shape of Western European leaders of mass parties. Schooled in the politics of the trendy dead Italian Antonio Gramsci rather than in a dusty reiteration of Marxism–Leninism, men like the Sardinian aristocrat Enrico Berlinguer and the hero of the Spanish underground, Santiago Carrillo, mapped out a new politics. One that no longer owed anything to the Soviet Union, that required no awkward dancing around the reality of how dissidents were treated, or how socialist democracy was, in the socialist countries at any rate, oxymoronic. People like me, sons and daughters of Party people, drank down Eurocommunism like desert-stranded adventurers drank down oasis water in the movies.

Ostensibly this was about Russia, as so much about Communism was. So in 1977 when the Party split, it seemed a good split at the time.

One of the peculiarities of Party life was that the most hard-line, pro-Soviet and 'proletarian internationalist' members of the Party were to be found in places like Oxford, Hampshire and Surrey. The District Secretary of Surrey since 1950, Sid French (called by one disgruntled Surrey member 'The Stalin of Surburbia'), even lent his name to the 'Stalinist' faction in the Party, known as Frenchites. As John Gollan stood down as General Secretary in 1976, opening a debate on inner Party democracy, the strangled content of which I cannot bring myself to recall, French took it as the cue to walk out of the Party and to take the un-terrifying class warriors of the Home Counties with him. Some 700 Party members followed and became the New Communist Party. Remarkably the NCP still exists, just. Its few dozen elderly members travel to places like North Korea and discover great joys and achievements that other travellers contrive to miss.

I loved Eurocommunism. It seemed the perfect way of squaring the circle of my upbringing. It was inclusive, democratic, progressive, pro-feminist, anti-racist, liberal and everything else that I instinctively leaned towards. Eurocommunists ran the Party's theoretical journal, *Marxism Today*, and organised an ideas festival called the Communist University of London every summer. (Aged twenty I was responsible for the evening events at the 1975 CUL. They were something of a fiasco. I held a film show of an interminable movie called *Born of the Americas* about Castro, Allende and Che. It was a warm night, the sound failed, and we sat there for three hours in the University of London Union watching revolutionaries mouth silent heroisms at each other.) In the year of the Queen's Silver Jubilee – also 1977 – the Party ran a People's Jubilee at Alexandra Palace, with clowns, face-painting, ethnic foods, discussion and speeches: 11,000 people attended at some point or another.

If Eurocommunists had a fault, it was a tendency towards intellectual abstraction. Our positions were not easily sloganised (What do we want? Hegemony! When do we want it? As soon as we have built the ideological conditions for an alliance between the working class and other key social strata!) One summer all my Eurocommunist colleagues would talk about was a French philosopher called Louis Althusser, whose greatest work was called 'Ideology and Ideological State Apparatuses: Notes Towards an Investigation'. Always something of a young empiricist, I judged that if I couldn't understand a word of what someone said, then the chances were that the masses wouldn't either. It came as a wicked relief at the time when, in 1980, Althusser went mad, killed his wife and was committed. Knowing what I now know about mental illness I am rather ashamed at my callousness.

I suppose my assumption had been that the things in which I was interested – race, feminism, democracy, international freedom – would complement working-class militancy, in a grand alliance of 'progressive forces'. And there was a lot of working-class militancy around. I was on the picket line outside a photo-processing plant called Grunwick's in North London when the Yorkshire miners arrived to lend their physical presence to the strike by mostly Asian workers. In 1977 working days lost through stoppages tripled from their 1976 figure, remained at the same high level in 1978 and then, in 1979, tripled again. All this under a Labour government.

At a facile level this was surely grist to the true socialist mill. The Party bigwigs at or near the top of major unions professed themselves pleased with all this militancy. Organised labour was on the march. But more thoughtful people in the Party had begun to wonder where this march was heading.

If you want to trace the australopithecus to New Labour's *Homo sapiens* you can probably find it in a lecture given by Eric Hobsbawm at the Marx Memorial Library in March 1978. In polite language, but unmistakably, Hobsbawm told those enthralled by trade union militancy that – in political terms – their strategy led nowhere. He noted the twenty-five-year secular decline in electoral support for both Labour and Communist Parties, the rise of the white-collar workers, the paucity of working-class people going on from militancy to political activity, and noted that striking to get yourself higher wages did not seem to inculcate a sense of wider class responsibility. Quite the opposite, such activity 'may at times set workers against each other rather than establish wider patterns of solidarity'.

The lecture was called 'The Forward March of Labour Halted?' and caused a row that rippled beyond the Party. Though Hobsbawm didn't set out his ideas for rebooting the Left machine, one obvious conclusion to be drawn from his words was that piling resources into automatic support for each and every pay strike was unproductive.

A critic of Hobsbawm's new thinking was the Marxist academic, Ralph Miliband, a man who had usually stayed aloof from practical politics and who was made famous after his death by the accession of his son, Ed, to the leadership of the Labour Party. Miliband senior was much more upbeat about strikes and walkouts. He saw 'advance in comparison with an earlier epoch, where he [Hobsbawm] sees stagnation and retreat'. Hobsbawm was being defeatist, thought Miliband, since his 'perspective of decline obscures not only the many positive developments which have occurred in the trade union movement: it also produces a debilitating under-estimation of important developments which have occurred in other areas'.

That winter the people of Britain saw images that transcended anyone's capacity for complex explanation. Uncollected mounds of rubbish appeared in London landmarks like Leicester Square. Petrol stations closed, trains stopped, ancillary hospital staff and ambulance drivers went on strike and, infamously, in Liverpool gravediggers downed shovels and bodies piled up in a rented factory. And all this over pay demands. At some point during this awful parade I slid over from enjoying strikes to hating them; from hoping they would succeed to praying that they would just stop.

That too was the view of the Eurocommunists and they and Hobsbawm and I received horrid vindication four months later when the Labour Party was turfed out of power by an epically underestimated leader of the Conservative Party, Margaret Thatcher. An essential part of her constituency were skilled workers who had been thoroughly scared during 'the winter of discontent', and rallied to her assurance that under her the Forward March of Labour would be reversed.

Thatcher turned the assumptions of the Left upside down and inside out. She did things that had been considered impossible, undo-able. Venerable state monopolies were sold off. Controls on capital almost abolished. In 1984–5 she smashed a strike by the most powerful union in Britain, the National Union of Mineworkers. She and her friend, the new American President Ronald Reagan, helped rearm a renewed Cold War. And every time she did these unimaginable things, she was rewarded at the polls.

The result was a collapse of morale and faith in a British Left which had imagined that *it* represented the threat to the post-war consensus. And pure Thatcher-hatred – though cathartic – simply wasn't enough to replace what had gone. The long march towards New Labour began: Foot to Kinnock, Kinnock to Smith, Smith finally to Tony Blair.

In the course of this journey, where it became increasingly pessimistic about the use of old methods to combat a phenomenon like Thatcherism, the Party started to play the role of John the Baptist to the delayed Messiah. It was a Party miners' leader, George Bolton, who first said the unsayable about the miners' strike – that, in effect, the whole thing was a catastrophic mistake, however heroic the strikers and their families had been. The Labour leader Neil Kinnock, whose electoral defeats now obscure his considerable political courage, openly agreed.

Unsurprisingly, two things resulted from the new strategy. First, as members died or dropped out, not enough new recruits were being found to take part in this slightly obscure jihad. Second, a section of the membership that liked the things the old working-class way became increasingly restive. By the mid '80s the Party was writhing in schism. I recall attending a branch meeting in Hackney, where I was living, which was characterised by such mutual loathing between old comrades that we narrowly escaped without punches being thrown.

The end came remarkably quickly. Or perhaps, objectively, it should have happened years earlier. In 1988 the Party split, with the *Morning Star*, for Byzantine reasons, being taken over by the new 'hard-line' Communist Party of Britain. Perhaps more noticed by the peoples of the world, however, the Soviet Union went from mightiness to dissolution in the space of a doctorate. Its collapse between 1989 and 1991 was the triumphant apotheosis of Thatcherism and Reaganism.

It wasn't, of course, that the Party had been banging the drum for Russia for some time. It was the realisation, as the Stasi files were opened and the Securitate fought in the tunnels under Bucharest, that there was nothing whatsoever to recommend real, existing socialism. The health service wasn't better. The society was not, in a peculiar way, more spiritual. It was, rather, cynical, backward, disillusioned and poor.

By 1991 almost everything a Communist could do he or she could do better somewhere else. The rump of good-natured feminists, Greens and democrats who had taken over the Party now dissolved it and set up a ginger group cum think tank called Democratic Left. The journey begun in Cannon Street Hotel had petered out after seventy years.

As for me, in my head I left the Party in around 1980, and in reality in 1987. I'd got my degree at Manchester, become immersed in student politics, and ended up as the first President of the National Union of Students to have Mrs Thatcher as Prime Minister during his entire term of office. I had friends who were in the Labour and Liberal and no parties, and by the time I left the student world I was meetinged out, demo-shy and political commitment averse. Around 1979 it occurred to me that there was nothing to be learned from the great leader Lenin and after that, though I liked *Marxism Today* and some of their thinkiness, I drifted off.

I became a journalist first in television and then in newspapers. When I moved from a producer's job in ITV to one of editing a new politics programme for the BBC I was told, in effect, that a condition was that I must leave the Communist Party. They couldn't really be doing with the adverse publicity if a paper like the *Daily Mail* discovered that I was still a Commie. So I left. But because Lavender and I were, at that moment, in the same Hackney branch, I couldn't not tell her. We'd driven down for a walk by the River Lea, but I waited until we were in the car on the way home. Her reaction was as full of hurt at my betrayal as I had feared it would be. In my emotional confusion I reversed my Ford Escort at speed into the back of a geographically incongruous Porsche. The Porsche was undamaged: the Escort cost £100 to fix.

By then – for reasons that we will discover later – Lavender and Sam had lived apart for over a decade. She occupied a flat above Sabrina in Stoke Newington, kept a dog, went to writers' classes, tended her roof terrace and was a valued member of the Older Feminist Network. Lavender stayed in the Democratic Left until it too disappeared.

She had her first heart attack in the early 1980s, recovered, but then – through her late seventies – began to suffer from arthritis, circulatory and digestive problems. She saw six grandchildren and two great-grandchildren into the world, and died, aged eighty-two, from a stroke. Lavender had a 'green funeral' as she had requested, on the day in July 2005 when we heard the news that London had won the right to stage the 2012 Olympic Games; her funeral procession was punctuated by the cheers of her grandchildren when the news was received by text.

Sam had been dead for seven years by then. He had followed his Oxford doctorate with a rise through academia – a rise that he knew to his frustration was limited more by his age than his ability. He became Professor of Business Studies at a London polytechnic, set up a think tank, and – for twenty years – worked as hard as he ever had in politics. He wrote books, served on the Party's Economic Committee and travelled the world taking in the marvels that, for fifty years, he'd missed out on. He never stopped being in a hurry. He never stopped learning.

In 2003, five years after his death, Britain invaded Iraq alongside the Americans. After months of internal debate I had decided that I didn't want to oppose the removal of what I saw as a fascist dictator – they shall not pass, and all that. As I was a writer for the *Guardian* and the *Observer* this meant that my family, friends and old comrades, many of whom would profoundly disagree with the invasion, would not be able to miss my apostasy.

Predictably, the letters and messages of excommunication arrived. One upset me more than most. It was from the old East End Communist Solly Kaye, who as a child I had watched every year doing his witty appeals for money at the *Daily Worker* and *Morning Star* rallies. I always enjoyed the memory of him though I hadn't heard a thing from him in twenty years, but now he wrote to tell me that my father, whom he had known very well, would 'never have tolerated such posturing'.

Was that true? Actually probably not. Sam was always in the business of escaping the last set of shackles that held him. In late middle age, Sam had taken up running (at sixty-six he ran the Bury St Edmunds half marathon in 1 hour 55. Look it up. It is a very good time!), and would drive, as I said, halfway across Europe to see one picture in a south German gallery. He fought any and every effort on the part of the polytechnic to retire him and was still fighting when complications of liver cancer killed him at the age of seventy-eight. Three months before his death he held a huge party for people from all epochs of his life at a club on Exhibition Road. I don't think anyone who was there that night will ever forget it. At one point his children and his younger friends held him aloft while seated on a chair, while a klezmer band played the music of a youth he'd not quite had.

So, by July 2005, Lavender, Sam and the Party were all over. And that – and you may think this odd – allowed me to begin thinking about telling the real story.

PART III

MESSAGE TO THE UNBORN

Introduction

Ihr, die ihr auftauchen werdet aus der Flut
In der wir untergegangen sind
Gedenkt
Wenn ihr von unseren Schwächen sprecht
Auch der finsteren Zeit
Der ihr entronnen seid.

You, who shall resurface following the flood
In which we have perished,
Contemplate –
When you speak of our weaknesses,
Also the dark time
That you have escaped.

Bertolt Brecht, *To the Unborn*, 1939. Translated
by Scott Horton

People make their own history, Marx famously wrote, but not in circumstances of their own choosing; the traditions of dead generations weigh down on the living like nightmares. And most of the time they don't even know it – as he should have added. The child certainly doesn't know. He accepts what he finds around him and fills in the gaps with pictures and explanations of his own, ones that he's almost unaware of seeing or making. I imagined, without ever once consciously thinking any such thing, that the world – especially my parents' world – more or less began at my birth. What they were was what, allowing for age, they had always been. However difficult life could be there was no weighing-down nightmare.

Naturally, this was wrong. The assumptions that formed the foundations of the house in which I lived had been fashioned before I entered it. The adults knew part of that prehistory and either recited in full the episodes they liked in the form of anec-dotes, referred to them gnomically or felt no need or desire to speak about them at all.

For example, the books already on our shelves and the books no longer on our shelves were – had I but known it – almost archaeological evidence of how things had come to be. Lenin was everywhere, but Stalin existed only in a remote bookcase in Sam's study. The books were just like the friends my parents had and the friends who were not friends any more.

What I have written up until now is – roughly – what I knew at the time or what I easily gathered. It is a history of the apparent. But what became increasingly obvious to me as I researched this book was that the explanations I sought for *why* things were as they were, were to be found either in the past or in the things left unsaid. When I knew how to look at what was there – and what wasn't – a story began to appear.

In addition to her diaries, which I inherited on her death in 2005, Lavender left letters and fragments of memoirs going back to the 1930s. The diaries also allowed me to cross-reference what was in them against my own memories, other accounts of the time and – in one extraordinary episode – the case history of a family published by the therapist who dealt with them. The case history of my family.

Biographies, academic studies, websites and, finally, the National Archives enabled me to build up a picture of Lavender and Sam, of us their children and the hopeless, hopeful, sometimes heroic and sometimes unpleasant and stupid reality of British Communism. This, then, is the history of what I did not know; the history I never saw and the biography I never quite lived. It explains almost everything.

9

Party Spies

**This is not to say that all Communists would be
prepared to betray their country; but there is no
way of separating the sheep from the goats.**

Cabinet Committee on Subversive Activities, 29 May 1947

Serendipity provided the photograph and the letter. The picture,
in black and white, was on the back cover of a history of Britain in
the early 1950s. It shows a family sitting around a kitchen table
in somewhere that is not suburbia. The room is thin, high-
ceilinged, with a tiled area and a stove at one end. On the table
is a pint of milk and some plates. Facing the camera, with a mug
in one hand, is a man and next to him a small girl of about seven.
Another two children, a boy and a girl, sit at the ends of the table
and a woman faces the man, her back to us.

The letter – marked 19A – was in the National Archives, and
had been in a file kept by the secret services. It had been sent on
29 August 1951 and a note at the top acknowledged its receipt five
days later. The letter was typed, with only the beginning ('My
Dear Bill') and the signature being handwritten.

My Dear Bill,

   This may prove to be complete nonsense so I am committing
the mild impropriety of sending it to you privately.

   My mother, as I may have mentioned to you before, lives in a
flat on the third floor of a shabby-genteel Victorian street in
Hampstead called Belsize Park Gardens, NW3, No 62. In the first

floor flat there is a happy family of Communists, obviously activists rather than sentimental adherents or communisants. It is apparently a rather amorphous, or at all events, changing household, but the central figure is a Mrs Brigitte Long (now Nicholson). She is believed to be Viennese and what her maiden name is, I know not.

It is without social rancour that I say that they are a scruffy lot but they are as busy as bees and Nicholson's navel is enormously distended by carrying banners in Trafalgar Square.

The letter's writer now moved from social observation to the purpose of his communication. Was it possible that these Communists were up to no good? He continued:

The other day my mother found in the entrance hall of the house two sheets of paper on which the Communist children had been drawing – for all the world as if they were little capitalists. My mother was merely making a despairing effort to keep the place tidy but found herself interested in the curious hieroglyphics on the papers, and they found their way eventually to me.

The author could see that the 'hieroglyphics' were the drawings by small children of semi-anthropomorphised animals – probably dogs. Perhaps these intrigued his communally minded mother, but what interested him was typescript, on the reverse side, concerning economic statistics in Britain's African colonies.

I make no comment on them but you may have African experts to whom all will be made clear. Although I have no evidence to support it, it may well be that the Nicholson ménage may be either a channel for sending propaganda to Africa or for making contacts with Africans here.

Yours ever,

Nigel.

The photograph is now part of a collection of pictures by the photographer Henry Grant held at the Museum of London. And the family round the kitchen table is the same family as the family in the Dear Bill letter, at almost exactly the same time – 1951. Jock Nicholson, railwayman and Communist candidate in St Pancras North – whom you met earlier in the book as the man who thought Sam would have made a better London District Secretary than Frank Stanley – is the man with the mug. The little girl next to him, Laura, was one of my sister Sabrina's closest friends. The woman is the woman I always knew as Bridget Nicholson, the one who took paying customers on 'Marx and Engels' walks around North London. There they are captured in the photograph and captured in the secret file.

There is very little about Bill's correspondent that is not mildly repellent. He is exactly the thing he says he is not – socially rancorous – yet nevertheless is content to have his mother living in a 'shabby genteel' flat with awkward neighbours. He is snide and pompous and inclined to fill in gaps in his knowledge with bad guesses (Bridget – Viennese?). And he is palpably wasting everyone's time. But he knows a man in MI6 or Special Branch and he clearly enjoys writing to him with some possibly important information.

You can look at the picture and then at the letter and, on their own, they would confirm almost everything I thought about the way that people, including officialdom, imagined Communists. Obviously just normal men and women with kitchens and children – families we knew and liked – were regarded as aliens, as we were. Like the Nicholsons we were a scruffy lot, we carried banners, we drew pictures on waste paper. Sabrina thinks she remembers the kitchen in the photograph and played in the hall of that building. We as a family were spied on and discriminated against and Sam was also, in the sense that Nigel meant it, 'Viennese'.

I remember being told when I was about eleven that our phone was tapped. A Post Office engineer had been treated by a Party doctor (one of the practitioners where Lavender worked) and, in a moment of grateful contrition, had divulged that he worked in the department that did the interceptions. All leading Communists' phones were tapped, he said. A couple of years later, when I was at home on my own, a telephone engineer arrived out of the blue. The handset at our house was not working, he said, and he had with him a new one, which he proceeded to install. No one had called the Post Office and in those days it was common to have to wait some time for an engineer. Perhaps we had been lucky, but we doubted it.

In the mid '70s the newspapers (and not just the *Morning Star*) carried the report on how workmen replacing woodwormy panelling in the meeting room at the Covent Garden HQ came across a small electronic device which proved to be a hidden microphone. As we have seen, at some earlier date state-licensed housebreakers had obviously got access to the room and installed bugs. The idea that the secret services were wasting their time in snooping on the perfectly legal (and often fabulously tedious) activities of a political party seemed to suggest to me that they simply weren't very good at their jobs.

But this was of a piece with the strange way that people regarded Communists. It was a background theme to our lives: something had happened, something had been said, someone hadn't got a job, because of being a Party member. You couldn't work at the BBC and be a Communist. You couldn't work in the Civil Service and be a Communist. You couldn't be an academic and – Christopher Hill's later success notwithstanding – hold the top positions, however brilliant and well qualified, and be a Communist. In almost any situation, except in the greater labour movement, being in the Party was a handicap. The only possible way round it was to be 'twice as good', twice as brilliant, twice as conscientious at any job, and then they might let you be.

In essence it was just unfair. We weren't the puppets of a foreign power they took us for. We weren't subversive. We just had strong opinions and cared about things like poverty, peace and the working class. That, when you render it down, is what I thought when I was young.

It was true that there had been one senior Party man who had sent British secrets to Russia, I knew that, as did other Party people. I also knew that the Party had not known what he had been up to and had expelled him when he was discovered. I was aware of it partly because the case involved – bizarrely – our dentist, our babysitter and my father's second wife.

Dave Springhall had been a movement hero, an organiser for the unemployed during the Depression, and a veteran of the International Brigades in Spain, wounded in 1937 at the Battle of Jarama where the British Brigade lost more than half its men. For just over a year, after his return to Britain, Springhall was the editor of the *Daily Worker*, and then went to Moscow as the Party's representative to the Communist International – the Comintern. After Britain declared war on Germany, Springhall came back to London to become part of the argument as to whether the Party should continue to support the war effort.

By 1943 he was National Organiser of the Party, effectively number three in the hierarchy. With Britain and the Soviet Union now the staunchest of allies and the warmest of comrades, the Party had never been so popular. The events it organised – Springhall organised – calling for a 'Second Front' attracted crowds, money and what passed in those days for celebrities. In one year, between December 1941 and Christmas 1942, Party membership rose from 22,000 to 55,000. A small 'cadre' – based party was on the verge of becoming a mass party.

And then Springhall was arrested and charged with espionage. The flatmate of Olive Sheehan, a woman working in the Air Ministry, overheard a conversation between Sheehan and Springhall that she thought was suspicious, and informed the authorities. When they investigated they discovered a small number of Communist sympathisers in the Ministry who had been handing a range of technical secrets to Springhall who, in turn, had passed them on to the Russians. The trial was held in secret, but Springhall's sentence – seven years in prison – was public.

It then turned out that the Air Ministry ring was only one of Springhall's clandestine enterprises. In October 1943 a young captain in the London office of the Special Operations Executive (SOE) was charged with having passed on secret military information, including the entire operational structure of SOE, to Springhall. Captain Ormond Uren (the surname is Cornish) was court-martialled and sent to prison, also for seven years.

The Party had – I was always told – known nothing of Springhall's activities, which were a terrible embarrassment to everyone. He'd been freelancing, quite possibly using Soviet intelligence contacts he'd made in Spain and Moscow, and had, in effect, betrayed his British comrades for the sake of the Greater Cause. Many comrades would doubtless have seen it that way, but the Party distanced itself from his activities, sacked him (and his wife, who worked for the *Daily Worker*) and expelled him.

In his biography of the Party General Secretary Harry Pollitt, the historian Kevin Morgan says that Pollitt was so furious when he heard the news about Springhall 'that he spent that night cursing the Russians in his sleepless rage. What, after all, did they care for his efforts if they could behave in such a scandalous and irresponsible fashion?'

Springhall was released from prison in 1948, and went abroad, ending up in Prague working for the Chinese Information Bureau. He died in 1953, leaving his wife and an adopted Chinese daughter. It was this daughter, a quiet, kind, broad-faced girl, who – a decade later – was our babysitter. Which was how I got to hear the story.

The SOE part of the saga touched us even more closely. Captain Ormond Uren had a sister, Kirstine, who – as you may remember – became Sam's second wife in 1948 (and the mother of my older half-sister, Frances). And Uren married a Frenchwoman and wartime *résistante*, Rose, our eccentric Party dentist and near neighbour.

Some of this I knew by the time I was eleven or twelve, so it was interesting to pick up a copy – just before writing this chapter – of Sasha Abramsky's book, *The House of Twenty Thousand Books*. Abramsky's grandparents Chimen and Miriam lived within 100 yards of us and their daughter Jenny was another childhood friend of my sister. The Abramskys had left the Party after 1956 and a *froideur* had crept in between the adults of the families, for which each seemed to have blamed the other. Somehow, though, the normally highly judgmental orthodontist had retained her friendly contact with the Abramskys, and makes a spirited cameo appearance as the eccentric Communist in Sasha's book. But nowhere does he mention that her husband was imprisoned for spying for the Russians. Somehow no one told him.

The reason I am telling you this is that as a child I thought that Springhall was, if you like, a rogue operative, not a conspirator. In circumstances when the Soviet Union was our ally and facing the bulk of Hitler's Wehrmacht and Luftwaffe, it was understandable (if wrong) that some comrades would want to help in any way they could. Even so, the Party itself had condemned such illegality, and no one could pretend that they weren't aware of the position. We were clean – and had been for years – yet despite this we had the wire-taps, the steamed letters and the surveillance. It was harassment. It was a way of keeping the spooks in a job. It was also a waste of time and resources.

That's what I thought as I arrived at the National Archives in Kew, to look through a number of security files released into the public domain, with characteristic arbitrariness, by the security services. I had wanted to know whether my family's MI5 or (more likely) Special Branch files, almost certainly held on at least two of us, had survived or been released. They hadn't. A few years earlier I'd discussed this with the then Home Secretary, Jack Straw, who – by accident – had seen his own parents' file, which had revealed the existence of an informer in their local CP branch. The name had been redacted, but it was possible to work out who the informer had been. It was to protect such informers – who, after all, had thought that what they were doing was patriotic – he suggested, that such files could not be released.

So I settled for a fishing expedition on members of our local Party branch, hoping that some reference to Sam and Lavender would emerge. From the brown cardboard files with their reference numbers written on the outside came a jumble of memoranda, pictures and reports which, at first, seemed to more than vindicate my scepticism about their purpose. Here was a picture of a thin youngish man in baggy trousers walking along a street, clearly taken from a first-floor window and marked as a being a 'Surveillance photo of John Gollan leaving a meeting of CPGB Central Committee, 30/1/42.'

I came to the Dear Bill letter in an oblique way, having asked to see the file of Frank Loeffler, the pipe-smoking retired lawyer who had been an affable presence in the Party branch, together with his German-born wife, Sabine, an intelligent if slightly nervy woman. Strangely there was quite a lot of information in Frank's file, but it wasn't really about him. His file seemed to exist mostly as a depository for cross-references to other files, and to one in particular. This belonged to one of the two adults in Henry Grant's photograph and mentioned in the Dear Bill letter. But to my complete surprise it wasn't to the file of Party candidate, rail union activist and friend of my father's, Jock Nicholson. It was to his wife, Bridget, or – as the files called her – Brigitte.

So I asked for her file. Bridget Nicholson had, by virtue of previous marriages, once been both Lewis and Long (Long I'd known about – since her daughter Laura had kept that surname), but by birth was Brigitte Kuczynski. She and her family – father, mother, brother and four sisters – had fled from Germany when Hitler came to power, and had settled in the Belsize Park area of

London, close to Hampstead Heath. One of the sisters was the Sabine who had married Frank Loeffler.

It became apparent that MI5 and the Special Branch of the Metropolitan Police had thrown everything they had at Bridget, which was completely perplexing. And their surveillance of her had started early. Short reports from someone who had obviously been along to Party meetings noted her presence at a discussion in Drummond Street near Euston station in the summer of 1938 at which sixty people 'about 10% of whom were Jews' talked about Air Raid Precautions. A year later she was at the AGM of the St Pancras Party where 'there were 70 persons present of whom about 50% were Jews'. Given that religious Jews were unlikely to attend Party meetings in kippah and sidelocks this informant clearly possessed a highly developed if topical talent for Jew-spotting.

In December 1940 a W. Ogilvie of Special Branch writes to MI5 that he is 'anxious to establish the identity of a girl called "BRIDGET" who is in close touch with leading members of the Communist Party'. She lives in Bristol, he says, 'but she comes to London from time to time and stays at 4, Lawn Road Flats. She was at this address on 14th to 16th October and 12th–13th November last. I wonder whether some information could be obtained about her – possibly from the Hall Porter at Lawn Road Flats?' Someone – at MI5, I think – adds a note at the bottom, 'The suggestion of the hall porter is in my opinion superfluous'.

The Lawn Road Flats in Belsize Park deserve a book to themselves, and recently got one.*

The building – also known as the Isokon – was an extraordinary piece of art deco architecture put up in 1934, four storeys high, white and resembling a passenger liner, including a communal club and restaurant. Agatha Christie lived there for a time in the 1930s as did the writer Nicholas Monsarrat and the architect

---

* David Burke, *The Lawn Road Flats: Spies, Writers and Artists* (Woodbridge, Boydell Press, 2014).

Maxwell Fry. Some BBC employees had flats there too, including the famous producer Lance Sieveking and a man called Anthony Lewis. As it happened, the pre-Jock Brigitte – whose family lived in a house opposite the Isokon – was visiting her lover Lewis at the time.

It appears that Special Branch had found out about her visits by opening one or more of her letters, but hadn't spied on a regular enough basis to make sense of the information that they had. By the following winter Bridget was herself working for the BBC and a note was sent by the secret services to the Corporation to recommend that – since she was an active Communist – she be given 'work of a routine nature which excludes any possibility of access to secret or confidential information'.

For a few years the file is thin. Then, at the end of the summer of 1947, the files thicken again in serious fashion. There are suddenly pages of verbatim telephone intercepts. For example on 1 September 1947 Bridget, now living in her own flat in Belsize Park, calls someone identified as LONG – obviously her second husband, from whom she is now estranged. She tells him the money has not arrived and demands 'How do you think we are going to live?' Eventually he rings off. She then phones LEWIS (presumably her first husband who had lived in the Isokon) and, in the words of the eavesdropper, 'putting forth all her charm asks him if he will come round and have dinner with her'.

There begin to be reports of physical surveillance – of a proper tail – not just on Bridget but on people she meets or who visit her. On one occasion in September, she is followed on a local shopping trip to a local left-wing bookshop. Her 'tail' evidently follows her inside and stays close, since her conversation with the bookseller is reported. Or perhaps she is being tailed by two agents since, in a local shopping street, 'she met a young woman with whom she talked for 20 minutes . . . The woman from whom she parted was followed to 19 Eton Villas, where she entered by the basement side door. Age about 22, 5' 3" in height; well built; black hair; very fresh complexion; Jewess. She was dressed in a white woollen jumper, red skirt and brown leather sandals.'

In this period Bridget was under direct surveillance from about 9 in the morning to 10 at night. And, for all the detailed descriptions, the Jewesses and the black hair, nothing happened.

This spy-thriller level of scrutiny seems to have been the work of MI5, since Special Branch's knowledge of Bridget was much less detailed. A Special Branch document sent in November is an updated report on her parents and siblings. Since August, it says, both parents, Robert and Bertha, have died. Sabine is married to LOEFFLER ('he is active in the legal profession and is an associate of PLATTS MILLS' – a former Labour MP and far-Left QC). Renate is in Lowestoft with her husband who works in the Ministry of Agriculture. The oldest sister, Ursula, 'lives at The Firs, Great Rollright, near Chipping Norton in Oxfordshire with her husband . . . both are active in the affairs of the local Communist party'. And Bridget is 'apparently acting as secretary of the Adelaide branch of Hampstead CP though it is known that she is reluctant to continue in this capacity . . .' What a lot they knew, I was thinking, and to how little avail!

Another report a year later gives Bridget's address as 64B Belsize Park Gardens (the 'Dear Bill' flat) and notes that she has been finding it hard to make ends meet since her parents died. 'At present,' the writer observes, 'her circumstances are somewhat reduced and she looks after the children of neighbours as an additional source of income.' But, puzzlingly, this document goes on to say that Bridget 'came to notice in November 1948 when she wrote to the Town Clerk, Hampstead Town Hall, protesting against the Council's decision to ban the use of the Town Hall to the Communist Party when she described this decision as "undemocratic".'

Another year later and there was another file entry, this one dated 16 December 1949 and in every way a Cold War classic. An officer writes:

Toni MUNSTER who runs a nursery and kindergarten at 10 Lawn Road NW3, has said that BN brings her small son by a previous marriage to the nursery every morning and fetches him back in the evening. Every time she comes she spreads Communist propaganda and distributes or sells something from the CP.

The file contains a rather jolly looking brochure, printed in white, black and red, for an event at St Pancras Town Hall (the Labour council clearly far less bothered by Communists than Conservative Hampstead). There are drawings of a festive kind – bottles, cakes, bunting, and legends like 'COME EARLY FOR THE BARGAINS! STAY LATE AND ENJOY YOURSELF!' Next to the brochure the office has typed, 'The attached ticket for the "Daily Worker" Christmas Bazaar was sold by her to Toni MUNSTER a few days ago.' Mrs Munster had done her duty and told the authorities about this insidious attempt to sell her wooden toys from Poland or a tinny samovar from Tula.

In February 1950 Bridget has 'left her child [sic] in the care of "Olga" at 19 Lambolle Road' and gone off to Scotland to work on the election campaign of one of the Party's two MPs, Willie Gallacher (and to be with her new husband Jock Nicholson). In August dockets sent to the office of the Postmaster General 'authorize and require you to detain, open and produce for my inspection all postal packets and telegrams addressed to Bridget Nicholson, née Kuczynski'. He is also requested to 'record all telephone conversations on telephone number PRImrose 6217.' The – to me – absurd reason given for this was that 'she and her husband are active communists and BN is connected with people who have engaged in espionage with a foreign power'.

Bridget? Espionage? Then why are the files full of intercepts of everyday ordinariness? The Dear Bill letter seemed an appropriately snide endnote, a record of almost utterly pointless and remarkably intrusive snooping on a woman who was clearly nothing more than an activist, albeit one who offended the Nigels of 1950s Britain by leading a slightly unconventional personal and political life. She was as much a spy as my mother was.

But just in case, out of curiosity and because research delays the peculiar pain of having to write, I began looking at the files on some of the other members of the Kuczynski family. Sabine I had known, and Renate seemed to have moved to Suffolk and faded from view. Barbara appeared in a recorded phone call and not again. But the name of Ursula, the oldest Kuczynski sister, appeared again and again in the Archive, not in the text, but as a file cross-reference, in black or red capitals. Bridget, it almost seemed, was an adjunct to the Ursula story, whatever that was – a Rosencrantz to Ursula's Hamlet.

And Ursula, it turned out to my amazement, was a bona fide Russian spy. She was not in one of those nebulous 'Our Man in Havana' categories that peppered the papers in the 1980s and '90s, such as 'agent of influence' or 'intelligence asset', meaning that someone in the KGB could claim expenses for having met up with them. She was a decorated officer in Soviet military intelligence, an honorary colonel in the Red Army, twice awarded the Order of the Red Banner and, from her final domicile, the German Democratic Republic, the Order of Karl Marx. She was a spy like Kim Philby was a spy.

Her autobiography, *Sonya's Report*, first published in East Germany in 1977 – carefully curated to avoid incriminating anyone living – is a not unhappy account of a life spent in clandestine service of the workers' state. An epilogue in the edition I bought, added after the fall of the Wall, admits some misgivings about the excesses of Stalinism. But Ursula was not in the NKVD or KGB so was not part, it seems, of the apparatus of purging, executing and imprisoning. Overall an uncomplicated sense of modest and morally necessary heroism permeates her account of collecting top secret intelligence for the GRU, the Red Army outfit, for twenty-five years.

Her career as a spy had begun in New York where she was living as a young woman in the late '20s. In 1930 she was sent to the Chinese port of Shanghai to be part of the network headed by the legendary Soviet spymaster, Richard Sorge. In that roiling international entrepôt Agent Sonya, as she was called, collected information on the Chinese, the Japanese and the Americans. In 1935 the Chinese began rolling up the foreign spy networks and Ursula/Sonya fled with her two small children, ending up in London where the rest of her family was living.

From there, in September 1938, the month that Chamberlain went to Munich to sign an agreement that Communists everywhere saw as the prelude to an eventual attack on Russia, Ursula was sent to Switzerland. There she played a leading part in the so-called Lucy ring, which received German military intelligence concerning plans for an attack on the Soviet Union, and passed them on to Moscow. (There is a satisfyingly complex if unlikely theory concerning whether or not the ring was itself later infiltrated by British intelligence – with the objective of passing on true information to Stalin which he would not have accepted had it come from an Allied source.)

But four months before Operation Barbarossa made allies out of Britain and Russia Ursula returned to wartime Britain. Now divorced and remarried, to a British Communist called Len Beurton, she went to live in Oxfordshire, first in Kidlington, then in Oxford itself and finally in the village of Great Rollright. And there she remained into the Cold War, until, towards the end of 1950, she and her family decamped to East Germany.

But what had 'Sonya' been doing in Britain? Had she retired after leaving Switzerland, her job done, or had she come to Britain to spy? And what had any of this to do with her sister Bridget in particular, rather than any of the other Kuczynski sisters?

Special Branch was interested in all Communists as 'subversives', and maintained a steady level of surveillance on all activists and many members. That included Bridget as much as Sam, Johnny Gollan and other Party people. But in 1947 and again after

1949, MI5 became very much involved and so the level of scrutiny went up dramatically. Why?

In the spring of 1947 a Soviet agent crossed over to the British sector of Berlin (this was before the Wall was built) and defected. But this man was no Russian. His name was Allan Alexander Foote, a Yorkshireman and former International Brigadier who told his debriefers that he had been working for the Soviet Union since 1938. His first assignment, he said, had been to Geneva where he had joined Ursula as the radio operator for the Lucy network.

In that year, back from Spain and anxious to help the movement, Foote told his handlers, he had gone to the CP headquarters in King Street and met with his former comrade in the Brigade Dave Springhall, currently the Party number three. Subsequently he had a second meeting, this time with another former Brigadier and Party official, Ben Copeman. Copeman gave Foote a telephone number to call. When Foote called the number, a woman answered. She invited him to lunch at an address in Belsize Park – 4, Lawn Road Flats. Six days later he was invited round again and this time asked whether he would be prepared to 'undertake a job in Germany'. If so he was to take some money (she gave him £10) and travel to Switzerland where he would meet another woman – the first woman's sister. This latter was Ursula; the former, of course, was Bridget. The job was espionage.

Did Bridget know what the job entailed? Foote thought she did, and if so, this was before the war, and at a time when defence of the USSR from fascism seemed a moral act to any Communist. In any case putting Foote in contact with agents spying on a third party (Germany) in a foreign country (Switzerland) would hardly have felt treacherous. All the same it wasn't something Party members were supposed to do. In her autobiography Ursula notes that when she returned to Britain – most assuredly to spy – she 'kept strictly away from the British party, in accordance with the rules' – the rules being those, one imagines, of Red Army intelligence.

However, Foote's account of his activities to MI5 suggested a
role for Bridget as late as 1941. In October of that year he found
himself unable to contact Moscow Centre, and sent a telegram
(he said) to Bridget in London telling her that he was worried
about not having heard from 'Joe'. A week later he received a
reply from Bridget, now in Bristol, saying that she had forwarded
his message. By then Ursula was in Oxfordshire, and had resumed
her intelligence work for the Russians. It seems a reasonable
assumption that Bridget acted as a go-between for Ursula, who
was able to contact Moscow using a secret transmitter she had
hidden in a wall of a house in which she was living.

MI5 were obviously now very interested in both Ursula and
Bridget, and Foote's arrival explains the subsequent 1947 surge of
surveillance, letter-openings, phone-tappings and followings,
which petered out after a few months.

In *Sonya's Report* Ursula tells of how – in September 1947 –
she was visited in Oxfordshire by two men from the security
services. A few weeks earlier her mother had died of a heart
attack in the same house while on a visit, and her ailing father
was still there. Ursula's memoir suggests that the men were
clumsy and rather laughable in their attempts to get her to tell
them about her role in Soviet intelligence. They went away and
life resumed.

In Bridget's file is a memo from the legendary spycatcher
William Skardon, who seems to have been one of the Oxfordshire
visitors. The memo, dated 19 September 1947, admits that MI5
had got 'little positive information' from Ursula, but then goes
on to say that 'there is reason to suppose that Mrs BEURTON
gave up her agency for the Russians on ideological grounds when
they behaved so badly, from an anti-Fascist point of view, at the
beginning of the war and [she] agreed to some extent that she
was disappointed with the Russian policy in 1939/40.' The report
concluded that 'we are reasonably satisfied that they [the sisters]
are not at present active, and there is no reason to suppose that
they have been for some years'.

However true this was for Bridget – and all her spies and phone-tappers, presumably looking out for Soviet contacts, dead drops and chalk marks, had come up with nothing – it was much more debatable when it came to Ursula.

However, in 1949, as the files showed, MI5 were back. People imagine that code-breaking is a one-two business of discovering what a code is and then reading everything. In fact encoded messages have to be intercepted, deciphered and, finally, read. And by the autumn of 1949 the security services had just got down to reading a job lot of encrypted Soviet messages and cables, dating as far back as 1940. This cache, known as Venona, suggested that towards the end of the war plans for the American atomic bomb had been passed on to the Russians by a British scientist who was involved in the project.

The man the secret services suspected as having betrayed the secrets of the bomb was a German expatriate called Klaus Fuchs. A Communist since 1932, Fuchs had fled Germany in 1933 for Paris, then Britain, before eventually, as a theoretical physicist, finding a teaching post at Edinburgh University. Briefly interned at the outbreak of the war as an enemy alien, Fuchs was released and taken to work on the British atomic bomb project based at Birmingham University. Towards the end of 1943 he travelled to New York to become part of the Manhattan Project, then, in the summer of 1944, joined the team at Los Alamos in New Mexico. After the dropping of the atomic bombs on the Japanese cities of Hiroshima and Nagasaki had helped bring about the end of the war, Fuchs went to work at the British atomic research facility at Harwell. In the late '40s he had access to British and American atomic secrets through his membership of various joint Allied scientific committees.

Fuchs was the most important atom spy there ever was and the information he passed on to the Russians changed post-war history. Yet, when he was arrested and interrogated in early 1950 by the same William Skardon who had questioned Ursula, Fuchs confessed readily enough. As early as 1942 he had conceived of it as his duty to assist the Soviet Union to be an equal player in the post-war world. So, in that year, he had contacted an old comrade from the German Communist Party to help put him in contact with the Soviet Embassy. That comrade was Bridget's brother Jürgen Kuczynski and, in the first instance, his contact was to be Jürgen's other sister Ursula, aka Agent Sonya.

When she wrote about her liaison with Fuchs in her memoirs, Ursula will have revealed only what she thought MI5 already knew. By 1942 she was ensconced with her family and her transmitter in Oxfordshire, where she and her husband made contact with various people in the armed forces apparently anxious to help the Russians. An RAF officer called 'James', for example, gave her details of new aircraft technology because, she wrote, he felt he was 'aiding the allied country that was fighting the hardest and bearing the heaviest sacrifices in the war against fascism'. Others passed on information about new submarine radar and seaborne tank landing technology.

Her embassy contact was a man she dubbed 'Sergei' and they met in Hyde Park and other public places or else at her parents' or sisters' homes but only, she stressed, when her family were not there. 'My sisters were out at work,' she emphasised, years later, 'and knew nothing of this.'

Her brother, though, clearly did. At the end of 1942 'a comrade with worthwhile military information [who] had lost touch with the Soviet Union for quite some time turned to Jürgen for advice. The name of this comrade: Klaus Fuchs.' Ursula became Fuchs's go-between, cycling to rendezvous in the countryside around Oxford. The first meeting was in Banbury where 'we went for a walk arm-in-arm, according to the old-established principle of illicit meetings'. Fuchs would pass files over – in one case a 'thick book of blueprints more than a hundred pages long', and Ursula would travel to London, signal via a chalk mark to 'Sergei' that she had something for him, then meet him that evening and pass it over.

This happened a number of times, and then in 1943 or '44 she was asked by Sergei to suggest a place for Fuchs to meet a new controller, this time in New York where she had once lived. This she did and, she leads the reader to imagine, passed out of contact herself with the atom spy. When Fuchs resumed his activities in post-war Britain Ursula had, by her account, ceased her clandestine work and was now a bona fide uncloseted Party member.

The Venona cache of intelligence led MI5 to Fuchs, and Fuchs, believing that MI5 knew far more than they did, made a full confession, which – among other things – led the spooks back to Ursula. They now knew that their earlier assumptions about her having ceased work for the Soviets after the Nazi–Soviet Pact were wrong. She had clearly been a Soviet spy as late as 1943. And – if so – perhaps Bridget had continued to help her.

A memo from a J.C. Robertson (head of the department dealing with Soviet espionage) written in March 1950 argued that both Ursula and Bridget should be 're-interrogated'. Both could, he thought, 'tell us more than they have yet told about their connection with Soviet Intelligence . . . The FUCHS case has reminded us of the value of renewed interrogation at suitable intervals.'

But the number two at MI5, John Marriott, wrote a rebuttal to this suggestion. Bridget had never been interrogated in the first place and nothing was gained from Ursula the first time round. 'Moreover these two ladies differ from FUCHS in that unlike him they are immune from any form of sanction at our hands. I think, therefore, that it is exceedingly unlikely that either of them will talk . . .'

Unsurprisingly, however, they re-interviewed Foote, who – penurious – had by now published an account of some of his Soviet activities called *Handbook for Spies*. In the interview, on 18 May 1950, Foote added a story of an encounter after the war. 'At about the end of 1947 or the beginning of 1948,' the account runs, 'he met Brigitte Lewis by accident in St John's Wood. She seemed very surprised to see him as she did not know that he was in the country, and confided to him that her sister, Ursula Beurton, had recently been visited by two policemen. She added that Ursula was very upset by this visit and was so scared that she had been obliged to break off and not go to a very important rendez-vous which she was due to attend the next day.'

It is possible that MI5 didn't believe Foote. But if what he said was true, then Ursula had certainly been telling her sister about her secret work and about her brush with the secret service. And if Ursula really was frightened off an assignation in 1947, it is at least possible that this meeting was with Klaus Fuchs. Who, at that stage, was still one of the most important spies Moscow ever had.

On 1 March 1950, after a very short trial, Klaus Fuchs was found guilty of breaking the Official Secrets Act (not treason, as the Soviet Union was not classed as an enemy when the offences occurred) and sentenced to fourteen years in prison. The day before the Fuchs trial opened – and closed – Ursula Beurton, née Ursula Kuczynski, alias Agent Sonya alias Ruth Werner, left Britain and travelled to East Germany, where she remained until it (not she) expired in 1989.

The trial appalled senior Party people. A bug in King Street picked up a conversation between Reuben Falber and Peter Kerrigan, who had succeeded the disgraced Dave Springhall as National Organiser. The transcript records Kerrigan, clearly reading from a press report of the trial that Fuchs was not 'known at any time to have associated with British members of the Communist Party' and adding, 'Well that's a bloody let off!' To which Falber responds with a 'Phew!'

It seems very unlikely that Kerrigan or Falber or any other senior Party official knew the story of Ursula, or indeed of Bridget. But Bridget was a Party member and, after 1949, was – as we've seen – married to a senior Party activist and Party candidate, Jock Nicholson. She was well known to every active Communist in London.

Of course Bridget's secret activities might have begun and ended with her organisation of Alexander Foote to get to her sister in Switzerland. But to believe that you have to accept Ursula's protestations that her sisters were unaware of the wartime assignations she arranged in their houses, some of which will have concerned atomic secrets.

This is hard to believe. Would Ursula really have run the risk of incriminating her family without ever warning them? In her memoir she admitted to her brother Jürgen's role, but she made the admission knowing that he was then safely living in East Germany. Her sisters were not. They were in Britain and in their sixties and even if the government did nothing the British newspapers could be expected to find the story very interesting.

The Dear Bill letter was ludicrous, but the file it was in was not. Our family friend and comrade, Bridget Nicholson, had been a Soviet agent, albeit a junior one. As a Party family we were only two degrees of separation away from the biggest spy story of the century. And if Bridget, then – in the eyes of a prudent secret service – why not Sam or Lavender or any other Party member, given the chance to serve the movement?

In the United States two of those discovered passing on the secrets of the atomic bomb to the Russians (one of their handlers also dealt with Fuchs) were executed by electric chair. The Rosenbergs became an infamous part of Cold War history. The Kuczynskis did not. But, in questioning the loyalty of Communists and in keeping them under surveillance, the security services had perhaps not behaved with the punitive irrationality that I had always assumed. If later their blanket spying on Party members came to seem excessive even to them, then at least it has to be admitted that it had once seemed merely sensible. How loyal, after all, were we?

10

Blind Man's Buff

**For me and for millions of Communists throughout the world
the collapse of the Communist Party of the Soviet Union was a
shattering blow. It has affected me physically and mentally. I
now suffer from chronic depression. Is everything that I lived
for and worked for only a mirage? Why was I so blind to what
so many people were saying about the CPSU? How could I have
been so wrong for so long?**

Jock Nicholson

On the first day of October 2012 the historian Eric Hobsbawm
died in London. Usually the demise of a ninety-five-year-old
scholar of international standing – in particular one whose interpretation of what he referred to as 'the long nineteenth century'
and 'the short twentieth century' became the predominant understanding of modern Western history – would be unattended by
any controversy other than whether or not there should be a
special programme on the BBC. In Hobsbawm's case the tributes –
and there were plenty – were accompanied by a minor chorus of
dissent. The dissenters hit one recurrent theme: however excellent
a historian Hobsbawm might have been (and some were found
to doubt even that), he had been for most of his life a Communist
and, furthermore, an *unrepentant* one. It was not the Communism
itself that damned him (Hobsbawm had been a Jewish boy growing
up in a Berlin where the Nazis were about to come to power, so
his youthful politics were forgivable) but the fact that he had not
properly disavowed his beliefs.

The British historian of Nazi Germany Michael Burleigh wrote in the *Daily Telegraph* of the dead man's 'implacable refusal to recant', describing Hobsbawm, a man who had actually managed to be British for two decades longer than Burleigh had been alive, as one of the 'foreign gurus' at whose feet the British academic establishment had a tendency to worship. In the even more declaratory pages – paper and web – of the *Daily Mail* the novelist and biographer A. N. Wilson argued that Hobsbawm's past beliefs tarnished not only his own reputation but that of anyone who was too enthusiastic about him. 'What is disgraceful about the life of Hobsbawm,' wrote Wilson, 'is not so much that he believed this poisonous codswallop, and propagated it in his lousy books, but that such a huge swathe of our country's intelligentsia . . . made him their guru. Made him our "greatest historian".' In addition to using the word 'guru', Burleigh and Wilson also cited the same television interview from the mid '90s, in which the Canadian writer Michael Ignatieff interrogated Hobsbawm about his politics. This interview, sometimes described as 'infamous', is invariably reduced to the moment when Hobsbawm immediately replied 'yes' to the question whether the deaths of 20 million or so people in Russia and elsewhere would have been justified had Utopia been achieved.

Given this account it is not surprising that one recurrent dissenting theme was the assertion that an unrepentant but brilliant old Nazi would not have been given the same adulatory send-off as the unrepentant old Communist Hobsbawm. The conservative journalist Douglas Murray penned a parody obituary in the *Spectator* for just such a National Socialist who considered the Holocaust a price worth paying to usher in the Aryan paradise. The left of centre writer Bryan Appleyard agreed. 'If Hobsbawm had been a right winger who supported and continued to support Hitler,' he wrote, 'the coverage today would have been very different, yet, in my terms, there is no difference.'

The rhetorical vigour of such a comparison stands in contrast to the moral logic-chopping that must seem to accompany any attempt to refute it. The Nazis, militant ideologues of the middle of the twentieth century, murdered and starved tens of millions. So were and did the Communists. Both claimed to be secular John the Baptists of a coming Kingdom of Heaven on earth, and if there were idealistic and humane Communists, then so were there Nazis fired by a concern for humanity (albeit Teutonic humanity) benefiting from their efforts. 'Struggle' or 'Kampf' – the idea of an almost blessed conflict – was inherent to both National Socialism and Communism and inspired the two kinds of partisans to systematic acts of barbarism.

To argue otherwise – to argue that Communism perhaps killed fewer people directly, or that the people who killed in the name of Communism regretted the necessity more, or that the Communism of Russia and China wasn't even proper Communism – must always seem like an exercise in sophistry. Of course it was possible that good people had been badly wrong; had been gulled by their own history or the temper of the times as Hobsbawm was; but ultimately good people would accept the fact that they had been terribly mistaken and, as a corollary, that it would have been better had they made other choices.

In the early 1990s, as the Soviet Union disintegrated and its old apparatchiks faced the judgements of oppressed peoples in the newly liberated countries of Eastern Europe, the conservative British philosopher Roger Scruton called for a trial by public opinion of cosy Western supporters of Communism before 'the page of history is turned':

> The majority of those who were caught up in the crimes of the Communist Party could plausibly argue that they had no choice. The same excuse cannot be offered by those in the West who promoted and apologized for Soviet communism. Should not they too be facing their day of reckoning?
>
> . . . Surely the time has come to call these villains to account. Witch hunts are indeed unjust, since there are no witches. But there are plenty of communists, and plenty of apologists: Our

unwillingness to hunt them down has been one cause of the Great
Socialist Experiment's longevity.

At least let us henceforth insist that the term communist is a
term of abuse, that anti-communism is not a crime but a duty
and that those who speak the language of communism are as
much apologists for mass murder as those who speak the language
of the Nazis.

It is hard for someone with my history not to take Scruton's
excoriations personally. Even if the actual British Communist
Party of the 1970s bore almost no relation to the one he was
depicting, it arguably did in the years before I joined. Should Sam
and Lavender have been 'hunted down', then, before their deaths?
Put, perhaps, on some newspaper list of those who had not properly repented? Made, in a rhetorical sense, to wear the pointed
hat of those accused by a modern (but enlightened) Inquisition?
Had they been Nazis that is probably what would have happened
to them after all.

Even as I write this, after years of agonising, wondering and –
yes – psychoanalysis, I feel a powerful urge to turn Scruton's
excruciating arguments back on him. If we entered his ideological
mansion and searched its cribs and corridors, noisily flinging open
its closets, what might we find? What has Scruton encompassed
either openly or (this being the way of conservatives) tacitly that
is as reprehensible as anything Sam and Lavender supported or
excused?

I suspect that the Scrutons, as a class, were either champions,
tolerators or beneficiaries of Empire. Were they ever among the
few who sat out the First World War in prison, protested against
the massacre of Indians in Amritsar, worried about the Lascar
seamen in the East End, wrote anguished letters to the Colonial
Secretary about the famine in Bengal, or resisted all common
notions about the natural superiority of the white race over the
others? And what about the supposed 'friends' of their country,
the despots and bastards who supplied us with oil and attended

our coronations, while imprisoning and torturing those who
opposed them? To whose British account are those services to be
charged? If it was criminal to have been a believer in Communism
and an apologist for Russia, then why was it less criminal to have
been a believer in colonialism and an apologist for racism?

You can see how easily this is done. I suppose that a few decades
ago I would have thought myself satisfied with it. But both
Scruton's formulation and my response to it are in fact ways of
evading rather than enriching thought. If Scruton had said that
a lifelong Western Communist must have had a curious way of
dealing with the gulfs between beliefs and outcomes, then he
would have been on to something interesting, an extreme example,
possibly, of a universal tendency.

Let us return to the great historian to illustrate this point.
Early in his interview, Ignatieff took Hobsbawm back to the
fact of his Jewishness in a country that had voted to give power
to those who most hated Jews. Had Hobsbawm been afraid
when Hitler became Chancellor in 1933? 'That is a private matter,'
Hobsbawm replied. This was an extraordinary enough answer,
but the next was almost as odd. How had members of his family
fared under the Nazis? This is, word for word, how Hobsbawm
responded: 'Some got out. Some got into concentration camps
and died.' And that was it. This refusal of sentiment, of any
expression of feeling, indicated that he spoke not as Hobsbawm
the Red or even Hobsbawm the Man, but as Hobsbawm the
Olympian. The historian took the long, cool view over the Ages
of Revolution and Extremes. He was there to analyse, not
to weep.

So when Ignatieff asked whether knowing the scale of suffering
under Stalin would have made a difference 'to you as a Communist?'
this is what Hobsbawm said:

This is an academic question to which an answer is simply not
possible. [PAUSE.] I don't actually know that it has any bearing
on the history that I've written. But if I were to give you a

retrospective answer, which is not the answer of a historian,
I would have said probably not . . . In a period in which, you
might say, mass murder and mass suffering are absolutely
universal, the chance of a new world being born in great
suffering would still have been worth backing. Looking back as
a historian I would say that the sufferings of the Russian people
were only marginally worthwhile. The sufferings were excessive
by almost any standards. That's because it turns out that the
Soviet Union was not the beginning of the world revolution.
Had it been, I'm not sure. Do people now say we shouldn't have
World War Two because more people died in that war than
died in Stalin's terror?

It was at this point that Ignatieff posed his celebrated question
as to whether 'the loss of 15 to 20 million people might have been
justified?' had 'the radiant tomorrow' come. Yes,' Hobsbawm
replied. 'This is exactly what people said about World War One
and World War Two. Most people ended up by saying it was wrong
in World War One, very few say it was wrong in World War Two.'
Later in the conversation Hobsbawm described the deaths under
Stalin as 'inhuman, indefensible', adding, 'there's no way you can
minimise it'. This codicil is never cited when the interview is
mentioned. Possibly because the professor's critics felt that it was
an insincere attempt to put the lock back on the stable door. What
is clear is that Hobsbawm had taken Ignatieff's thought about the
loss of life as a serious intellectual proposition. I once interviewed
the American novelist Nicholson Baker who had written a book
proposing that fighting the Second World War had not been worth
it because of the scale of suffering involved in confronting Hitler.
He regarded my British obduracy on this point as being as callous
as anything that Eric Hobsbawm had ever said about the aftermath
of the Bolshevik Revolution. In any case the discussion for both
of us involved a calculus of human destruction that was coldly
academic, to say the least.

*

The interesting and completely unacademic question for those British Communists who were most active in the Party between the late '30s and the '60s was not 'what if you had known?' It was rather something on the spectrum of 'how could you not have known?', 'how did you manage not to know?' and 'why did you choose not to know?' For the moment, as we have seen, Sam and Lavender were not spies – even if they knew a few people who had been – and they had not known about or been enriched by Moscow gold. They had denounced no one to the authorities and they had led lives of considerable sacrifice for the sake of the movement.

In his interview with Ignatieff, Eric Hobsbawm suggested that the excoriation of British Communists was misdirected. 'We in the West,' he argued, 'never had very much to reproach ourselves with. We never got into government and did the things that we might have been expected to do. What we did was, on the whole, on the right side. When we talked about Russia, which was neither here nor there as far as our politics were concerned, we were either fools or liars or naïve.' So British Communists, crucially, were not murderers or torturers or gulag operators. They were people who cared about the downtrodden and the oppressed and who, as a result, enjoyed ostracism rather than power.

But there are reasons for finding this formulation problematic. If it is true that the British people were never mad enough to let their native Communists discover whether they could have been as repressive as their counterparts in the 'socialist countries', that constitutes meagre exculpation of the tendencies that might have led those Party members to sentence dissidents to slave labour in the Welsh salt mines. And though it was one thing to be naïve, it was another to be a liar, particularly if the lie did service for a crime.

When I was a child, I understood Sam's work in the Communist Party to have been rather, well, *jolly*. As Cultural Secretary of the Party at a time of real political and cultural upheaval, he had helped bring the great American black singer, Paul Robeson, to Britain and was photographed with him. Famous actors who were associated with the only true working-class theatre, Unity Theatre, knew Sam, as did the Brendan Behans, the Ewan MacColls, the E. P. Thompsons and the Christopher Hills. And insofar as this did not square with Doris Lessing's depiction of a 'grim and sardonic' cultural commissar, then this must certainly be due to her use of authorial licence. Or, as Lavender much later put it, to the fact that the great novelist was a 'bloody liar'.

Then, a few years ago, I came across an Internet reference, a single loose skein to Sam's work as Cultural Secretary that unravelled, in time, the old carpet of my comfortable assumptions. In 1955 the British Parliament passed the Children and Young Persons (Harmful Publications) Act, designed 'to prevent the dissemination of certain pictorial publications'. The 'pictorial publications' in question were horror comics imported from the United States. These had titles such as *Tales from the Crypt* and *The Haunt of Fear*, and often featured animated deliquescing corpses or bizarre murders sufficient to produce horrified delight in almost any adolescent. Supporters of restriction worried – in the words of the Act – that such an image could 'corrupt a child or young person into whose hands it might fall (whether by inciting or encouraging to commit crimes or acts of violence or cruelty or in any way whatsoever)'.

The legislation had been drawn up by the Home Office under the aegis of a Conservative Home Secretary and passed easily with the help of the large Conservative majority in the House of Commons. But the political origins of the Act lay in a completely different part of the political world – the Communist Party of Great Britain and its Cultural Secretary, Sam Aaronovitch.

In 1949 a Communist Party member called Peter Mauger was on a train between the Thames-side town of Pangbourne, around which much of the *Wind in the Willows* is supposed to have been set, and Paddington station, in transit, as it were, between the two great anthropomorphisms of British children's literature. A boy of ten or eleven sat reading in the same compartment as Mauger, who observed the child to be so transfixed by his books that he didn't so much as look up for an hour. Mauger – a teacher – knew that such concentration at that age was unusual and before the journey ended asked to see what the boy had been looking at. 'I was absolutely horrified,' he later said. The boy had been reading American comic books with lurid pictures and stories. Mauger's determination to fight this previously unknown scourge began there.

The campaign, as it evolved, was run by a body called the Comics Campaign Council, itself largely an arm of a charity, the Council for Children's Welfare. The founder of both was a Party member called Simon (Sam) Yudkin, an idealistic North London paediatrician. And urging the campaign along was the Cultural Committee of the CPGB and its secretary, Sam Aaronovitch.

'The whole point of the campaign,' Sam recalled years later, 'was to draw in people with no interest in left-wing politics.' He was speaking with a British academic, Martin Barker, who was fascinated by this earlyish example of what we now call a 'moral panic'. Barker had discovered to his surprise that, though many of those involved did not know it (and some were quite irate when he told them), the dynamism of the mini-crusade came from the Communist Party. In effect, the Comics Campaign Council was a quasi- 'front' organisation.

Barker asked my dad what evidence the campaigners had had for the assertion that comics corrupted. The reply was that, back then, there had simply been no sophisticated media analysis to draw on. (Sam had asked Peter Mauger to write a full study, but Mauger hadn't had time.) About which reply Barker noted in a book, the one to which my late-night Internet sleuthing led me, 'I do not want to dismiss this argument, but I doubt its explanatory power.'

Barker was right to doubt it. This battle was part of a much bigger, almost global war about values and civilisation. British Communists were as sincere in their belief in the corrupting possibilities of American comics as were the more usual Tory apostles of censorship. Barker saw this in the writings and speeches of Peter Mauger and others. At a Communist Party cultural symposium in 1951, titled 'The American Threat to British Culture', Mauger concluded his anti-American address with the peroration that 'it is by appealing to the best instincts of ordinary, decent people that we can stop this American vulgarisation, this degradation, this perversion, of our young people'.

Sam presided over this conference. He arranged for a number of distinguished speakers including the historian E. P. Thompson, the writer and librettist Montagu Slater, the geneticist J. L. Fyfe, the novelist Jack Lindsay, and the documentarist Ralph Bond. Each speech contained its own condemnation of the new barbarism of the United States. Thompson described the present-day 'American dream' as 'childish and debased'. 'Its poison can be felt in every field of American life,' he said. The journalist Rose Grant talked about the need for more 'written and spoken exposures of the American threat' if ever the 'Yankee marauders in our cultural life' were to be defeated.

In a moment, I'll get to Sam's speech, the lengthy ideological washing line – over twenty pages – on which all these various garments hung. But first we need to note the origins of this hysteria. On 31 August 1948 Andrei Alexandrovich Zhdanov, chief of the Soviet Communist Party's cultural affairs department, died in Moscow aged fifty-two. A career Bolshevik who had survived the purges to become a possible successor to Stalin, Zhdanov had turned into something of a drinker and the habit may have undermined his health. Even so, before the vodka claimed him, he had succeeded in creating a doctrine that was all his own.

The *Zhdanovshchina* was in part about getting rid of abstraction and pessimism in art. 'Elitist' Soviet writers and composers found themselves under attack for wasting the people's paper and canvases on work bereft of ideologically improving meaning. Under Zhdanov some of Russia's greatest artists and composers were persecuted by talentless bureaucrats or assaulted in print by envious fellow artists, and sometimes forced into humiliating statements of repentance for their bourgeois, intellectual ways. Naturally, since it was a Soviet doctrine, it affected to some extent all the other Communist parties' attitudes towards art. They were bound at the very least to discuss it earnestly.

But an attack on artistic innovation and experiment was only one half of the Zhdanov doctrine. The other was pure anti-Americanism. What Zhdanov did was to openly extend the politics of the Cold War into the cultural field. American imperialism, the doctrine argued, was not just about military invasion. Much more insidiously it was about the aggressive and intentional use of American popular culture to entice nations away from the socialist camp, rendering them helpless before US foreign policy demands. To counteract this incursion, Zhdanov encouraged alliances of 'national forces' to resist the hegemony of Yankee dollar-funded culture and to defend the authentic cultures of their homelands. In other words the Communist was to become the ultimate cultural conservative.

Sam was naturally keen to distinguish the Party's stance from anything as repellent as chauvinism or xenophobia. His was not to be understood as a rejection of America as such, but of a kind of America. The good America was that 'which represents the

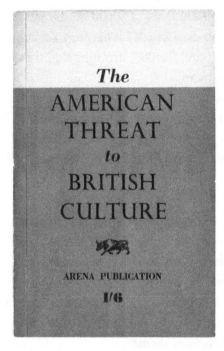

The
AMERICAN
THREAT
to
BRITISH
CULTURE

ARENA PUBLICATION
1/6

struggle of the American people, the America of Emerson and Whitman, Theodore Dreiser, Paul Robeson and Howard Fast'. Unfortunately the 'real rulers of America' – the bad America – were the plutocratic families, 'the Fords, Morgans, Du Ponts and Rockefellers'. This was a ruling class that was not even gentled, as the British ruling class had been, by the experience of feudalism and *noblesse oblige*, but had been formed in the jungle of capitalism. And these were the people, said Sam, 'who attempt to impose their way of life on other countries and who therefore threaten British culture'.

But what was the British culture that was threatened? Was it the comedy of *The Goon Show* or the melodrama of *The Archers* (both first broadcast on radio that year)? Or was it the quintessential English and Scottish FA Cup Finals? Sam, of course, knew little of these. No, British culture was (as he listed it) Chaucer, Shakespeare, Robert Burns, Shelley, Byron, Dickens, William Morris, George Bernard Shaw and the Scottish socialist novelist

Lewis Grassic Gibbon. It was Constable, Hogarth, and – his latest named artist, who died exactly a century earlier – Turner. It was the music of Byrd and Purcell, brought slightly up to date by 'our folk songs and dances'.

Now, Sam warned, this solid, consensual patrimony was drowning under a tide of imports from America. These products tended towards the lurid and the violent, and they did so for a reason. Here his address vaulted from the superstructure and landed squarely on the base:

> The American trusts, desperate to expand in a shrinking capitalist world, have fostered an unprecedented growth of the worship of violence and brutality since they see only a violent solution to their problems. But it must be sold abroad. How otherwise are the British, French and other peoples to be persuaded to fight for American trusts or watch and not resist their national independence being taken from them?

One primary medium of this cultural barbarism was American cinema. Hollywood was producing movies with the objective of selling the idea of war to naïve foreigners. Its films were means of

> converting other peoples to the ideas of American big business, creating illusions of American world leadership, in Stalin's words, 'enmeshing their minds in lies'. The more their war plans develop, the harder they press our outlook upon us, caring nothing if it destroys our own national culture.

Sam estimated that 70 per cent of American films were 'preoccupied with crime or sex. Almost all are pervaded with violence.' He didn't quite explain why films that aimed at assisting preparation for war should be full of sex and crime, but I imagine that he could have come up with something about desensitisation.

As pernicious was the effect on the remains of the British film industry that had survived the Hollywood onslaught. In Sam's view the police film *The Blue Lamp* – in which an avuncular police sergeant is shot by a delinquent Dirk Bogarde and which won the BAFTA award for 1950 – followed this almost degenerate obsession with violent malefaction.

Meanwhile British songwriters were being pushed out of business by American commercial dance music. Sam quoted an article in the *Daily Mirror* lamenting the fact that 'out of twenty of the most popular current songs seventeen are American, one is French, two are British . . .' The American songs, said Sam, were full of characteristics that were deceptively damaging. All that wish on a star stuff?

> Wish fulfilment, sloppy eroticism and similar features are not harmless simply because we take them for granted. They are useful aids in drugging the minds of the people while US big business goes about its plans.

After this unlikely description of the work of Bing Crosby, Nat King Cole and Rosemary Clooney, Sam ploughed on through sociology, psychology, military and other scientific research, before turning to the implied question of what might constitute good art. The answer was 'socialist realist' art. If anyone was not clear about what that might be, Sam was ready with a definition.

> What is it? It is an artistic method which not only shows things as they are but in the process of change; more than that, which reveals the causes, the contradictions leading to that change. And because it illuminates this for us, helps us, shall we say, moves us, to take part in changing what is portrayed.

Socialist realism therefore was art that furthered the struggle, as defined by those who truly understood what underlay the causes of and need for that struggle. And who understood it better than the students and teachers of scientific Marxism

who were to be found in the Communist parties? It was therefore for them to tell the artists what was good and what was
not. Then,

> Socialist realism can become a powerful artistic method for us in
> Britain insofar as our own writers and artists really strive to apply
> it to our own conditions and stage of struggle.

But the problem, even allowing for the American influence, was
that there existed a coterie of British writers and artists who were,
in effect, bought creatures of the American empire. Seduced by
the false grittiness of Americana they had become enemies of
their own culture.

> [They] lean instead on the slum or tough naturalism imported
> from the States of a Hemingway and a J. T. Farrell. And from this
> they are led to desert their own country . . . We produce an Orwell
> or an Aldous Huxley. America puffs them up, mass produces them
> and re-exports them back to unlucky Europe . . . Clearly if we
> wish successfully to combat the 'American way of life', we must
> also expose its fifth column in Britain.

Sam ended his speech on a belligerent note. These revelations
about 'the US "way of life" and its invasion of Britain', he thun-
dered, 'can only rouse disgust and shame in the hearts of the
British people'. Which was a claim made easier by a lack of
analysis of how exactly these shamed and disgusted people had
come to be listening to the songs, reading the comics that 'take
up British paper resources' and buying tickets for the films. In
any case the point was that, in the future, this would not persist.
Britain's 'long and powerful traditions of struggle present a
barrier which these arrogant gum-chewers will not be allowed
to destroy'.

Am I being somehow Oedipal in making so much of this
dreadful speech? The man who ended his days in a sunny room

in a North London hospital two years shy of the millennium was nothing like that orator from whose mouth poured forth the full Stalinist declension – spurious authority, feigned outrage, conspiracy theory pretending to be deep analysis, difference characterised as treachery and, if necessary, distortion amounting to outright lying. Sam claimed to be sympathetic to ordinary Americans but in that last 'arrogant gum-chewers' jibe he fed the not-so-sly chauvinism that had emerged from Britain's post-war feeling of relative weakness and its barely suppressed envy. Had he forgotten that the sons and brothers of the gum-chewers had, just seven years earlier, bled on European beaches to help free the world from Nazism? His speech lacked only the declaration of a death sentence or two.

Sam's portrait of a degenerate culture determined to export war was a caricature, and one drawn for effect. It was true that Mickey Spillane's Mike Hammer was hard-boiling his way through the bestseller lists. But the top grossing films in the United States in 1951 included *The African Queen, An American in Paris, Strangers on a Train, Show Boat, Quo Vadis* and *A Streetcar Named Desire*. More egregious was the cultural policing implied by Sam's stance on socialist realism. To describe Orwell and Huxley as 'fifth columnists' was to accuse them of treachery. Sam's words were an invitation to almost any self-respecting artist, writer or composer to join anyone but the Communists.

In his role as Cultural Secretary did Sam put these Stalinist precepts into practice? Not one of his many old comrades ever said or hinted to me that my dad had once been a small-minded zealot, but perhaps I too easily dismissed Doris Lessing's description of him in *The Golden Notebook* as being sardonic and almost cynical. A throwaway line in a biography of a fairly obscure Communist writer had one Party poet refer to Andrei Zhdanov as 'the Soviet Sam Aaronovitch', and the other replying, 'Do you think he's really as awful as that?' A Scottish playwright recalled that his work for Unity Theatre had been censored by Sam in 1946 for not being sufficiently close to the Party line, for being in fact (though it isn't clear whether the words were Sam's or a précis) 'a hotchpotch of anti-Party, anti-working class confusion'.

In 1979 E. P. Thompson recalled – with something like horror – being present for a 'disgraceful meeting' in the late '40s at which the chairman of the Cultural Committee, Emile Burns, scolded two Party writers for their various political incorrectnesses and, in effect, closed down the Party literary magazine, *Our Time*. 'I had allowed myself to be made use of as part of the team of uncultured yobbos and musclemen under the command of the elderly Burns,' the famous historian said. Perhaps, on that day, Sam – also youthful – was busy doing something else. But actually it is almost inconceivable (and I wish it were otherwise) that one of those musclemen was not my father.

There is something worse, though; something I never heard anyone talk about during my childhood and that only became clear to me while researching and writing this book. That is the story of the Party's attitude towards the series of show trials in Eastern Europe that took place between 1948 and 1953.

The wartime meeting of the Allies at Yalta in the Crimea had reached a broad agreement on the division of Europe into Soviet and non-Soviet spheres of interest. Hungary, Czechoslovakia, Rumania, Bulgaria and Poland – all liberated by the Red Army – as well as the eastern part of what remained of Germany, were soon declared to be people's democratic republics with socialism as the official state politics.

Two socialist countries had not been liberated by the Red Army. Albania freed itself from the Italians after which its largely Communist resistance movement won the single-party election with 93 per cent of the vote. It was a mountainous and difficult country, too small to be of strategic significance in the burgeoning Cold War and sufficiently far from the Soviet border to worry even the anxious men in the Kremlin.

Its larger neighbour Yugoslavia was another matter. Not only did the country of the southern Slavs not owe its deliverance to

Stalin, but in its self-grown liberator, Josip Broz Tito (who later took the rank of 'Marshal') it had a figure who could compete with the Soviet leader for recognition in the Communist world. And whereas Stalin's burnished biography had him as the wise and eternal figure who succeeded Lenin and won the war, Tito was an actual soldier, a real war hero with a mythology around him that was potent and romantic. He could quite easily become a second pole of the European Communist world.

By 1948 Stalin and Tito were beginning to have disagreements. Tito was explicitly in favour of supporting the Greek Communists in the Civil War there, whereas Stalin had consigned Greece, more or less, to the Western zone of influence. Then too Yugoslavia had begun to develop some idiosyncratic economic and organisational policies, and these effectively rejected the model favoured by Soviet orthodoxy. In an exchange of letters Tito told the Kremlin that the Yugoslavs were 'developing socialism in our country in somewhat different forms'. Different forms, to Stalin, suggested worse forms.

On 28 June 1948 representatives of eight Communist parties – six of them Russian or Eastern European – met in Bucharest and agreed to expel the absent Yugoslavia from the Communist Information Bureau, which had been set up in 1947 to bring the large Communist parties of Europe together under Soviet leadership (the Comintern having been abolished in 1943 as an act of goodwill towards Russia's capitalist allies). Overnight Tito went from being a hero of the Communist movement to being an enemy of the international proletarian struggle.

This sudden switch of category – though not unfamiliar to those who had endured the Nazi–Soviet Pact and the sudden abandonment of the war against fascism in 1939 – had to be explained. In Eastern Europe, in the complete absence of a competing narrative, that was a relatively straightforward if unsatisfactory process. In the West it was more difficult. How could Communists be expected to understand why the marvellous Tito was now one of their most hated foes?

The job of selling the new line to the British movement was not an enviable one. Its difficulty is illustrated by the fact that it took two years for the definitive Party tract on the wickedness of Tito to be written. But when it did arrive it was at least from a source who could claim a deeper knowledge of Yugoslavia and its leadership than almost anyone in Britain. The title alone – *From Trotsky to Tito* – told British Party members what to expect: that the Yugoslav leader was the successor of the arch-traitor Leon Trotsky, whose Russian followers had sought to sabotage the young Soviet Union in the 1930s, whose international supporters had undermined the struggle against fascism in Spain and whose British supporters were even now a noisome addendum to otherwise good demonstrations and rallies.

James Klugmann, the author of the tract, had been central in edging Britain's wartime government away from support for the Serb nationalist Chetnik insurgency, and towards Tito's forces. During the Second World War, he joined the Royal Army Service Corps and worked in the Yugoslav section of the Special Operations Executive, a job for which he was dropped behind the lines and made contact with Tito himself. Eventually it was decided in London, on Klugmann's recommendation, to concentrate all British military efforts on assisting the mostly Communist partisans.

When the war finished and Tito was consolidating his power in Yugolsavia, Klugmann worked in the region for the United Nations Relief and Rehabilitation Administration. Then he returned home and joined Sam as a full-time Party official in London and as one of its leading intellectuals. By 1950, according to his pamphlet, Klugmann had made a shattering discovery. His old Yugoslav comrade had actually been a renegade all along. The Titoists, for example, 'were putting forward a theory of smooth and peaceful transition to socialism, in the style and tradition of the Mensheviks and Ramsay MacDonald'. So they were right-wing. They also encouraged 'kulaks' (wealthy peasants) to join the Yugoslav Communist Party. 'What policy could more openly violate the principles of Marxism Leninism and the experience of the Soviet Union?' Klugmann railed. Titoist degeneracy caused its adherents to react badly to the guidance of the Cominform, and the party leaders of Russia, Bulgaria, Hungary, Italy and France. 'Is it possible to think of an honest Communist who would not be proud to receive criticisms from the Parties whose leaders were Stalin, Dimitrov, Rakosi, Togliatti or Thorez?' A true Communist, he implied, would fall over himself trying to rectify the errors that such exalted men had generously identified.

Klugmann then prefaced his Stalinist transition from political difference to criminality with an appeal to precedent. Communists knew – who better? – that the enemy was always active.

> All the open, overt methods of capitalist oppression – police, army, reactionary press, fascist thugs and vigilantes – are complemented by the secret, covert efforts of capitalists to penetrate, spy on and disrupt the organisations of the working class and progressive movement from inside, through spies and agents.

It had been thus when Trotsky's agents were active in the pre-purge Soviet Union. It was true now, as evidenced by the trials of Party traitors in Eastern Europe. As evidenced indeed by some writers questioning the validity of these people's tribunals! There were people who were so far gone in enmity to the cause as to describe Stalin as 'the real deviationist'!

This, said Klugmann, was an international conspiracy. Ostensibly and outwardly its 'trumpeters' – people like the left-wing Labour MP Konni Zilliacus – promised a '"new kind of Communism", or "national Communism" as it is sometimes called'. But in fact this was 'of the same order as the "new kind of socialism" or "national socialism".' Having now completed the intellectual feat of linking Tito to Hitler, Klugmann cast the Yugoslav leader as a kind of Nazi comeback, except 'with the control and leadership

passed from the hands of Himmler of the Gestapo into the hands
of Hoover of the FBI'.

It only remained for Klugmann to call the faithful to arms. 'In
the interests of the international solidarity of the working people,
of peace and of socialism,' he wrote. 'the combating of Titoism,
instrument of imperialist rule – is urgent and just.'

In reality, Klugmann's tract was less a battle cry than an apologia
for a process already under way. This work in progress was the
purging in Eastern Europe of old Communists, many in the
leadership of their own parties. And many of them known personally by members of the British Communist Party.

By the time the Party imprint, Lawrence & Wishart, published
Klugmann's screed, it had already produced a 124-page discourse
on *Tito's Plot Against Europe: the story of the Rajk conspiracy*
written by one Derek Kartun, a CPGB member and foreign
correspondent for the *Daily Worker*. In September 1949, at the
headquarters of the metalworkers' union in Budapest Kartun
attended the eight-day trial of László Rajk, the Hungarian
Interior Minister and veteran Communist, who, along with
seven others, pleaded guilty to charges of espionage and treason.
Within three weeks of the trial's conclusion Rajk and four others
had been shot.

Kartun, like Klugmann, faced the difficulty of the likely initial
scepticism of his potential readers. Rajk had been a Communist
folk hero, an International Brigadier in Spain. During the war –
unlike the Hungarian Party boss Mátyás Rákosi who was in
Russia – Rajk had led the underground party in the Hungarian
Resistance. Indeed Kartun had to acknowledge that Rayk had
been known as 'one of the finest members of the Hungarian
Communist Party'. Consequently it was necessary to try harder
to persuade the reader of the truth of what she was about to
read. Kartun began:

> So very much stranger than fiction is this narrative of the Rajk
> conspiracy that I feel it necessary to say a word about my sources.

I have not invented, assumed, elaborated or modified any of the facts in these pages . . . I was present at the trial itself, and I have been fortunate in being able to consult many people who knew Rajk and his associates well in the days before the discovery of the plot.

What Kartun had discovered was that Rajk, beneath the appearance of solid masculine virtue, had in fact – all along, in Spain and then in hiding – been a man of subtle, concealed vices. A man who:

> managed to keep his pride and ambition hidden well enough, and there was another trait in his complex character that he also managed to conceal. He was a coward . . . he believed in nothing but himself. He betrayed because he was terrified, because he had a contempt for his fellow man and because his flighty, unbalanced personality welcomed the thrill of playing a double game. He had the character of the international adventurer, the cosmopolitan.

The word 'cosmopolitan' had a very interesting Stalinist etymology. In the post-war Soviet Union it was a term used to deride any intellectual tendency regarded as un-national or remotely pro-Western. In Eastern Europe it extended to those who had significant contacts with people in the West – as, ironically, many of the Party members who had served in the International Brigades did. Soon, as we shall see, it began to take on a second meaning.

So, deep character flaws seduced Rajk (and, presumably, his confederates) into a series of improbably complicated plots, all of which were fully and – to Kartun's mind – voluntarily confessed at length. Rajk and his circle had proved themselves to be 'fascist police spies, traitors, American agents and organizers of what would have been the bloodiest military putsch in even Hungary's history'.

Of course, this being a Communist trial it had to be understood
that the wellsprings of treason rose as much in political theory
as in personality.

> Fundamentally there were weaknesses of mental grasp and know-
> ledge of Marxism which were to become obvious later and to
> give rise to the first suspicions among his closest colleagues.

And here Kartun took a swipe at unbelievers and Tito-lovers
on the non-Communist left:

> If those are the sort of people the *New Statesman* wishes to clasp
> to its bosom, one can only tell it regretfully to go ahead and be
> careful of the bloodstains.

Kartun's understanding of the Rajk trial was in every way
the same as his predecessors' understanding, over a decade
earlier, of the Moscow Trials. Then too Soviet sympathisers in
the West had clung to the credulous reports of naïve third-party
observers (often Americans), had convinced themselves of the
impossibility of confessions being coerced, and fitted the
supposed conspiracies easily into a history of past supposed
conspiracies.

The biggest show trial, nearly two years later, had the potential
to be a much more directly troubling affair for the comrades. As
Reuben Falber, then a Secretary of the Communist Party in Leeds,
later wrote, Czechoslovakia was 'perhaps the East European
country with which British communists had the greatest affinity'.
Before and during the war Czechoslovak Communists and anti-
fascists had fled to Britain. At the local HQ, Falber observed
volunteers who staffed a Czechoslovak club where exiles could
eat decent food at low prices until the war ended. 'A few days
after VE Day,' Falber wrote, 'we said goodbye to our friends who
were returning home to help rebuild their country.'

The same thing happened in London. In his autobiography *Muck, Silk and Socialism*, the fellow-travelling QC John Platts-Mills recalled being approached by a young Czechoslovak medical student called Otto Sling in the late summer of 1940. Sling had served with the Republican medical corps in Spain, where he had been buried alive twice and had been wounded by a bullet through the lung. The two men shared several different lodgings in London, and it was in London that Sling met his wife. 'Otto was a real inspiration to many young Britons,' wrote Platts-Mills, 'one of whom was a lovely girl called Marian'; or, as Eric Hobsbawm remembered her, 'the ever-reliable Marion Wilbraham from the pre-war Youth Peace Movement' and now a Communist named Marian Slingova.

The war over, like the Leeds Czechoslovaks, Sling returned home. And rose. As a Communist, he was elected to the first National Assembly and became its head in Moravia. In 1948, after the Communists took power, Sling stayed in Moravia, in its capital Brno, but obviously as a much more significant national figure. He and Marian maintained their contacts and he was visited by the Pollitt family (Harry's son, Brian, later remembered playing with the Sling children) and continued the correspondence with Platts-Mills.

In 1950, the anti-Titoist campaign caught up with Sling. After months of fearfulness, he was arrested, accused of treason, interrogated and re-interrogated. As Platts-Mills recalls, 'Marian was also arrested and their little boys were shunted from one children's home to another until she was released without charge two years later.'

Some of Sling's British friends attempted to intercede for him. In the matter of someone as obviously innocent as Sling, Platts-Mills determined that 'Stalin must have been mistaken and ill-advised.' As the trial approached, he decided to travel to Prague and testify on behalf of his friend. But Platts-Mills, despite having been a Labour MP and a staunch friend of the Soviet Union, was

denied a visa by the Czech authorities. Nonplussed he went to
see the General Secretary of the Communist Party, Harry Pollitt,
also a friend of Sling's. According to Platts-Mills, Pollitt listened
and then replied:

> 'I've heard of you. I'm told that you are ambitious, arrogant and
> conceited. You think you can get anything you want and always
> know how to go about it. Well, I was the same. All politicians are
> the same. The Czechs know better than we do what's happening
> in their country. They and their movement have suffered more
> than you or I will ever suffer and they must be left to decide these
> matters for themselves. Go and try if you want to, but I can't
> help.'

In fact Sling was relatively small fry – a regional Rosencrantz.
The big target of the eventual trial was no less than the General
Secretary of the Communist Party of Czechoslovakia, Rudolf
Slánský. Slánský was arrested in November 1951 and accused in
the Party press – along with Sling and twelve other senior figures –
of a variety of familiar crimes such as Titoism and working for
Western intelligence, as well as an important new one.

By now a novel enemy had arisen for the international proletariat to fight. In 1948 Stalin had supported the establishment of
the State of Israel. Czechoslovakia had been a major source of
arms for the Haganah – the Jewish defence force – which had
defeated the armies of various invading Arab states. But by 1949
Israel was gravitating towards the American camp and some of
the important Arab countries were slowly becoming friendly
towards Russia.

In this context the sin of 'cosmopolitanism' began to take on
an older colour. If any people had not been properly national,
had cleaved to themselves and their own customs, it was the Jews.
And if any people had a divided loyalty after 1948 it was the Jews –
to their old country perhaps but, of course, also to that new
country on the eastern Mediterranean shore. If, in addition to

being Jewish, a Party official had been in Spain, had spent time in the West and hadn't seen out the war as a guest of Stalin, then he or she had a CV that practically screamed 'Zionist-Titoist-Western agent!'

Of the fourteen who went on trial for treason on 20 November 1952 Slánský and ten others were Jewish. Whatever their origins, all pleaded guilty. In Sling's case his confession contained evidence of treachery going back to his days in England. Platts-Mills did not believe it. 'I was convinced that there was no circumstance in his life in London that gave the slightest opportunity for any of the intrigue and treason that he was persuaded to admit before his trial,' he wrote.

Platts-Mills's conviction availed his friend nothing. A week later, after the usual recitation of their complicated crimes, eleven of the defendants were sentenced to be hanged. Sling was one of them. In his final words from the dock on 3 December he wished 'every success to the Communist Party, the Czechoslovak people, and the President of the Republic'. But, he said, 'I have never been a spy.'

Artur London, one of the accused men who was not executed, later wrote about their treatment by the secret police. A Jew who had fought in Spain and the Czech resistance, whose mother and sister had been murdered in Auschwitz, London had been arrested after the Rajk trial and broken through psychological and physical torture and the use of threats to him and his family. In his book *The Confession* (turned into a movie by Costa-Gavras), he recalled being confronted by the infamous secret police officer, Major Smola. 'We'll get rid of you and your filthy race,' Smola apparently told him. 'You're all the same. Not everything Hitler did was right, but he destroyed the Jews and he was right about that. Too many of you escaped the gas chamber. We'll finish what he started.'

The bodies of Slánský, Sling and the others had barely been rendered to ashes when the next (and, as it happened, last) great story of conspiracy, treachery, arrests and confessions struck the

Communist world. This apotheosis of Stalinism was announced
on the front page of the Soviet Communist Party newspaper,
Pravda, on Tuesday 13 January 1953 under the headline 'Vicious
Spies and Killers under the Mask of Academic Physicians'. The
story began:

> Today the TASS news agency reported the arrest of a group of
> saboteur-doctors. This terrorist group, uncovered some time
> ago by organs of state security, had as their goal shortening the
> lives of leaders of the Soviet Union by means of medical
> sabotage.

The 'saboteur-doctors' had already done away with two senior
comrades, Andrei Zhdanov ('the Soviet Sam Aaronovitch' earlier
in this chapter) and Alexander Shcherbakov, former head of the
Writers' Union, as well as a number of military men. These deaths
had been accomplished by deliberately administering the wrong
drugs and incorrect regimen to them while they were ill in hospital.
Thus the crimes had been concealed by the appearance of death
from natural causes. The idea had been to 'remove Soviet and
military cadres from the power structure' and so weaken the defence
of the nation. 'Whom,' demanded *Pravda*, 'did these monsters
serve?' Then, as was customary, the writer answered himself:

> The majority of the participants of the terrorist group – Vovsi,
> B. Kogan, Feldman, Grinshtein, Etinger and others – were bought
> by American intelligence. They were recruited by a branch-office
> of American intelligence – the international Jewish bourgeois-
> nationalist organisation called 'Joint'. The filthy face of this Zionist
> spy organisation, covering up their vicious actions under the mask
> of kindness, is now completely revealed.

Had the plot not been uncovered, said *Pravda*, then other and
even more senior leaders might have been murdered, up to and
including Stalin himself.

The 'bourgeois press' in Britain and elsewhere had little doubt that this plot was a figment and the consequence either of paranoia or of some internal power struggle in the Soviet Union. Jewish writers and organisations round the world understood immediately that it was a variation on a deadly and ancient theme. The conspirators were Jews supposedly working for an underground Jewish cause. Unsurprisingly there were fears that this campaign would end in a state pogrom against the considerable number of Jews in the Soviet Union.

The British Communist Party was – officially – not worried. Pat Sloan, a long-time senior member, author of several books about the Soviet Union (including the 1937 classic *Soviet Democracy*) and now Secretary of the British Soviet Friendship Society, gave the line in March's edition of *Labour Monthly*:

> Ultimately with the passage of time it becomes generally accepted that the Soviet Government did, in fact, nip a conspiracy in the bud. The recent announcement of the doctors' plot discovered in Moscow has so far run true to form . . . So let the Press shriek 'fantastic' and 'frame-up' and 'anti-Semitism'. We've had it all before. But the facts will show, as they have shown before, that drastic steps must sometimes be taken by a Socialist state against capitalist conspirators and their tools.

'The facts will show'. Sloan was writing even before any trial could take place to test the evidence (not, of course, that any trial would have done so), but he knew – and he wanted everyone else to know – that the Jewish doctors would turn out to have been as guilty as Slansky, Sling and Rajk.

The British Communist Party itself had a significant Jewish membership, partly as a result of its record in the fight against fascism. And the leadership must have realised that the increasingly strident tone of the Soviet antagonism to 'Zionism' would discomfit many such members and supporters. What was needed to bring everyone into line was another pamphlet like

Klugmann's or Kartun's and so they cast around for someone
with good Jewish credentials to write it. Their first choice was
a Scottish Jewish mathematician and author of the wartime
pamphlet *Soviet Jews at War*, Professor Hyman Levy. Levy
refused.

The main job of explanation fell to Andrew Rothstein, whose
house on Hillway was a few yards away from Sam and Lavender.
In the same March 1953 edition of *Labour Monthly* as Pat Sloan's
defence of Soviet paranoia, Rothstein linked the ideological with
the conspiratorial. The working-class movement, he wrote, had
never been welcomed by 'petty Jewish capitalists', who had
wanted a way of diverting the Jewish proletariat from Marxism.
It had found just the vehicle it needed in Zionism. When it
seemed advantageous Zionists had collaborated with the Nazis,
but as Hitler faced defeat they had thrown in their lot with 'the
highest bidder' – America. As a result 'Jewish millionaires in the
USA took over in practice the leadership of the world Zionist
organization'.

So Zionism was inimical to socialism. Hence when a plot
involving Zionists was uncovered, neither it nor the shrieks of those
determined to deny it was at all surprising. Wrote Rothstein:

> The Zionist leaders of this and other countries have rushed into
> the press to attack the Soviet Union for arresting a few degenerate
> middle-class professional men whom thwarted class hatred of
> socialism (thwarted Zionism for some) has led into terrorist attacks
> on behalf of Wall Street.

There was, concluded Rothstein, 'but one road to safety . . . the
victory of working-class internationalism over bourgeois nation-
alism and Zionist racialism'.

Unfortunately for Rothstein hardly had the March edition
appeared than a great event happened, which sundered time
between 'before' and 'after'. On 5 March 1953, at his dacha in
Kuntsevo near Moscow, Stalin died. By the end of the month the

doctors had been exonerated (alas, two had already died in prison, probably as a result of torture), the charges dismissed and the entire business subsequently blamed on Stalin's Georgian security chief, Lavrentiy Beria, and his deputy, Mikhail Ryumin, both of whom were tried and shot.

How Andrew Rothstein, Pat Sloan and other Party members reconciled what they had just written about the plot with its rapid and complete evaporation is a matter of conjecture. I can find nothing from any of them explaining how such a thing could have happened. But in any case the rather sudden death of the giant of world Communism was probably their main preoccupation at the time.

It will occupy me in a few pages' time. But for now it is impossible not to ask questions, like the one Eric Hobsbawm asked years later in his memoirs, *Interesting Times*:

> How could one possibly believe the official Soviet line that Tito had to be excommunicated because he had long prepared to betray the interests of proletarian internationalism in the interest of foreign intelligence services? We could understand that James Klugmann was forced to disavow Tito, but we did not believe him . . . We knew he did not believe it either.

Who was this 'we'? It appeared again in a review by the Party historian Victor Kiernan of Alison Macleod's memoir of the 1950s, *The Death of Uncle Joe*.

> We had all admired the Yugoslav resistance to Hitler, and Tito's sudden excommunication seemed inexplicable. James Klugmann, who had served in Yugoslavia during the war, and came back talking enthusiastically of everything there, was – very tactlessly – commissioned by the Party to write a book explaining the *volte-face*. He could only make the shuffling best of a bad job. Someone told me of having seen him at headquarters, about to face the leadership over some question, looking distressingly nervous.

I and a friend, who had spent some time in Prague on scientific work, went to see him privately – we had known him well at Cambridge – and tried to make him see that some of the tales told at the trials, as at the earlier ones in Russia, were quite incredible. They meant that men who had risked their lives for years as revolutionaries had been wearing traitors' masks all the time, ready to be thrown off at a given signal. We could make no impression whatever.

By 1951–2 Hobsbawm, who said he hadn't believed the 1949 stories about Tito, found the accusations against Slansky and Sling, who were eventually rehabilitated in the 1960s, 'even less convincing'. Apparently now the Party's reflexive belief in the Soviet Union was waning. 'Party defence of the Czech trial seemed to show,' thought Hobsbawm, 'a certain lack of conviction.'

> Unlike what happened in the 1930s I cannot recall any serious attempt to compel Party members to justify the succession of show trials that disfigured the last years of Stalin, but this means that intellectuals like myself had given up the effort to be convinced.

Such may have been the mood amongst the Party historians (though they clearly kept it to themselves) but that such scepticism was not shared by Party members was demonstrated to me by a letter sent by Lavender to Sam on 27 January 1953, at the height of the furore over the Doctors' Plot. 'Dearest One', she wrote:

> Have just come back from the Pollitt meeting. It was not as well attended as it should have been, but 10 new recruits were made (alas not Gill among them) and £48 collected. The theme was 'socialism in our time' and Harry took the opportunity of dealing very clearly and firmly with the Czech and Moscow plots.

This was also the experience of the young *Daily Worker* journalist, Alison Mcleod. She remembered that in 1949 her colleagues
Derek Kartun ('clever, interesting, cultivated') and Peter Fryer had
'both sincerely believed the confessions of the accused to be
genuine'. Two years later when *Pravda* announced the Doctors'
Plot a colleague in the newsroom spoke for himself and others
when he said of the supposed conspirators and their masters,
'Gosh, they never give up, do they?'

And Sam, all this time working as Cultural Secretary? In Doris
Lessing's novel *The Golden Notebook* there is another episode
involving Comrade Bill, but this one does not appear in non-fiction
form in her memoirs. The heroine, Anna – being of Hobsbawmian
mind but possessing a more activist disposition – is shocked by
the East European show trials and in particular by the accusation
against an old friend. So she and a writer friend approach Bill,
who says he will make enquiries. Then . . .

> We went to see Bill again. Extremely affable. Said he could do
> nothing. Why not? 'Well in matters of this case where there might
> be doubt . . .' Bill hesitated, began on a long and manifestly insin-
> cere rationalisation, about how it was possible that anyone could
> be an agent, 'including me'.

If Bill is indeed Sam then he knows what Lavender obviously
doesn't – that the accusations are almost certainly untrue. In other
words, he is – for whatever reasons – a complete cynic.

But perhaps not so cynical because, according to my aunt Gill,
on hearing the news of Stalin's death that spring in 1953, Sam
cried. I never once saw my father cry in the forty-four years I knew
him – except twice, maybe, with laughter.

In the National Archive is a file on the Communist singer Ewan
MacColl. Intercepted letters in the file show that at the beginning
of the decade MacColl was in correspondence with Sam about,

among other matters, his new song, 'The Ballad of Stalin'. The last verse ran:

> *Joe Stalin was a mighty man and he made a mighty plan;*
> *He harnessed nature to the plough to work for the good of man;*
> *He's hammered out the future, the forgeman he has been*
> *And he's made the workers' state the best the world has ever seen.*

It later came be to an item of faith that what was known as 'the cult of personality' was a Soviet disease, inculcated by Stalin and his hangers on, and which, though influential, had never quite infected parties like the British Communist Party. They were not directly responsible for the idolatry, the pictures of an almost godlike Marshal in white uniform standing in a golden field of Soviet corn.

But MacColl's ballad suggests otherwise. Here Stalin is the quintessential Big Hewer of industrial mythology – half worker, half god. Elsewhere British Party members and leaders also assigned to him a unique intellectual and prophetic capacity.

The March 1953 edition of *Labour Monthly* – the same that held Sloan's justification of show trials and arrests and Rothstein's complementary attack on Zionism – also marked the 70th anniversary of Karl Marx's death. The editor was concerned to reconcile Marxism as a science with what had obviously been recent attacks by political opponents on the idolatrous nature of Stalinism. Written as little as two or three weeks before the General Secretary passed on, it is a masterpiece of aggressive apologism and of making an elephant look like an apostrophe. It has to be admired for its casuistry:

> Marxism is a science alike in the field of theory and action; and
> precisely because it is a science, and all the more because it repre-
> sents the highest level of science, it requires mastery; and mastery
> implies a master. For this reason Marxism finds its expression in

the living person, and its highest expression in the 'greatest head', the 'central figure', the genius whose perfect understanding and whose theoretical and practical leadership most effectively carries forward to the fulfilment of Marxism.

If a man was the 'greatest head' and the 'central figure', then it was not just the science of which he was master, but all its practitioners. It was no step at all to make Stalin a figure not of Pope-like authority, but something greater than that. From his pen came new scriptures, new commandments. Thou shalt not like Tito, thou shalt loathe Israel. Thou wilt strike agreements with social democrats. Honour thy Father above all things.

Sam quoted Stalin in each of his books until 1955, somehow shoehorning the Georgian into the text. E. P. Thompson cited Stalin in his biography of William Morris (the reference was removed after 1956). Stalin was the authority for everything. The ultimate superdad, in direct line of succession from Lenin. With Stalin around there would always be an answer. There would never be doubt.

And then he was gone and replaced in Russia by a triumvirate of gnomes. Malenkov. Bulganin. Khrushchev. The April edition of *Labour Monthly* was sombre but tearfully determined:

> Through all the storms of a thunderous dawn, of the dissolution of an old era and the birth of a new, he steered the ship of human hopes and aspirations with unflinching tenacity, courage, judgment and confidence. Now the road lies plain ahead.

Except it didn't. That's why the trials stopped, the doctors were freed and why – between early and late 1953 – Peter Mauger's speech about those dreadful comics moved from a concentration on crude anti-Americanism to a more ecumenical idea about promoting a world at peace. ('There is not one reference to American imperialism,' the perceptive academic Martin

Barker noted while reading a speech made by Mauger in the second half of 1953. 'The tenor has altered from a crude political anti-Americanism to a humanistic stance of war versus peace.') Stalin's death changed everything because they had all been Stalinists.

The Cold War went down a notch or two from appalling to dreadful, workers were shot in East Berlin, my parents married and I was born. Sam stopped being Cultural Secretary, Khrushchev visited Yugoslavia and made up with Tito, some prisoners of Stalinism emerged from Eastern European gaols to tell their stories (and to be accused of exaggeration), the battle against colonialism intensified and the class struggle carried on in Britain, albeit in a not completely uncivilised way.

If Eric Hobsbawm and Victor Kiernan or, for that matter, Sam Aaronovitch and Harry Pollitt and John Gollan had believed that Sling and Rajk and the others were guiltless, then at least that period was over and the edifice – the past leaders, Marx, Engels, Lenin, Stalin, the heroic Soviet Union and the international proletarian movement – still stood. When the Soviet Party Congress met in February 1956 there were early reports of complaints about a lack of collective leadership in the past and a suggestion that there had been a problem with a 'cult of the individual'. The release a year earlier of some of those imprisoned in the Slansky trial suggested second thoughts. Significant, perhaps, but the structure of Communist history and Communist belief was intact. Pictures of Stalin still hung on the walls of King Street.

But then it began to filter out in accounts in various countries, picked up by the British press, that there had been an unprecedented secret session at the Congress, and that this session had heard extraordinary revelations concerning the Stalin period. At the *Daily Worker* there was a continuing hum among journalists about the provenance of emerging stories of pardons and rehabilitations.

And then, in the spring and early summer of 1956, it was announced as news that the rumours of a closed session were correct and that at this session Khrushchev (now in a univirate with himself) had destroyed the reputation of Stalin. In May Harry Pollitt stood down as General Secretary of the Party and John Gollan took over.

On 10 June, without any warning being given to Party comrades, the *Observer* published the previously unseen full text of the speech which, boiled down, implied that almost everything that the capitalist press had said about repression and tyranny in Russia over twenty years was true and (an unsaid corollary) everything that the Communist Party and its members had said in response was not. The trials the Party had defended were all shams, the confessions were all false, the condemnations of old comrades as having been fascist hyenas and worse were all unjust, the executions all – in effect – judicial murders.

'Of the 139 members and candidates of the party's Central Committee who were elected at the 17th congress [of 1934],' Khrushchev told the delegates (and now the *Observer* told the world), '98 persons, that is, 70 per cent, were arrested and shot.' There was the 'most cruel repression' of many prominent Party leaders and rank-and-file Party workers, honest and dedicated to the cause of Communism, who 'fell victim to Stalin's despotism'. And so on for page after page. It was an exposition both of a systematic brutality and, for British Communists, of an equally systematic wrongness. 'Most comrades,' wrote Alison Macleod, 'could not believe what they were reading.'

Doris Lessing had left the Party earlier, and now anguished Party members were turning to her. 'I was joking, but then could no longer joke,' she said, 'that every time the phone rang another comrade had had a religious conversion, taken to drink, committed suicide, or turned into his or her opposite.'

Alison Macleod remembered that 'all around us the marriages of Party members were cracking up. Some couples stayed together only by never holding those discussions which to us were the breath of life.' At the turn of the millennium Eric Hobsbawm wrote – unusually dramatically for him – that:

Even after practically half a century my throat contracts as I recall
the almost intolerable tensions under which we lived month after
month, the unending moments of decision about what to say and
do on which our future lives seemed to depend, the friends now
clinging together, or facing one another bitterly as adversaries, the
sense of lurching, unwillingly but irreversibly down the scree
towards the fatal rock face.

In America the young Vivian Gornick, from a Party family (the
CPUSA bore some similarities to its comrade party in Britain),
fell out with an aunt in her kitchen. 'Millions of Russians have
been destroyed! Millions of Communists have betrayed themselves
and each other!' screamed Gornick. 'A Red-baiter!' my aunt yelled
back, 'A lousy little Red-baiter you've become. Louie Gornick
must be turning over in his grave that his daughter has become
a Red-baiter!'

These were the two poles of reaction. For some, believing
anything now coming from Russia or the Party was no longer
possible as it cast a backwards light on years of Soviet claims.
Alison Macleod's husband Jack, also a Party member, woke her
in the middle of the night saying, 'Do you realise the Russians
massacred those Poles at Katyn?' 'Yes, of course they did,' she
replied.*

Peter Fryer and Derek Kartun, the men who had been at the
Rajk trial and declared him a traitor who received a just punish-
ment, were desolate with guilt. They had embroidered and sold
the lie of the wickedness of innocent men. As Kartun wrote in
an article the following year, 'It has made puppets and parrots
out of us in the past. It has been bad for the Russians and disastrous for us.'

---

* It was another thirty-five years before the Russians admitted that the
  1940 mass murder of 12,000 Polish officers had indeed been their
  doing.

At the opposite end of the spectrum were some who defiantly maintained that Khrushchev was exaggerating. Platts-Mills had the same instincts as many in the Party when he said that, at the time and despite the denunciation, he 'couldn't accept' that Stalin had been instrumental in actions such as procuring the death of his friend Otto Sling. Others jumped the hurdle with a strange alacrity using a deferential logic. It was summarised by the staunch cadre who said that he wouldn't believe that the Russians had been wrong until they themselves said they had been wrong – and when they did say they were wrong then he'd believe that they were right about that, as they were about everything else.

Then there were comrades like Kim James, the bohemian veteran whom I talked to not long before he died and who, well into the twenty-first century, 'loved the whole idea of Marxism'. He had actually worked in Poland during the early '50s and spent a period in Moscow. James said, almost lightly even, that yes, he'd known this repression was dreadful and self-defeating, but it was all happening abroad and that there was work to be done for the working class in Britain – that was the important thing. While Eric Hobsbawm was distraught and Alison Macleod aghast, Kim James was undeflected. The real enemy – one that he hated with an impish pleasure until he died – was the British capitalist class.

The Party itself writhed. George Matthews was the urbane pleasant-voiced intellectual who was effectively number two in the Party from 1949 onwards. He was the same age as Sam and was yet another Party stalwart who could have done well for himself if he hadn't taken up the great cause as a young man. Macleod remembers several occasions, as the Khrushchev revelations unfolded, on which Matthews travelled the distance between Covent Garden and Clerkenwell to address the staff at the *Daily Worker* and answer their increasingly difficult questions.

The line as it developed was to suggest that, though what had been revealed was deeply troubling, the very fact of its revelation

showed that everything was on the proper track now. As summarised by Macleod (who started by accepting it), his argument was
that 'the vital thing is that the mistakes have been recognized and
put right'. Pollitt tried at first to make it sound as though the
Great Terror was in the normal range of error. 'Stalin was a very
great leader,' he told a meeting. 'But all great men make mistakes.'
His successor Johnny Gollan gave a very rare television interview
to the great BBC inquisitor Robin Day (rare because the Party
was almost never asked). Day wanted to know how Gollan
explained the terrible facts now admitted by the Russians themselves. The new Party leader reversed the blame. So paranoid had
the Russians been about the possibility of external attack (and
who could blame them?) that they had too easily mistaken friends
for enemies.

As to the British Party, it had itself been wronged, was sorry,
and would learn the lesson. It issued a statement that:

> On the basis of false information we, in all good faith, made a
> number of mistakes, as in our support for the accusation against
> the Yugoslav Communist leaders as traitors, and our condemna-
> tion of those falsely convicted . . . There is, in future, bound to
> be a more critical examination of policies, from whatever quarter
> they come.

This was apparently good enough for many comrades, who
said, in essence, as did one *Daily Worker* staff member, that they
were 'prepared to believe that the Party leaders knew best'.

What of Sam and Lavender? My mother, at least, was preoccupied. Two days after the text of the Khrushchev speech was
published my brother Owen was born, and now she had a ten-
year-old, a toddler and a baby to look after, and almost no money
on which to do any of it. I have no reason to doubt that Sam
went along with the Party line and, if he had doubts, kept them
to himself. In any case, that summer the Suez Crisis was more
often in the news even than the historical revelations from Russia.

Adjustments would have to be made, no doubt, but this too would pass.

What happened instead was the Hungarian Uprising. In October small protests in socialist Hungary became mass protests. The Hungarian leadership, itself riven by doubts after the secret speech, dithered. Troops refused to fire on protestors, who attacked secret police headquarters, acquired guns and lynched hated Party officials. At 2 a.m. on 24 October, acting on orders from the Soviet Defence Minister – none other than that fabled hero of the Great Patriotic War, Marshal Zhukov – Russian tanks entered Budapest. As the Red Army throttled the rebellion the insurgents broadcast increasingly desperate pleas for help, pleas which were heard in the impotent West.

Once again George Matthews appeared in the newsroom. 'As a general principle the Soviet Union should be presumed innocent until proved guilty,' he said. The British Party agreed with its Soviet comrades that the rebellion had been an attempt to destroy socialism and install a neo-fascist regime. In the next few months 20 per cent of the Party membership gave up their cards, including many of its best thinkers. Derek Kartun joined the Labour Party and became a thriller writer.

A fifth of Party members went. But four-fifths didn't. In a meeting Andrew Rothstein attacked 'groups of backboneless and spineless intellectuals who have turned in upon their own emotions and frustrations'. When I was a child there was a tag that was sometimes applied to a famous person whom Sam and Lavender knew or had known – 'they left in '56'. Or 'they left after Hungary'. Its connotation was almost that of someone who had been a good person but who couldn't stay the course, who somehow lacked the stamina.

Not all these departures happened immediately. A few doors down from the Rothsteins and an avenue away from our growing household, the Abramskys – Miriam and Chimen – left in 1956 and 1958 respectively. Lavender never forgave Miriam, who had been a friend (they may have 'had words', I don't

know), and whenever she spoke about the Abramskys afterwards there was an implied rebuke or criticism of them. Their
daughter Jenny, a friend of Sabrina's, said that my mother's
disapproval brought their friendship to an end. This is quite
possible. The sense of guilty relief on the one side and that of
being abandoned by your friends on the other, created some
poisonous moments.

1956 was the last moment, apparently and seen with hindsight,
when anyone who might want to be spared the stain of association with Soviet crimes could leave. Or so the literature seems
to suggest. Christopher Hill, E. P. Thompson, Hyman Levy (actually he got himself expelled) and Raphael Samuel among them.
Peter Fryer, covering Hungary for the *Daily Worker*, found his
reports on the Hungarian rebels suppressed or censored, and
angrily departed for the less compromised desert island of
Trotskyism.

But why 1956 and Hungary? Why not 1936–8 after the show
trials and the purges? Old Nellie Rathbone from Makepeace
Avenue had – I found out years later – been born Nellie
Cohen. Her sister Rose had been something of a beauty and
had been courted by the young Harry Pollitt, but had married
a Russian instead and moved to Moscow. Her husband, Max
Petrovsky, worked in the Commissariat for Heavy Industry
and Rose was foreign editor of the English-language *Moscow
Daily News*.

Early in 1937 Max was arrested and then shot. That August
Rose was arrested. Nellie turned to Pollitt and the Party to
intercede, which they did. According to the author Francis
Beckett, Pollitt said to one mutual friend, 'What can I do?
They've arrested Rose Cohen. I know she's innocent.' The
response from intermediaries in Moscow was, 'Comrade, it's
best that you don't pursue these matters.' Ivy, the English wife
of the Soviet foreign policy chief, Maxim Litvinov, suggested
later that Pollitt had asked Stalin directly for Rose to be allowed
to return to Britain. Stalin, she said, agreed. But by then it was

too late. Rose had already been tried summarily and sentenced to 'ten years without the right of visits'. In other words, shot immediately.

So, if not then, why not 1939 and the Nazi–Soviet Pact and the Party's headstand? Or 1948 and the Tito split which Eric Hobsbawm, after all, knew to be based on a falsehood? Or 1952 and the execution of Otto Sling, whose children had played with the children of Party leaders? Or 1953 and the anti-Semitic Doctors' Plot? Why not after the Khrushchev speech, but before Hungary?

In the mid 1970s Vivian Gornick, researching for her book on American Communism, interviewed a former Party member whom she named 'Max Bitterman'. She noted the old man's 'scorn for and hatred for anyone who had left the Party either thirty seconds earlier or thirty seconds later than he had'. Those who left before him were morally deficient and those who left after were intellectually impaired.

In a way everyone was right. It could be cowardly to leave and courageous to stay. The leavers no longer had to face those Cold War battles in which they were always on the wrong side of received opinion. The stayers, on the other hand, maintained their commitment in the face of everything the bourgeois media could throw at them.

But it could also be cowardly to stay and courageous to leave. The leavers went from the comfortable if constricting shape of a life in the Party, their certainties and their relationships all abandoned. The stayers carried on in the familiar routines, buying the Party paper, attending meetings, knowing exactly where they were on almost any issue in any country of the world.

And, to an extent, the longer you'd stayed already and the more you'd endured, the longer you would stay and endure. A famous piece of research by the American psychologists Aronson and Mills concerned students who were each asked to undergo an initiation process before being allowed to join what was promised to be a fascinating discussion group on the psychology of

sex. The levels of embarrassment in the initiation processes that
the students were asked to undergo varied from excruciating to
minor. There then followed a deliberately turgid, lengthy and
academic session on the topic of the sex lives of birds. The
students whose initiations had been painless tended to describe
the discussion as boring and pointless and the speakers as not
very interesting. Those whose initiation had been more taxing
and unpleasant, however, were much more likely to say that the
debate had been fascinating and that their colleagues had been
rather wonderful. This experiment was repeated in various ways,
but the result was always the same. If you'd suffered for the
cause, you thought more highly of it. This is one reason why
being rude to someone whose political ideas you think are
stupid – however truthful you are being or however satisfying it
is to do – is more likely to confirm them in their opinions than
change their minds. The greater the sacrifice, the greater the
commitment.

In a book written by a Party defector in the early 1950s, the
author, Douglas Hyde, described some of the extreme commit-
ments made by comrades. Like Jimmie, the one-legged factory
worker from Essex, whose supply of *Daily Workers* was
disrupted by bombing and who rigged up a one-pedal bicycle,
cycled to central London via the docks during the Blitz, and
back with two big rucksacks strapped to his sides. The very
fact of so many high-profile departures from the Party, accompanied by their public recantations, could cause members to
resist. Eric Hobsbawm hated the idea of joining the intellectuals
who had written for a famous collection of recantatory essays.
He 'was strongly repelled by the idea of being in the company
of anti-communists, because they could free themselves from
the service of *The God That Failed* only by turning him into
Satan.'

Strong in many Party members – strong in my mother – was
the idea of duty, linked of course to ideas of loyalty and sacrifice.

Gornick tells of an elderly Communist setting out in a snowstorm for yet another rally in Madison Square Gardens. 'If I didn't go,' he demanded, 'who will be there?' It was, as Hobsbawm told Ignatieff, 'a lifetime commitment and a total commitment'. It was a search for meaning in a meaningless world. It was the opium of some people.

In Arnold Wesker's play *Chicken Soup with Barley*, written in the aftermath of the events of 1956, the mother, a lifelong Communist, is confronted by her son's rejection of the Party. Her reaction is a beautiful distillation of the feelings of people like Lavender when faced with the challenge to their world.

> If the electrician who comes to mend my fuse, blows it instead, so I should stop having electricity? Socialism is my light, can you understand that? A way of life. A man *can* be beautiful. I hate ugly people – I can't bear meanness and fighting and jealousy – I've got to have light. I'm a simple person, Ronnie, and I've got to have light and love.

I can hear these words of Wesker's running as an emotional subtext through this letter, sent by a man who used to come to our house when I was a boy and published in the *Guardian* newspaper half a century later:

> Sir, as an 88-year-old who joined the Young Communist League on leaving school in 1936, graduated into the Communist party of Great Britain a few years later, and remained a member until it ceased to exist in 1991, I am angered by the attacks made on it by John Morrison in his letter throwing mud at Eric Hobsbawm (Review, February 24). We believed the Soviet Union to be socialist. It certainly had some features of socialism: social ownership, low rents, a state health service and state education. Yes, we made a terrible mistake over Stalin, and we have paid for it. But is the world a safer place without the USSR? I am proud to have belonged to a party which created

the International Brigade, organised by the worldwide Spanish aid campaign, helped push Churchill to launch the second front and has always been at the forefront of anti-fascism.

Hyman Frankel

Frankel died a couple of years later. And Lavender, I think, would have expressed much the same defiant sentiment. As one old woman told Vivian Gornick, no one was coerced in the West into being in the Communist Party, or into staying in it. 'You know,' she said, 'people never understand that. They say to us, 'The CP held a whip over you.' They don't understand. The whip was inside each of us. We held it over ourselves, not over each other.' They had a choice.

The Party was a church, not a cult. There was no psychological game played to keep members docile and loyal. Its strength was that it was about belief and faith as much as about intellect. No – more than it was about intellect. Because if it had been in any way 'scientific', if it had involved a cold appraisal of the truth, then how could Party members have been so obtuse as not to see what was so apparent to others?

'It is anachronistic,' wrote Hobsbawm in *Interesting Times*, 'to suppose that only genuine or wilful ignorance stood between us and denouncing the inhumanities perpetrated on our side.' Or, he might have added, stupidity. Though there was indeed a kind of stupidity among some people – including people who held on to important jobs and had had expensive educations. John Platts-Mills, the QC and erstwhile Labour MP, whose country house was sometimes a venue for the annual get-together of the British Bulgarian Friendship Society, remembered a reunion with the former Labour colleague Konni Zilliacus, who had been accused by the Soviets of being a Yugoslav (and hence an American) stooge. Men had been executed on the basis of their imagined contact with Zilliacus. But Platts-Mills recalled that years after he had finally became convinced that Stalin had been occasionally very badly behaved, 'I sought out Zilly and made a suitable obeisance. He laughed, put an arm round my shoulder and said, "My dear boy, we all learn in time and it is never too late".' For Rajk, Slansky and thousands of others, of course, 'too late' is precisely what it was.*

Hobsbawm cannot have meant that Party members told themselves all along that Stalin was a murderer, that Tito was traduced, that all those agents, traitors and enemies of socialism were innocent, and that the hyenas of the capitalist press were the tribunes of truth. Because they clearly didn't. Derek Kartun believed in the guilt of Rajk, even if Hobsbawm did not. So did many, many others.

But when Lavender went to see Harry Pollitt, 'dealing very clearly and firmly' with the absurd conspiracy theories about Agent Otto Sling and the murderous Zionist doctors, she came away having heard what she needed to hear. She accepted it because she had to, because anything else would bring the edifice down around her ears. There had to be one Father – Stalin, or the Party – who was steadfast and utterly reliable, and in whom you placed your trust.

The French Marxist historian, Maxime Rodinson, recognised the psychology at work, when writing about how Communists reacted to the Doctors' Plot. There can be a

> visceral need not to renounce a commitment that has illuminated one's life, given it meaning, and for which many sacrifices have often been made. Hence the reluctance to recognize even the most obvious facts, the desperate para-logical guile to which one resorts in an effort to avoid the required conclusions, the passionate and

---

* It is hard to believe – it really is difficult – that someone could be that stupid. But readers of Platts-Mills's astonishing autobiography will also find the following passage: 'Mentioning that I am on the nominating committee for the Muammar Gaddafi Annual prize for Human Rights tends to leave people rather stunned. This is an award given for genuine and deep-rooted commitment to the struggle for freedom and democracy, as defined by the Libyans.'

obstinate blindness with which any idea of any change is rejected, the refusal even to examine any document, any argument, that could imperil the delicate balance one has achieved in one's inner being.

That is why we couldn't have Orwell in the house. He was a one-man imperilment of delicate balances. So he became a fifth columnist, a man whose words were automatically to be discounted. They never needed to be read, let alone thought about.

This process of banishment was not purely a product of a time and place. Any of us, I now realise, can do it and most of us will.

Three years after Lavender died I appeared on a BBC programme called *My Dad Was a Communist*. Various people talked briefly about their experiences of being 'red diaper' babies, including Arnold Wesker, the comedian Alexei Sayle and me. It was a slight programme, but mostly affectionate, during the course of which I talked about the bazaars and jumble sales and mentioned Lavender's reaction to the invasion of Czechoslovakia and – more seriously – the execution of Otto Sling.

A few days later I received a bitterly angry letter from the daughter of a former senior Party figure, now (of all things) an Episcopalian minister in the far north of Scotland. The same age as Sabrina, she had been our babysitter sometimes and I had liked her.

She had, she began, 'probably experienced a far more intensive party childhood than you', and then accused those appearing on the programme of 'betraying their own parents in a way I found quite disloyal'. Our childhoods hadn't been so bad, she went on (I had never said they were), and 'at least we were given some guidelines to live by, some form of discipline and something to aim for, unlike so many children today, who don't really know who they are or where they are going'. She had 'ended up feeling

insulted on behalf of your parents – especially your mother –
where was your loyalty?'

The reader will notice that there was no complaint that anything
that had been said was untrue. The issues were disloyalty and
betrayal. Then came this remarkable passage:

> I also thought the reference to Otto Sling was unnecessary. Yes it
> was a bad event but there were many more and did anyone give
> a thought to my dear childhood friends Jan and Karel Sling and
> their mother Marian Slingova/Fagin [*sic* – actually Fagan] who is
> still living – they suffered enough without it being dredged up to
> suit the producers' ideas. Certainly there were unpleasant things
> that people tried to brush under the carpet but nothing really has
> changed.

In the former *Daily Worker* journalist Alison Macleod's book
she wrote about how a comrade told her much later that in 1951–2
he had gone to see Harry Pollitt and the letter-writer's father to
try and convince them that Otto Sling was innocent. He had come
away without succeeding.

The idea that Marian Fagan would have been upset by a reference to her dead husband's judicial murder, when she wrote an
entire book on the subject, is almost an epic in unconscious
disingenuousness. Rather, the person who is discomfited to have
the affair recalled is the one who – her father dead – carries the
most guilt about it. She was angry with me because, if she really
allowed herself to think it through, she would be impossibly angry
with the parents she loved who stood by and – in public –
applauded the hanging of her playmates' father. I – clumsily, no
doubt – momentarily imperilled that delicate balance, which her
letter was set on maintaining. A balance she may have taken to
God and the Highlands to maintain.

The perspicacious Alison Macleod wrote that, 'looking back
I can see that I insisted on being lied to'. But that means that she

both knew and didn't know. The thing she wanted not to believe was still there – perhaps half a dream, a sudden anger, an unexpected doubt – so she had to try even harder not to know it; until the point where it could no longer not be known. Which for some people arrived too late or never arrived at all.

But this wasn't and isn't a human trait confined to politics. It's also what we do with each other. It's what Lavender did with Sam and what I did with both of them.

II

The Referred Patient

But you, when at last the time comes
That man can aid his fellow man,
Should think upon us
With leniency.

Bertolt Brecht 'To Those Who Follow in Our Wake',
translated by Scott Horton

If my childhood was not much fun it had nothing to do with the Party. Something in our family didn't quite work and little tended towards joy.

Sam was rarely at home and, when he was, his attention was not given easily or willingly to his children. He didn't read to us or play games with us and an outing with him would be to one of his Party offices where we'd sit, Owen and I, at a table and draw or read. If Sam was in the house in the evening his main desire seemed to be that we children should go to bed. Wrongly I thought that this was a drive prompted by an officious (if remote) concern for our well-being. Later I discovered that it had another cause.

Most of what we now call 'parenting' was done by Lavender, and she was fed up a lot of the time. There was no money, her attempts to earn some from part-time jobs were undermined by the constant series of illnesses we all seem to have suffered from, and she had to deal with three children – two of them boys very close in age.

Lavender operated at a constant low level of crossness with flare-ups of anger, minor violence and spite, and – even more occasionally – small episodes of hilarity and enjoyment. When I was nine we watched a BBC adaptation of *Jane Eyre*, and I recall thinking even then that being confined with my mother was sometimes like being up there in the attic with the first Mrs Rochester. However, holidays were even more purgatorial. At least at home, if the weather was good enough, you could escape Thornfield Hall to the Heath, or the garden, or to your friend's house. But on holiday you were cribbed with the family – surly father, neurotic mother, bored brother, semi-detached sister.

I think Sam might have liked me had he taken the time. He might have identified with me. My mother, however, preferred my brother Owen. As soon as I was articulate, my exaggerated notion of what I thought was fair was made more alienating by a precocious capacity to argue the case. Lavender admired and hated this prodigious verbosity. Her way of dealing with it was to know my weak, emotional points, my tendency to become enraged, and to play on them. The slightest sign of rage was held to invalidate any argument. After a while the safest way of dealing with the depressed family was to withdraw from it.

I wasn't hated, or neglected, or starved or regularly beaten. Now, with children of my own, I see the sad truth that Sam and Lavender didn't seem to get anything out of having me for a son. I was supposedly the brightest kid in school, but that appeared to give them no great pleasure. I read anything and everything. I was interested in the world, and yet the main thing about me was that I was a problem. My 'jealousy' of my younger brother was a constant feature of their conversation concerning me and the main accusation made to my face. And it was partly true. Though in fact we shared a solidarity in the evening bedroom that they never really understood (as adults

rarely understand what is going on between siblings), nevertheless the quarrels between us and the fact that I was the oldest
created a dynamic in which I ended up resenting Owen and
looked for signs that he was indeed preferred. Then I would

behave badly and so I became the imagined grit in the family clockwork.

What anchored me before adolescence and tempered my loneliness was the fact that I loved my primary school, liked the teachers and had a best friend there who was loyal to me and to whom I was loyal in return. But then the time came to leave, put on blazer and tie and go to secondary school.

Easily the nearest was 400 yards away, and was next to the girls' school where Sabrina had gone. It was a slightly old-fashioned school where rugby, not football, was played and had a reputation for a '50s academicism. It was where my best friend and some of my other classmates, including another Party child, went.

But William Ellis was a grammar school and organisations like the Campaign for Advancement of State Education (of which Lavender was a member) were now actively promoting the cause of comprehensives. It wasn't just a matter of thinking that the division between grammar and secondary modern schools, to be decided by selection at age eleven, was pernicious (it was indeed, as Sam had discovered in 1930), but also of believing that the new comprehensives represented something better in themselves. Everybody would benefit. So, somehow it was decided that I would want to be part of this new movement. When it was put like that, my ten-year-old self was attracted by the idea.

The process of deciding which of the local comprehensives I should go to is obscure to me now. I didn't attend the closest, which was co-educational (rare in those days) but fetched up being admitted to a large boys' comprehensive school located a mile and half away from my home, among a series of council estates between Camden Road and Brecknock Road, and not far from Holloway Prison. There had very recently been a celebrated cell of Party teachers at Holloway County (blazer motto 'Persequere' – which gave us the unwanted nickname of the 'Percy Queers'), but the year I arrived they all left. Not one of my primary school-mates went to Holloway.

At Holloway there was a core of committed teachers, part of the school was housed in a relatively new building, and the institution's ambition could be seen in its mounting of school musicals and concerts at an extraordinarily high level. The head of music, a considerable force, even managed to create a fund for a school organ, whose sad, disused pipes I saw in the school when I visited it thirty years later.

The classes were 'streamed' for ability (though no one actually told us this). In the first year I came top in almost all the subjects, and made friends readily enough, though only two of them lived within walking distance. But after that it all began to fall apart.

Eleven-year-old boys are biddable; thirteen-year-old boys are mad. Whatever the teachers tried to do, the overwhelming peer culture at the school was hostile to study. Football and fighting, messing about, disrupting class, seeing how quickly you could get a supply teacher to leave the room in tears – all these became more important than the learning being done.

We were madder too because attitudes to authority were now changing very quickly. The summer of 1967 was the Summer of Love in San Francisco. There were beautiful girls there, people who did not wear ties or get told off because their kaftans were dirty, and documentaries on the television told us about communes in Haight-Ashbury and raised questions about the youth of today. Communes sounded marvellous. A group of Ilford mods in a band called the Small Faces captured it precisely. The BBC was persuaded that the words did not mean what they transparently did mean and 'Itchycoo Park' was played on Radio 1 (established that year) and performed on *Top of the Pops*. I remember hearing it on the radio of our school coach as it trundled homeward from an improving Nature Studies field trip.

*

The lead singer Steve Marriott was only seven years older than me. And even if you weren't quite sure what getting 'high' was, you certainly understood the idea of bunking off school because it was a waste of time. It was an illustration of how things were changing in ways that did not much help teachers or parents.

There were plenty of mods but no hippies at Holloway. Though the lovely family of my nearest 'friend' took me fishing once and to a point-to-point meeting, his way of settling arguments with a punch in the face unsettled me. Then, sensing that fighting was not my forte, his younger brother also punched me in the face. That was enough.

Isolated at school, I hung out with some old primary school friends who lived nearby. Together we met girls. My first girl-friend's parents were a pair of Tory bohemians. He was an Australian picture-frame maker with an Antipodean attitude towards individualism. She was a minor artist of the practical 'sell to live' school. And as far as she was concerned it was common sense that people had different aptitudes and that if they were, say, clever, they'd go to clever college. And stupid people would go to the stupid place. She was my first Social Darwinist.

Young as I was, their flat – ten minutes away – was a refuge to me. They liked my loquacity and I didn't have to accept their politics to accept their help. Gradually they told me what I half knew, which was that I wanted to leave Holloway and that if I wanted to, I should. I became more openly rebellious at school.

Soon my teachers became alarmed at my alienation. I think the proximate cause of their alarm was an essay for my English teacher and form master which more or less repeated some of the pithier observations of the Australian frame-maker. The teacher's diagnosis, which was shared with me, was that they were facing a classic problem of the bright child who wasn't (in the language of the time) being 'stretched', and who might be happier somewhere more academic. However, just in case something else was going on in my psyche they called in an educational psychologist.

When my mother died in 2005, as well as her diaries I inherited some of her books. One was an unprepossessing red trade paperback with a Dutch sculpture of a family on the cover, whose author was given as A. C. Robin Skynner, MB, MRC Psych, DPM. Published thirty years earlier, it was called *One Flesh, Separate Persons: Principles of Family and Marital Psychotherapy.*

I knew of Robin Skynner in two ways. First, by reputation from his famous collaboration with the actor and comedian John Cleese, which had made Skynner something of a colour supplement psycho-celeb. Together they had written two books: *Families and How to Survive Them* and *Life and How to Survive It*, the first of which sold over 350,000 copies in the anglophone world. The success of these titles helped the book I inherited to remain constantly in print.

The second way in which I knew Skynner was that I was in the book. We all were. After sixteen chapters of theory and its application, the seventeenth chapter of *One Flesh* (to me, an interestingly repulsive title) was entitled 'Outline of a Family and Marital Treatment'. It is a case history of a family therapy, recorded, the introduction says, with the family's permission. 'Needless to say,' Skynner found it necessary to say, 'the identity of the family has been thoroughly disguised.' Perhaps more pertinently, the family did not give its permission. Sam and Lavender did, and that is different, but it's the kind of difference you never notice until you are the subject. I have no real complaint about it. How could I? I'm writing this, after all.

The book had been published in 1976, which, as we will see, was ironic in itself. But the history of the family therapy it recorded over thirty-two pages had begun in the autumn of 1967 and ended seventeen sessions later in January 1969.

Skynner's account began with a dramatis personae under the heading of FAMILY STRUCTURE. We were:

A middle class intelligent family with a bias towards an intellectual approach to problems. Both parents in their early forties.

> *Father* – a teacher in a practical subject at a polytechnic school, devoting himself more fully to his work than was in the family's interest, and perhaps somewhat disappointed that he was not teaching at an academic level.
> *Mother* – had a part-time job as a book-keeper.
> *Mary* – aged 18, a daughter by mother's previous marriage, was away at a university at the time of the series of interviews.
> *Matthew* – aged 14, the referred patient.
> *Mark* – aged 11.
> *Luke* – aged two.

In our real world Sam had just gone up to Oxford to study, Sabrina was twenty-one, I was thirteen, Owen eleven and Ben was three. I kept no youthful diary that year, and can recall only moments and episodes. But for the year of therapy I can now cross-reference those recollections with Skynner's account (which apart from names, occupations and ages was completely undisguised) and with Lavender's own diaries, including her cryptic comments on the sessions herself. It creates a 3-D picture of a time long gone.

The background to our therapy, according to Skynner, was that I (or, rather, the doppelgänging Matthew) had been 'failing to work anywhere near his capacity. The teachers felt he should be transferred to a more academic environment. Father said to be opposed because of strong egalitarian principles. Mother didn't want him transferred because of younger brother attending the same school. The boy is said to be extremely argumentative and arrogant.'

Skynner was wrong about Sam, having encountered him at a previous event and having assumed that his political position was decisive here. In fact my father had no very strong views on grammar schools – plenty of Communists sent their children to them. The person who was opposed to any idea of my moving school was Lavender. It was letting people down – the teachers, the parents she had met, the other boys; it was disloyal, it would end in tears. She had set her face against it.

Before I was sent for therapy Sam and Lavender travelled to a preliminary interview with Skynner at his office in a community health centre in the bucolic-sounding Woodberry Down area of Hackney. Skynner recorded that Lavender was 'quite agitated. Her relationship with Matthew had "always been an unhappy one". He first changed after his brother was born and became "a very difficult toddler, to a point where she found herself hating him".'

But she was anxious that I would feel – young as I was – pathologised. So Skynner recommended family therapy which was – given that he was at this point developing a specialist family therapy practice – fortuitous. My therapy could be subsumed in the family's. My mother's diary commented that she thought it 'a simply marvellous idea'.

She missed the first session, on a dark Wednesday evening in mid-November, because she'd had a varicose vein operation that week. We found ourselves – Sam, Owen and me – in a bright, cheerful toy-strewn room with the tall, tweedy Skynner and his collaborator, a white-haired and smily woman whom we only knew as 'Miss Roberts'.

I simply remember that I hated it and I hated them. I didn't want to be there and I couldn't see what good it would do. I saw it as another imposition by parents who, once they had conceived a view about something or someone (in this case, me), would not change it. It was an invasion of my head. Skynner interpreted this as 'depressive anxiety' caused by a 'rivalry with his father which he could not face'. Sam – often very charming – he saw

as a 'cheerful outgoing man who talked easily and fluently'.
When my father reported back to Lavender she wrote, 'I feel
much happier now we have someone to help us.' To help them
with me.

Three weeks later we were back for the second session, this
time with Lavender present. 'Father reported the situation much
improved,' wrote Skynner, though my parents also complained
about 'constant fights between Matthew and Mark, because
Matthew was so jealous'. It also emerged that Sam felt guilty
because he was rarely at home and rarely available for his children. Or as Skynner put it, 'the father admitted that he was, as
it were, married to his work and had never wanted Mark. This
was news to mother, who looked quite shocked.' I imagine Owen
was a bit surprised as well. Lavender, however, did not confide
any shock to her diary, mentioning only that she had felt 'artificial
and silly'.

Skynner's method was not that of conventional psychoanalysts
and psychotherapists of the time. Their training taught them to
sit and let the patient guide the session, listening hard and offering
an interpretation only towards the end and then only if it seemed
helpful. Skynner's view was that it was better to have a dialogue,
in which he offered a running interpretation. What this meant
was that he would often 'lead' the discussion with his views. But
since those views were necessarily provisional, the patient could
sometimes be baffled by the speed and changeability of Skynner's
analysis.

After number three Skynner felt that 'throughout this session
we had been on the verge of open expression of the oedipal
conflict' – i.e. my dislike for Sam and my feelings of guilt towards
my mother. Lavender obviously enjoyed it, because she wrote
that the 'interview progressed rather more than usual. I wonder
if it's being a help to David? Dr Skynner looked quite pleased.
All kinds of things are coming out.'

On 10 January, on leaving school in the afternoon, an older boy
with a mod haircut and Martens punched me as hard as he could

above the right eye for no reason that I could fathom, other than he had conceived a dislike for me. By the time I got home a bump the size of a chicken's egg had risen on my eyebrow. I know it was the 10th of January only because there is an entry about it in Lavender's diary.

Consider all the ways she could have reported this incident to herself. 'A bigger boy hit him in the eye', or 'David was the victim of a bully who punched him', or 'Will write to school about older boy who hit David'. But instead the entry reads, 'David had a bash on the head at school.' She adopted this passive tense to avoid saying that a bigger pupil was violent towards me – a pupil from the school where she wanted me to stay. So she didn't admit it to herself. In fact this boy did it again a fortnight or so later, following it up with a kick in the ribs as I lay on the playground tarmac. This time I complained to my form master and my asymmetrical enemy was caned and warned of possible expulsion.

On a Saturday ten days after the 'bash on the head' Lavender's diary recorded that she and I had 'a row about homework'. Lavender was not confident enough to help with our homework and so measured our diligence by how long we spent visibly 'doing' it. I'd probably been out all day and she had raised it when I got back. An argument became a fight. In the diary she recalled that I had called her 'fucking mad' and then she added sadly, 'I agree with him, really.'

She'd missed something out. I called her 'fucking mad' after I had so annoyed her that she'd hit me over the head with the carpet sweeper and broken it. For some reason she didn't want her diary to know about this. But four days later we were back with Skynner, who did write about it: 'The mother recounted how she had broken the broom over Matthew's head during a quarrel one day when the father was out.'

Clearly such an occurrence was a common enough feature of the '60s for it not to worry Skynner in the least. All over London, it seemed, mothers were breaking household implements over the heads of their thirteen-year-old sons.

Lavender's version in her diary (which was now let in on the sweeper secret) was that we had all gone 'off to Dr Skynner. David v rude at the start, all hunched up in his coat and gloves but after I had discussed my attack with the carpet sweeper etc we were quite cheerful'.

I wasn't cheerful about that. I was cheerful about something else that happened that evening, something that again was missing from Lavender's account. Skynner saw it clearly. 'The father now,' he wrote, 'seemed to be making an attempt to open up the subject of the marital difficulty.' Then, 'we seemed over and over again to be approaching the parents' marital difficulties but they behaved as if they could not see this implication at all.'

In other words, for once it wasn't about me. It wasn't about my jealousy, my quarrelling, my impossibility, my Oedipus complex, my under-achievement and surliness. It was about them. Sam and Lavender. I remember, as Sam hinted at problems with Lavender, a feeling of enormous relief. Sabrina had mentioned that something was wrong during her Christmas break from university, and I had felt – for a second – that someone was on my side.

'A week after this interview,' Skynner continued, 'the father wrote to say, "The sessions have acted as a catalyst with regard to our own relationship. The position is very difficult. We are both anxious to put it right but cannot do it without outside help. Are you in a position to discuss this with us separately?"'

The next two sessions happened without Owen and me. We had no idea what was said in them. The first child-free session began with Sam . . .

. . . describing an affair he had had five years previously, after which the wife had withdrawn from him as well as suffering frequent depressions. From this point on the sexual relationship had become unsatisfactory. It was clear from the wife's account that she had not wanted to know the truth and had avoided recognizing what was happening at the time, though she now realised she had sensed something and feared she had taken it out on the children, particularly Matthew.

Lavender wrote merely that, 'We felt rather unburdened and were able to be much more free with each other.' In the second session, poignantly, 'the mother described how, much of the time, she felt like a child wanting to remedy the deprivation she suffered in her own family through arranging happy family outings which the father spoiled'. 'Mother herself' wrote up this exchange as, 'I had the textbook thrown at me. Little girl looking for a father figure. Came home utterly depressed.'

That month, March, my mother fought a rearguard action to stop me from leaving Holloway. Don, one of the doctors at the GP's practice, was enlisted as an ally (his own daughter went to the local girls' grammar school) as was a Miss Cowdie, the head of the childcare committee of the borough of Camden, whom Lavender knew from working for the social workers at the centre. But Sam had finally decided. I wanted to go, the teachers thought I should, there was not much question but that I would be allowed into the local grammar school, and it must have seemed to him that keeping me at a school that I'd come to hate was perverse. And so the parental alliance was broken. 'We discussed the school,' wrote Lavender. 'I am defeated in spite of Don's efforts and Miss Cowdie's opinion'. Next day, 'I felt frozen re school. Don said he was sorry. He is going to talk to Skynner.'

He didn't. Or if he did Skynner didn't record it, and I think he would have. At the end of the month, after a full family session Skynner noted that 'father had gotten his way and Matthew had been moved to a school more able to cater to his high potential'. He added that he and his collaborator noted their impression from Owen and me that we were now 'resisting an attempt by the parents to make them the focus and project the marital conflicts on to them'.

For months we kept on going – a Wednesday evening every four weeks. I had changed schools in April, and though I had found the grammar school to be no nirvana, nor was it the constant misery that I had begun to experience at Holloway. But now I just didn't see the point in us all traipsing out to Woodberry Down to talk about things that I more than intuited had little any longer to do with us. At session 11 in the summer 'both father and mother said they had found the meetings very helpful and felt they had been able to see things in a different light. Matthew said he did not want to continue.'

Now, however, a crisis approached. In the first year of his time at Oxford Sam had mostly been in London. For the next couple of years he would spend half his time in Oxford, coming back in termtime only at weekends. In September, with weeks to go before his departure, his and Lavender's anxiety intensified.

> Father spoke of mother's brief periods of elation, which he said were always followed by trouble. In this interview for the first time the mother's problems have come fully into the open, particularly her depression and her rage at rejection. In the past the family has repeatedly colluded to avoid facing this and to present some other issue on which to focus attention . . . [now] the children were also able to refuse to let the marital problems be displaced on to them.

In the first week of October, just before he left for the beginning of Michaelmas term, in a parents-only session, Sam had a vision of the Apocalypse. 'The father said the mother was too complacent. The marriage could go on the rocks. He declared he often felt fed up with it and wished it could end.' To Skynner this candour represented an advance. 'For the first time they appeared to be listening to each other,' he wrote; 'this interview seemed to be a breakthrough.' Lavender didn't see it like that at all. 'I feel they disapprove of me so thoroughly,' she told her diary. 'Felt very tearful.'

The breakthrough continued. The following month, 'Father began to complain about the present marital relationship saying that it was "almost non-existent" and that they only stayed together because of the children. I called the father a "puffed up windbag".'

I can only imagine Sam's look of hurt surprise when Skynner – who had always been more sceptical about my father than people usually were – used that word. Lavender was nervously delighted. 'Skynner said Sam talked a lot of hot air!' she wrote.

And then it was over. At the beginning of 1969, at what turned out to be the final session of the journey in therapy that had (lest we forget) begun with my educational psychologist, my parents told Skynner that they now wished to 'terminate' the sessions. Somehow all the problems that I, we, they had had were now resolved. 'Both parents looked more relaxed and comfortable and a better relationship was evident throughout the session,' wrote Skynner. 'Mother agreed that they now felt closer together. They both reported that the children also improved. They left with warm expressions of gratitude. And we felt equally warm feelings of pleasure at the outcome of the work we had done together.' The 'referred patient' was not referred to by therapist or parents. 'Cycled through the rain to Skynner,' Lavender wrote. 'Had a really conclusive happy discussion. Felt very peaceful and relaxed.'

I now see why Lavender had to believe this. But how could someone like Robin Skynner think that it was all so easy? Perhaps because one of his beliefs was that the denial of emotions was itself the primary cause of low-level mental illness. So when Sam had openly said that he often wanted his marriage to end, that was a catharsis. And now the thing was in plain view, it could be resolved. He, Skynner, had helped get it out in the open and was consequently free to receive the gratitude of the patients and chalk up the fourteen months of therapy as a successful enterprise. That was the story Sam and Lavender told each other, told him and that he now seems to have told himself.

Robin Skynner was, almost everyone agreed, a good man and a good therapist. And yet, over the space of all this time, I remain almost as angry with him as when, aged thirteen, I sat there 'hunched in [my] coat and gloves', wishing I could be anywhere else and with anyone else in the world. Why did he not just tell them to let me stay at home? I am still furious with that roomful of dead adults. It is interesting to me just how much, by then, I wanted not to be the focus of their attention and not to know anything about their intimate problems. And yet they made me.

Also, by the time I read 'our' chapter I knew how the story ended and Skynner didn't. I don't imagine he followed up his patients, and that may have been wise. If he had he would have discovered that, in the year he published his book, with its case history ending in such warmth and gratitude, my parents' marriage was in the process of breaking up, almost in the worst possible way, and in so breaking up fucking up the lives of anybody unlucky enough to be caught in the vicinity.

I felt I had myself solved the original problem for which I had been referred. I (not Sam) took myself out of my school and then I detached myself as much as I could from my family. I never went on holiday with them again and when Sabrina left home in the summer of 1969 I got my own room at last where I read and read and read, and at school I made a friend who was to be my inspiration and consolation throughout my adolescence. After Skynner I protected my mental space with a minefield of negativity that even Lavender, with her instinct for what hurt people, could not often penetrate. I didn't reject Sam's or Lavender's politics; they were what I knew and what made sense of the world to me. But I rejected them.

Why am I telling you all this? In the 1970s the phrase 'the personal is political' became ubiquitous on the Left. It was partly a goad to those traditional socialists who could fight the class war all day long and then come home to demand their dinners from their

oppressed wives. That thing that happens at home or any time
there is an exchange between a man and a woman? That too is
political. And so it is.

Yet the reverse is also true. The political is personal; our politics
are an extension of our personalities. We like to think that they
inhabit a different mental realm to that of our emotions, having
been chosen by us rationally and as a consequence of argument
and perception. It also follows that politics is a process governed,
if you like, by the front of the brain. Emotional sometimes, of
course, but always conscious.

But what the sincere and ardent Communists of the early Cold
War tell us – mostly without ever knowing it themselves – is a
story of denial, of the state of 'knowing' something really, but
also ensuring that it is not known. Of suppressing – of needing
to suppress – reality because of the agonising consequences of
acknowledging it. Of telling themselves stories sometimes right
up to the point when the roof and the walls fall in upon them.
And even then insisting that they could always see the sky from
their living-room sofas.

I had been the referred patient in the same way that someone
can suffer a referred pain. The problem was somewhere else.

FIVE YEARS BEFORE SKYNNER . . .

On 25 March 1963, with the children in bed (my youngest brother
was born the next year), Lavender sat alone and watched the BBC
programme *That Was the Week That Was* satirising the Profumo
affair and, as she wrote in her new diary, probably the next day,
'Hoped Sam would be home, but not. V. late back'.

There was nothing very odd about that. Sam was often home
late, driving the Party van back from a meeting or from staying
late to finish a report or draft a leaflet. The next evening, the 26th,
there was a lobby of Parliament, though the diary doesn't say
what it was about (the diary was a very small page-per-view affair
that could only hold about sixty words). 'Sam not home until

3 am,' Lavender wrote the following day. 'Thought he'd been arrested. Had been to see lobbiers off.'

The next day was a Wednesday and clearly Sam had stayed at home and perhaps caught up on a little sleep. Anyway the diary entry for that day is out of keeping with anything that has gone before. 'Wonderful morning with Sam. I felt such passion for him that it was like our courting days. So happy. Life is marvellous,' Lavender had written, apparently ecstatically.

I say 'apparently' because the pen used for this entry is the thin blue pen used for the next three days, and this entry seems to have been written at the same time as the ones that follow. And these do not at all tell a tale of happy families. They are about the realisation of a betrayal.

On the Thursday a young woman called Elizabeth who worked with my father in the London Party offices took an overdose. Lavender reported this then added, 'Sam involved. He's fearfully worried. On tenterhooks till he came home. She's OK, v. drowsy but not going to die. Must get it all straightened out.'

I can only guess at what had happened that day. Perhaps on the Tuesday night when he was home so very late, Sam had told his lover (because there was no doubt, even from that entry, that this is what she was) that he wouldn't be leaving his wife. Then this Elizabeth popped a large number of pills, left a note and though failing to die had managed to draw attention to the affair.

We – Owen and I – knew Elizabeth. She was a slim, dark-haired, nervous-looking young woman who shared a large flat near the Camden Road with an older Party woman called Delsey. My mother had joked that Delsey had a crush on Sam – which had always seemed improbable to me, for the very bad reason that Delsey looked like a gigantic frog, with over-large glasses, a wide mouth and a liking for green. In fact Sam had sometimes taken us both to Delsey's and left us there with the frog for a few hours while he did Party work. Presumably with Elizabeth and presumably horizontally. But I was eight and Owen was six, what did we understand?

On Saturday Lavender 'got thoroughly tight and tackled Sam. He's been unfaithful to me with Elizabeth for several months. At the moment I feel completely desolate that Sam with all his high principles should do this. I'm shattered. No doubt we'll weather it all, but O, if only it could all be wiped out.'

The 'life is marvellous' entry was almost certainly written at the same time as the 'completely desolate' one. Lavender had clearly described her feelings about their great happiness after she had found out about his infidelity. This was a diary that only she would read, and yet – for herself alone – she reshaped the past as some Edenic existence which only now had been imperilled. This does not qualify, I think, as 'lying to oneself'. It belongs to another category of delusion altogether. I weep for this Lavender.

Over the next few months some details of the affair were gradually revealed: most of it, Lavender wrote a week later, 'took place in the back of the van'. It is even possible that while we were upstairs at Delsey's playing or drawing, Sam and Elizabeth were double-parked outside.

My father assured my mother that it was over, and that the suicide bid had marked its end. She believed him, she said both to him and to herself. A few weekends later they left us in Sabrina's care and drove off to a small hotel in the New Forest on what Lavender described as a 'second honeymoon'. 'I can't understand, but can only marvel at my feelings,' my mother told herself. 'All my old passion for Sam has been revived.'

But this was only one of her narratives. The other was of the profound depression that would break in on her when she was not expecting it. She had been betrayed. On a long-planned solo trip by Russian liner to Leningrad (she had never visited the Soviet motherland before, and never did again), via Copenhagen, Lavender asserted herself – against character and conviction – by having an affair with a Party member called Harry. As the ship neared Southampton she wrote, 'I don't know if I shall tell Sam about Harry, but at least I feel no more misery about Elizabeth. I hope I'm not deluding myself.'

A day later she wrote that she had indeed told Sam. And a day after that she also knew that she had been deluding herself. And the day after that that she hadn't. 'Very depressed in the morning' would be followed within a week by, 'Cheerful again, hope and think depression gone for good!' My father got the job in South Essex and soon would no longer be bumping into Elizabeth during the day.

Even so, jealousy tortured her. 'Got home completely exhausted and black depression descended on me. Wish I could control it, but unbidden mental images of Elizabeth in Sam's arms came to me, his special loving look directed on her, her black hair around his shoulders, and I'm lost.' This would be a recurring cry in her diaries for the next three years. Over and over and over again.

That summer Lavender discovered that she was pregnant with a baby that would be due around her forty-first birthday. A week or so later at my father's farewell party from the London District she encountered the other woman. Until then she had been 'thoroughly enjoying myself when there was Elizabeth in long green gloves and very green eye make-up. She was drunk. Told her that I was pregnant, which was rather catty as I know she cannot conceive.' A few days on, 'Hate being pregnant, feel at such a disadvantage against the Elizabeth/anyone else set-up.'

One afternoon in July, over three months after the affair was supposed to have ended Lavender 'had a terrible presentiment when he wasn't home at teatime. Tore to Elizabeth's on bike and there he was sitting in the van in the rain. Heartbroken, but as I cycled home he caught me up and explained that he couldn't bear to break off, but that he really would. This must have gone much deeper than ever I thought.'

This time he finally did end the affair. On her birthday he drove Elizabeth down to Chichester to see a performance of *Uncle Vanya*. It is to be hoped that she was impressed by the cast (Laurence Olivier, Sybil Thorndike, Michael Redgrave, Joan Plowright) because on the way back Sam did what had to be done. Elizabeth moved and I never heard of her again. On 31 December my mother, testifying in her personal court to the survival of her marriage, wrote, 'So ends the worst year of my life, but also nearly the best.'

For nine months, as detailed in her diary, Lavender was alternately depressed, despairing, furious and jealously obsessed. Even when she insisted that things were marvellous, it was a peculiar form of deliberate self-deception, not unlike trying to have a nice thought before you go to sleep, so as to guide your own dreams. And it never worked. The fear and the betrayal came back, unbidden, time after time. It was still there in the Woodberry Down Centre with Skynner five years later – the demon in the corner.

But what about the rest of us who shared a house and a life with her? Who were, in fact, with her more than Sam was? What did we know? In 2005 – the year in which Lavender died – I was persuaded by a good friend of mine who is a practising psychoanalyst that I might benefit from seeing an analyst myself. So for five years I walked down the hill three or four days a week to lie in a peaceful room and talk to someone who was there to listen and to help. At some point we talked about Sam and his affair with Elizabeth. 'So what did you feel about it at the time?' my analyst asked. 'I didn't know about it,' I replied, 'I was a child.' My analyst seemed genuinely surprised. She wondered how the intense emotions of the Elizabeth period, the depressions Lavender described, the urgent late-night recriminations and protestations in the bedroom next door, could have gone unregistered. When, at Delsey's, he disappeared with Elizabeth, what did we imagine?

Nothing. I knew nothing. I imagined nothing. But her suggestion, I think, was that somehow I chose to know and imagine nothing. At first I took her mild incredulity as a criticism of my own selfishness. Had I not always been selfish? Had I not sought to leave my family emotionally at the age of fourteen, while remaining, until I was twenty-one or twenty-two, to sleep and sometimes eat at home? I took what I wanted and rejected the rest.

She wasn't saying that. In any case Sabrina, then seventeen, knew nothing either. At some point that summer she travelled up to Edinburgh and came across Sam and Elizabeth together in a café (God alone knows what story he'd told Lavender), and even then suspected nothing. Yet I can imagine the look on Sam's face when he saw that Sabrina had broken in on his tryst.

I think we compartmentalised our perceptions and our feelings. Lavender's moods were so precarious at all times that all of us, in our own ways, sought to insulate ourselves against the agonies she often felt. And we simply didn't know Sam that well. He was, I think, unstimulated by small children and could always imagine something more urgent to do. Write a book. Address a school. Go to a play with someone other than us. Later, when we were growing up and he was no longer responsible for us, he was much more interested.

There was nothing unique about this for the times. For many of my generation our fathers were semi-detached and our mothers were miserable. There is one wonderful series of black-and-white pictures of Sam holding my baby self and looking genuinely delighted with his son. I don't recall seeing that look turned on me again for another twenty-five years. So, there was nothing to be noticed in his behaviour.

But again, there was something happening which we suppressed all knowledge of. Owen and I were made to go to bed earlier than anyone else I knew. Teatime was hardly over, an hour of playing or television, and it was time to go upstairs. Then it was lights off by seven. The bathwater would run, and Owen and I would talk and if we made too much noise we'd be told off, and if that didn't work then Sam – if he was home – would come in, shout at us, and 'wallop' us through the bedclothes.

I just assumed that this was about a battle of wills that he was determined to win and that no other explanation was needed. The alternative, true story would have appalled me. But it became obvious from reading Lavender's diaries all those years later that, Elizabeth (and any other unknown dalliance) notwithstanding, my parents' strictness over early bedtimes was not about us being tired, or enforcing house rules, but almost invariably about enabling them to have sex, or 'love' as Lavender always described it to herself. Which they did, in the evening, pretty much whenever Sam was home early enough. Even at the height of his affairs, on the days when he didn't get back too late, the 'marital situation' was addressed. Without me 'knowing'.

In February 1964 my youngest brother was born, and babies do not understand being told to go to sleep or else. Bedtime was liberalised, and my relationship with both parents grew steadily worse. Sam lost his study, which became the nursery (not a word we ever used) and went to libraries to write.

Not long before she died Lavender told me the story I recounted earlier about the teachers at my primary school saying that I should try for a scholarship at Westminster School. This was never put to me, and – when my mother eventually and not at all shamefacedly revealed it to me – I had just assumed that the reasons were ideological.

Then finally – almost between that chapter and this – it occurred to me that formal learning had played a very small role in my parents' lives. Sam had left school at fourteen, Lavender (more or less) at sixteen. I am not at all sure that they could have coped with me getting an education that was so much better than theirs had been. Only when Sam was at Oxford in his own right could he bring himself round to thinking about what was best for me.

AND SEVEN YEARS AFTER SKYNNER . . .

So I pulled away. And I decided to believe that, in my half-presence and half-absence, Sam and Lavender were a happy enough couple, even if my relationship with my mother was always fraught. They went off on foreign holidays with my brothers, often to Italy, and it all seemed amicable enough and I imagined that we were just more content apart. Them. Me. Frictionless.

Because when we were together it didn't stay happy for long. My mother hectored me in every school holiday to get a job, and often – for a while – I did. Every now and again one of these sessions would turn into a full-scale shouting match and she would tell me I ought to move out – despite my still being at secondary school – and I would seriously think about where a seventeen-year-old could move to. And then it would pass over.

But now life was not miserable for me. I was doing well at school again, I had good friends, and eventually I had lovers. Instead of being pulled away from the Party, however, I pulled them – those who 'needed' pulling – towards it. Communism was a state of something, after all, whereas most people existed, politically, in a state of nothing very much. So there were my Communist parents and I chose to imagine about them that things were now settled, that I didn't have to worry about them, or feel guilty about my mother. I went to Oxford, I got sent down, I got admitted to Manchester, and in the summer of '74 went on a trip to Ireland with a group of friends and, by the time I got back, was as much in love with one of them as I could bear. I had no room for anything else but her.

What I returned to was an emotional disaster. Almost the moment that I walked in the door my mother – who had never confided in me before (and who often picked the moment of my return to find fault with my attitudes towards work or earning money), launched a trebuchet volley of revelation and despair into my unprepared defences. It went something like this . . .

Our family usually had a van. When I was seven we drove in a borrowed Bedford Dormobile through Scotland to Loch Morar, seeing the Highland Games at Glenfinnan, and nearly being swept into Loch Lomond by torrential rain. Elizabeth and Sam had conducted their affair mostly in the Party van. After that came our succession of second-hand Volkswagen camper vans, one of which was left behind by a generous young American Marxist – Erik Olin Wright – who studied with Sam at Balliol and then had returned to the US. We were in a constant state, if you like, of vanness.

Let me park the van for a page. On 8 September 1974, Lavender – now in her early fifties – recorded the usual types of event: she cycled to work, she shopped, she noted down something political (there was a minority Labour Government and we were heading for the second election of the year). This was all written with one pen. What followed was written with another.

By 1974 Sam was an academic at a London polytechnic and – as he never had done in his hard-working life before – was earning a proper salary; one that allowed decent shoes and a new jacket. But now he felt that time was against him. Had he started in academia a few years earlier he could have been a professor – a Hobsbawm of economics – but as it was he had to make his way quickly, and that meant hard work, long hours, evenings and weekends spent in libraries, at meetings or in the polytechnic, or addressing Party economics seminars. He would often be home late.

But this particular night he was too late. In a different pen and presumably at a different time, Lavender wrote, 'To bed alone. Sam joined me early in the morning – don't like to think what it all means.' Once again this was a diary entry written *ex post facto*. By the time she wrote it she knew exactly what it meant.

Sam arrived late the next night, but not quite as late as before. My mother, with peculiar aptness, had been watching John le Carré's *The Deadly Affair* on television, 'which was quite horrible'. When Sam arrived he had brought with him two bottles of Stingo's barley wine for Lavender – something he had obviously done before. This time, however, they didn't have the sedative effect that he may have been hoping for. 'Went to bed,' she wrote, 'but with my light on. Sam came in and switched it off. Then I heard him creeping about and he wouldn't come to bed. Felt disturbed.'

Lavender went downstairs. 'Sat in the sitting room and saw him creeping out via the back door and to the van, which was parked away from the house. Went out in my nightie and confronted him.' It was obvious that there was somebody already in the van, but – perhaps because she was not in a movie – my mother didn't wait to find out who. She went back indoors and wrote, 'Oh, it's all happening again, deceit and hate. Why can't he be civilised – such pain I felt. Took 3 Mogadon, heard him come back. Such misery.'

A week later, I came home from Ireland, light-headed from love and without the slightest idea of what was coming. Even now the awful tawdriness of it – the van (there was an American bumper sticker of the time that read, 'If the van's a-rockin', don't come knockin''), my dad's pathetic attempts to drug my mother, *The Deadly Affair* showing on TV as *The Tacky Affair* played out in real life – almost overwhelms me. Back then, as a very young man who was reading Neruda's poetry and thinking it was true what the poet said about love, the thing appalled me. 'Back home,' read my own diary (I wrote about forty entries spread across three years), then curtly, 'the bloody news.'

As soon as it was known – or as soon as Lavender chose or was forced to know it – it was obvious. Even if Sam had not been adulterous before (which, of course, he had), he had given all the classic and clichéd signs of being a middle-aged man enjoying a dalliance. He had taken up running, lost a lot of weight, had begun to wear clothes that my mother had never advised he buy. He was not often at home, but when he was he was solicitous to a fault. Today you would check the mobile phone of someone behaving like him. Back then, once he went out the door, who knew?

And then there was the kind of man he was – something I had never wanted to consider. A few years later, still in my twenties, I took a rather beautiful girlfriend round to see him. 'That was interesting,' she told me later. 'Your dad's a bit of a flirt.' The next time we went to see him I looked out for what he would do. It was like watching a heat-seeking missile locking on target. Around the same time I met the mother of a student friend of mine for the first time. She had been at Party weekend schools during the late '40s and early '50s. 'Your dad!' she said, smiling, and practically winked at me. 'Your dad!'

The poet Jackie Kay's adoptive father, Ian, had known Sam up in Scotland and then, later, when they were both Party full-time workers. We met up listening to his daughter perform at a book festival in the Scottish borders. Sam was dead by then but almost the first thing Ian told me was, 'Aye, your old man was a one for the ladies.' It was no longer a strange thing to hear.

The affair had been going on for months with the much younger mother of my ten-year-old brother Ben's best friend, a woman who had also been, for the last year or so, one of Lavender's closest friends. Worse, it rapidly became obvious that just as taking Owen and me to Delsey's was a cover for his affair with Elizabeth, so taking Ben and his young friend out on trips was a cover for Sam's most recent adulteries. It would be almost impossible for a bad genie to devise a curse as psychologically damaging to the victim as the details of this affair were for Lavender.

For the moment, she was spared – or had spared herself – the knowledge of who the co-respondent was. Even so the next day she wrote in a mixture of agony and delusion: 'How I hated waking up to that same misery I had 11 years ago. Suddenly felt so weary. Drank whole bottle of wine and little bottle of rum. Sam acting as though nothing had happened. I can cope with another woman as long as I know when they are meeting so that I'm not sitting at home speculating. Keep wondering who it is.'

Of course, she couldn't cope with another woman. And when she did find out who it was, she was sent into a cycle of false hope, jealous obsession, black depression and even violence. For an impossible period – over a year – they cohabited in a mad ménage. He would go to meet the girlfriend, come back at 2 a.m. to make love to my mother until five, then both would try to act normally in front of family and friends. 'Does he feel that this affair is going on for a long time?' my mother asked her diary in the early days. 'We talked about separate holidays, etc. I hope he doesn't mean that we will never again go walking together? I was hoping for a happy, companionable old age.'

On some nights, when he was out with his girlfriend, Lavender would take the van herself and, in a strange act of counter-defiance, sleep on the fringes of Hampstead Heath, leaving my eleven-year-old brother in the house alone. 'I'm full of terrible mood swings. Sometimes I think I can cope and manage and other times I feel utterly defeated and find myself in tears.'

In many of her diary entries she imagined that my dad was suffering from a temporary illness from which he might recover. 'A beautiful day. I loved having Sam beside me. If only he could get better and we could all be happy again.'

'All' had never included me. Probably it had never really included anyone. But compared with this, it had been heavenly. So terrible was the atmosphere at home – he all pacifying and pleasant while obdurately maintaining his love affair, she all pained and held together by false hopes and real drugs – that I found ways of spending vacations anywhere else at all.

Month after month they tormented each other. They quarrelled; she insisted; he resisted; his affair continued. But they made love two to three times a week and she blamed not him but the other woman. From time to time she'd win a victory over his love-making timetable – force him to stay with her rather than making his late-evening pilgrimages to the other woman – and she'd imagine, briefly and crazily, that she was in the ascendant. Then the ceiling of her jerry-built emotional home would come crashing down.

When it did, new, almost unimagined Lavenders appeared. Ten months after the affair was discovered, my mother, in a fit of anger over some missed domestic arrangement or a lie my father had told (and most of what he told her was now lies, because they were the only things she could cope with), sought out the other woman, who was walking her dog. 'Picked her up,' my mother exulted. 'She was still so completely egocentric, so gave her a good hiding. She fled, leaving part of her halterneck and a sandal behind! Felt great! Judith [a friend] said I should have done it long ago.'

A week later, 'Fearful row with Sam, he knocked me to the floor, hope Ben didn't hear it'.

At the end of July – over ten months after the discovery – on a ghastly pony-trekking holiday, during which my mother noted the breaking of a scandal about Harold Pinter and Lady Antonia Fraser, they finally told my poor brother that they were splitting up. My sister recalls that, before this event, she and her husband took Ben for a day away by the seaside, and as they walked on the front he banged his head repeatedly on a wall.

He was eleven. Ben told me much later that one of his memories of this time was being chased out of his friend's house by the enraged, impotent husband of my father's lover. My mother wrote it up like this: 'When Ben came home he burst out talking about emotional violence, the effect of family stress on children, etc, but later when I tried to question him he told me not to worry, it was just a mood. Can't think what can have happened, Sam unwilling to discuss. Blamed it on me.'

All this time Robin Skynner was writing his book and, as he published it, complete with those warm expressions of gratitude, even my mother – who held on to her dead marriage as though her own life depended on it – could bear no more. Sam moved out to his flat and the impossible daily self-crucifixion of their relationship became the more usual decade of constant bitterness on her part and defiant guilt on his. Lavender almost forgave Sam over the following three decades, but never forgave the lover.

At her funeral, among the items she had requested be played or sung by her family and the many members of the Older Feminist Network who turned out for the occasion, was Gloria Gaynor's 'I Will Survive'. I think Lavender had imagined, after a heart attack in her early sixties, that she would be the first to go, and pictured my father having to listen to 'Now go! Walk out the door!' in front of her reproving friends. Unfortunately, he beat her to the Styx by seven years. I said in my little speech that I thought 'I Will Survive' was an ironic song to have at a funeral. One by one the OFN stood up to tell me why I was wrong. Then we sang the Internationale.

My parents' politics were inseparable from their psyches. So are yours. I have been asked by one of the brightest men in the land, in tones of genuine incredulity, how could my mum and dad have been Communists? How could they have remained Communists? What, he implied, was wrong with them?

They were human, is what was wrong with them. You can surely see how they stopped their sessions with Skynner, not because they had reached the point where everything was uncovered and recognised, but precisely because had they continued everything would have been uncovered and recognised. The therapy ended because it was getting too dangerous. It was broken off exactly at the moment of catharsis, when Skynner was getting a bit too close. Lavender simply could not bear the idea of the marriage finishing – would not countenance it even unconsciously – and I have a terrible feeling that though he may have thought about it, it didn't suit Sam either. I'm not saying that he ever made such a calculation, but the only asset our family had was the house in a nice area of London given to my mother by her guardian. And it belonged to her, not him. Later, after the discovery of the second affair and even when he was earning more money, it seems apparent that he was reluctant to find himself back in some garret.

Both stood to lose too much from admitting the truth – even to themselves. About the Party, about themselves. My mother was a constant source of reproach for things that we had done or hadn't done – quite a few of these reproaches being entirely vicarious and entered on the behalf of absent third parties. Many of these reproaches had something to do with a supposed failure of duty or proper love. My fault was either selfishness or it was jealousy. But jealousy was what had tormented Lavender since her girlhood. Jealousy of her younger sister, jealousy of the new family, jealousy of her own daughter as she grew up. So, almost as soon as I was old enough to be a credible receptacle for her own projected feelings, I became not just jealous, but *the* jealous one.

Lavender was reproachful and notoriously prone to blaming people for infractions, because she blamed and reproached herself. When you're rejected by your parent as early as she was, I think it becomes almost impossible to imagine yourself loveable. For the same reason abandonment was her greatest fear, and the only bandage for this wound was to imagine that she could create the ideal family that she had lost and bind Sam to it. She would blame herself intensely if this wasn't accomplished.

So it was probably bad luck that they found each other in the Left London landscape of the '50s, almost certainly seeing in each other the opposite of what was true about each of them. My mother probably mistook my father's political ardency for true fidelity, and he may have thought that she was the perfectly understanding base from which he could launch and relaunch himself into the changing political world. He propelled himself out of his East End family as soon as he could and into the biggest world he could find – Communism. To him, a family was almost an abstraction. Early on he became an abandoner.

She was a Party member through thick and thin because it was a kind of family. He was a Party member despite everything because it was his bigger world.

I think about my own political evolution and my own innate prejudices – the direction I tend in before there has been a word of rational argument. And I find the same pattern endlessly. I am obliterated by pessimism and anger. I am made fearful by blame. I find myself resisting almost any political manifestation which is based on saying that it is all the fault of X or Y. Because, somewhere in my head, it is always me being blamed. When I'd completed *Voodoo Histories*, my book on conspiracy theories, which became a major tool for debunking them, I realised that it satisfied a need in me that also went beyond the rational.

My only advantage is that I know this about myself. Many people don't. What this does *not* amount to is my saying that everyone believes what they want to: rather that they believe what they do, and in the way that they do, because they need to. And the greater the need the bigger the gap you can sometimes bridge.

A first afterword, by way of illustrating the point. I first wrote about Sam's adultery in my newspaper, *The Times*. A few weeks later I received a letter, addressed from a suburban cul-de-sac in the Home Counties. The writer was furious. His brother Eddie, now dead, had been a Party colleague of my late father's, and he was sure that Eddie would have been hugely distressed by what I had written about Sam. The writer had also shown the article to his own daughter, who had agreed with him that I must be a thoroughly dreadful person. So there we were: someone no one in our family had ever met was full of rage and projected distress at what had been revealed in an article in *The Times*. You don't have to be a psychoanalyst to find such a reaction interesting.

And a second afterword, because there was one. Before Sam died in 1998, there had been a reconciliation between most of my family and the woman he had had the affair with and then, finally, settled down with. Lavender always disparaged this woman but over time most of us came to realise that she was tolerable, if a little erratic. They had some good years together, even if she was sometimes a bit careless of the fact that he was older than she. Indeed I once met someone at a conference who told me that he had rescued my father from falling off a glacier on a walking holiday that was rather more challenging than a seventy-five-year-old is normally expected to undertake.

In the period before he died we even became friendly. Then, after the funeral, she stopped speaking to any of us. She wouldn't return calls or answer the door. We asked intermediaries to get her to talk to us, but to no avail. It took months to get my father's will into probate, and one of the clauses of the will – that we should each be able to choose an object of his that meant something emotionally to us – was never fulfilled. None of us thought it was worth the distress of insisting on our legal rights. And we let it go. The woman is still alive and still in the house they shared. She almost certainly has her own story, but – of course – I don't know what it is.

Fifteen years after the funeral I received a letter. I had to read it three times before I quite understood it. It was from the undertakers who had handled Sam's cremation. They were very sorry to do this, but they had to inform me that my father's ashes were still on a shelf in a storeroom at their premises in Kentish Town. They had written to my father's lover many, many times at the address they knew she lived at to ask for instructions as to what to do with Sam's remains, but she never answered. Now they felt they really must do something about it. Knowing I worked for *The Times* they had phoned the editor's secretary asking for an address. Could I perhaps (though, they wanted to stress, I was under no obligation to) suggest what was to be done? And, of course, I could.

This next paragraph should begin, 'On a grey, wet, late October's day' – and indeed it does. On that day I drove down to the undertaker's, signed for Sam, took the heavy, green plastic urn to the car, and drove home. Two weeks later Sabrina, Ben, Owen, our spouses, our children, their boyfriends, scattered him in a trail, where once he had run, just before a late-autumnal dusk on Hampstead Heath.

Loss and fear of loss and making up for loss as best you can. Always, always, that's what it comes down to. Politics and love. Hence the need to be kind. A need I am always forgetting.

Acknowledgements

This book has consumed half a decade and the patience of almost everyone who knows me. I thank them for never grabbing me by the collar while shouting, 'Not another word about the bloody Communist Party!'

Clearly I owe my greatest debt to my birth family, Sabrina, Owen, Ben and Frances. This is a version of their stories too, but they would almost certainly have told it differently. They have been extraordinarily tolerant. I am grateful too to my aunt Gillian Aarons who gave up the best part of a West Country summer's day to help me when her judgement probably was that she shouldn't.

Dan Franklin at Cape and my agent Georgia Garrett have helped me through this with exemplary – possibly absurd – patience. My friend John Lahr offered hours and hours of advice – all taken – amounting to the proposition that the more I didn't want to write about something, the more I should. So I did. So it's his fault. Without knowing Stephen Grosz I would never have had sufficient insight into my own biases and proclivities to write this book. Jennifer Stahl, from far away, somehow performed the trick of making my words sing. The late Kim James gave me a hilarious and unrepentant afternoon near Northampton and Arnold Wesker a fascinating, literary one near Hay one spring. Two comrades from Sam and Lavender's branch – the late Pete Richards and his wife Elvira – told me things in their flat in the block where they'd lived for forty years, with its view over the railway. That great East-Ender Bernard Kops allowed me to quote from his wonderful poem. My thanks too to the staff at the wonderful People's Museum in Manchester for the assistance with riffling through their archives.

An unlikely source of encouragement (unless you know him) was my colleague at *The Times*, and Conservative peer, Daniel Finkelstein. 'When is the book coming out?' he would ask me regularly for at least the first three years. 'I want to understand why they did it!' Hopefully, Danny, now you do.

Permission Credits

Extract taken from 'The Waste Land' taken from *The Waste Land and other poems* © Estate of T. S. Eliot and reprinted by permission of Faber and Faber Ltd. Lines from from 'The Party', first performed 1973, first published by Faber & Faber in 1974. © Trevor Griffiths 1973. Used by permission of United Agents LLP on behalf of Trevor Griffiths. Lines from 'Whitechapel Library, Aldgate East' © Bernard Kops, used by kind permission of Bernard Kops. 'Hey Ho! Cooke and Rowe' written by Peggy Seeger, published by Stormking Music Inc., administered by Harmony Music Limited, used with permission. 'Which Side Are You On' written by Forence Reece, published by Stormking Music Inc., administered by Harmony Music Limited, used with permission. 'Alabama 58' written by Ewan MacColl and Peggy Seeger, published by Stormking Music Inc., administered by Harmony Music Limited, used with permission. 'The Banks of Marble' written by Les Rice, published by Stormking Music Inc., administered by Harmony Music Limited, used with permission. 'If You Miss Me At the Back of the Bus' written by Carver Neblett, published by Sanga Music Inc., administered by Harmony Music Limited, used with permission. 'Something in the Air' by John Keen © 1969 FABULOUS MUSIC LTD. Lines from 'The Delicate Dictator' translated by Robert Bly. Translation Copyright © 1971, 1993 by Robert Bly. Reprinted by permission of Georges Borchardt, Inc., for Robert Bly. 'I'm Gonna Be An Engineer' written by Peggy Seeger,